Pentecostals, Proselytization, and Anti-Christian
Violence in Contemporary India

GLOBAL PENTECOSTAL AND CHARISMATIC
CHRISTIANITY
Series Editor
Donald E. Miller
Executive Director, Center for Religion and Civic Culture,
University of Southern California

PENTECOSTALS, PROSELYTIZATION, AND
ANTI-CHRISTIAN VIOLENCE IN CONTEMPORARY INDIA
Chad M. Bauman

Pentecostals, Proselytization, and Anti-Christian Violence in Contemporary India

CHAD M. BAUMAN

OXFORD
UNIVERSITY PRESS

OXFORD
UNIVERSITY PRESS

Oxford University Press is a department of the University of
Oxford. It furthers the University's objective of excellence in research,
scholarship, and education by publishing worldwide.

Oxford   New York
Auckland   Cape Town   Dar es Salaam   Hong Kong   Karachi
Kuala Lumpur   Madrid   Melbourne   Mexico City   Nairobi
New Delhi   Shanghai   Taipei   Toronto

With offices in
Argentina   Austria   Brazil   Chile   Czech Republic   France   Greece
Guatemala   Hungary   Italy   Japan   Poland   Portugal   Singapore
South Korea   Switzerland   Thailand   Turkey   Ukraine   Vietnam

Oxford is a registered trademark of Oxford University Press
in the UK and certain other countries.

Published in the United States of America by
Oxford University Press
198 Madison Avenue, New York, NY 10016

CIP data is on file at the Library of Congress
ISBN 978–0–19–020209–5 (hbk); ISBN 978–0–19–020210–1 (pbk)

CONTENTS

ACKNOWLEDGMENTS

This book, like nearly every other, is the textual manifestation of mani-
fold collaborations, large and small. Most of them will, unfortunately,
go unacknowledged in the short paragraphs that follow, but I am grateful,
nonetheless, for every single one.

The majority of the research for the book was conducted during a year-
long sabbatical in 2011–12. Butler University, where I work, funded half
of that sabbatical, and to the university I am grateful for the opportunity to
engage in the kind of sustained scholarly reflection that sabbaticals allow.
Financial support for the other half of the sabbatical, as well as for a good
deal of research and travel support, came in the form of a grant from the
Pentecostal and Charismatic Research Initiative (PCRI) at the Center for
Religion & Civic Culture (CRCC) housed at the University of Southern
California, and from the John Templeton Foundation, which funded it.
Aside from the material support provided by PCRI, I would be remiss if
I did not express my gratitude to the CRCC staff for planning two utterly
stimulating workshops that brought together all of the PCRI grantees in
Quito, Ecuador, and Nairobi, Kenya. To all of the grantees I am indebted
for helping me grasp the global dimensions of the Pentecostal movement.
But I am particularly grateful to Donald E. Miller, Executive Director of
CRCC and Editor of the series in which this volume appears, and to Brie
"Aguardiente" Loskota and Richard "Fireball" Flory (Managing Director
and Director of Research, respectively, at CRCC), for their wit, wisdom,
and ongoing friendship and scholarly guidance.

In the collection of data, and in the arranging, conducting, translating,
and transcribing of interviews, I was aided by a small army of research
assistants, both at Butler University (Ariel Tyring, Katie Kilgore, Matt

Miller, Douglas Manuel, and Stephanie Cheuvront) and in India (Naveen John, Yehova Das, and Abel Raj). Without them this project might have never come to fruition.

For scholarly support, I am indebted to participants at conferences sponsored by the American Academy of Religion, the Conference on the Study of Religions of India, the European Association for South Asian Studies (EASAS), and the Society for Hindu-Christian Studies, who provided feedback on some of the material that appears in the volume. Among EASAS colleagues, I would like to single out Eva Ambos and Davide Torri for their scholarly friendship and support, and for their endearingly "mind-buckling" polylinguistic abilities. Similarly, I am grateful to fellow scholars of Indian religions, Jacob Cherian, Joseph Prabhakar Dayam, Satish Gyan, Paul Parathazham, Gyanapragasam Patrick, James Ponniah, and Nandini Ramaswamy, who influenced my thinking on the issues discussed in this book in various ways, and who provided me with valuable contacts and guidance throughout North and South India. Similarly, while I was at work on the project, Sarah Claerhout, Richard Fox Young, Robert Frykenberg, Brian Hatcher, Roger Hedlund, Arun Jones, Tamara Leech, Reid Locklin, Brian Pennington, Nathaniel Roberts, Charles Ryerson, and Kerry San Chirico stimulated my thinking, filled in gaps in my knowledge, critiqued my presentations, and read first drafts of sections of the book.

A reviewer at Oxford University Press provided invaluable comment on the entire manuscript, as did Corinne Dempsey, who regularly embodies the best of scholarly collegiality by combining thoughtful, informed, and careful critique with equally thoughtful and effusive encouragement. I am additionally grateful to Theo Calderara, editor at OUP, for his reasonable, calming, and thoughtful work with me on this project, and to OUP's editorial assistant, Glenn Ramirez (and his team), for their help in seeing it through to publication.

Engaging in research on this controversial subject required an attempt to sympathetically apprehend the views of prominent critics of Christianity in India, and in this regard, I am particularly grateful for the assistance of Koenraad Elst and Mihir Meghani, co-founder of the Hindu American Foundation (HAF). The latter helped me refine my understanding of HAF's positions on these matters (though I don't discuss them much in the book), and also put me in touch with R. Venkatanarayanan, former Secretary of the Hindu Dharma Acharya Sabha. I owe Venkatanarayanan himself a debt of thanks for a series of thoughtful and engaging conversations in Delhi, and for elucidating the statements of his close associate, Swami Dayananda Saraswati, who makes several appearances in these pages.

A number of pro-Christian and pro-Dalit leaders and activists in India spent time with me, corresponded with me, and helped me understand the topic from their perspective, and among them I would like to express particular appreciation for John Dayal, Richard Howell, and Asha Kowtal. Similarly, the data and analysis appearing in chapter 5 is better and more complete because of the assistance and advice of several Christian mission scholars and practitioners, among them Jonathan Bonk, William Burrows, Darrell Guder, Wilbert Shenk, and Erica Johnson.

I am particularly grateful to Cambridge University Press, for allowing me to republish material in chapter 2 that first appeared in the *Journal of Asian Studies*, and to Brill, for permission to reprint parts of my chapter that appeared in Richard Fox Young and Jonathan Seitz's *Asia in the Making of Christianity: Conversion, Agency, and Indigeneity, 1600s to the Present* (Boston: Brill, 2013).

I am, additionally, indebted to a number of friends and colleagues at Butler University. Members of my department, including our departmental administrative specialist, Mary Proffitt, helped maintain my sanity through professional collaboration, intellectual stimulation, and scholarly commiseration. I would also like to express my gratitude to Travis Ryan, for help with (metaphorical) breeding, and to Terri Carney, for regularly reminding me to keep my priorities straight, and for encouraging me—borrowing the words of another—to practice at failure.

Speaking of priorities, my first monograph ended with an acknowledgment of the "sisters B," who accompanied me through the often lonely hours of writing, and who just happened to be canine. Those sisters, sadly, have since then passed on. But my life now is perpetually enriched by the presence of a new pair of sisters, our (human) daughters, Annika Priya and Nadya Sonali, who surely made sacrifices for this book in ways they couldn't possibly know or understand. To borrow and adapt a line from a character in George Saunders's *Tenth of December: Stories*, all I want from my life is to feel, at the end, like I did right by those magnificent little creatures. And finally, both to *and* for Jodi, my wife, who may have known the many sacrifices she had to make, but who nevertheless made them with characteristic grace and poise, I am, as always, grateful.

ABBREVIATIONS

ABVKA	Akhil Bharatiya Vanvasi Kalyan Ashram
BEIC	British East India Company
BJP	Bharatiya Janata Party
BYM	Blessing Youth Ministry
CNI	Church of North India
CSI	Church of South India
DBC	Doon Bible College
EFEO	École française d'Extrême-Orient
EFI	Evangelical Fellowship of India
FCRA	Foreign Contribution (Regulation) Act
GCW	Gospel Christian Workers (a pseudonym)
GFA	Gospel for Asia
NGO	nongovernmental organization
OUP	Oxford University Press
PUCL	People's Union for Civil Liberties
RDT	Rural Development Trust
RSS	Rashtriya Swayamsevak Sangh
SC	schedule caste
ST	schedule tribe
UCFHR	United Christian Forum for Human Rights
VBS	Vacation Bible School
VHP	Vishwa Hindu Parishad

MAP

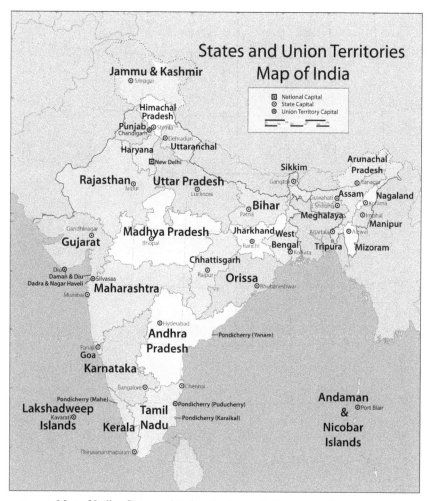

MAP I.I Map of Indian States and Union Territories (color removed)

SOURCE: From Creative Commons via Wikimedia Commons, available at http://commons. wikimedia.org/wiki/File:India_states_and_union_territories_map.svg.

Pentecostals, Proselytization, and Anti-Christian
Violence in Contemporary India

Introduction

THIS BOOK WAS AN accident of sorts. For nearly a decade I have been conducting research on violence against Christians in India. Examining and attempting to account for what I discovered was the disproportionate targeting of Pentecostal Christians in that violence was initially intended to be one small element of a larger, more general and theoretical book project on anti-Christian violence, a project on which I continue to work. But after spending some time on the question of the disproportionate targeting of Pentecostals, it became clear to me that it deserved its own thorough treatment. For this reason, in 2011, I devoted several months of fieldwork in India to this specific question, utilizing participant observation techniques and conducting around one hundred qualitative interviews with Christians and their critics in North and South India.

Very little has been written by scholars on anti-Christian violence in contemporary India, particularly in comparison with the amount that has been written on anti-Muslim violence. And less still has been written about Pentecostals in the context of Hindu–Christian conflict. For example, the most widely cited text on contemporary conversion controversies in India, Sebastian Kim's *In Search of Identity* (Oxford: OUP, 2003), deals very little with anti-Christian violence, and almost not at all with Pentecostalism. In fact, with few exceptions, most notably Michael Bergunder's *The South Indian Pentecostal Movement in the Twentieth Century* (Grand Rapids, MI: Eerdmans Publishers, 2008), few scholars have looked seriously and systematically at Indian Pentecostalism in any context. This book, then, is an attempt to contribute both to the general literature on Indian Pentecostals, and to our understanding of Indian Pentecostals' relationship to contemporary anti-Christian violence.

The series of Hindu–Christian riots that took place during 2007 and 2008 in Kandhamal, Odisha (formerly Orissa), received a great deal of attention from the media (and subsequently from scholars, activists, and human rights organizations).[1] During these devastating riots, dozens of mostly impecunious villagers lost their lives and thousands lost their homes. The victims were primarily Christian, but Hindus also died and saw their homes and other possessions destroyed in less frequent but still calamitous assaults by Christian mobs. And, of course, a brutal and fatal attack on the prominent and controversial Hindu activist, Swami Lakshmanananda Saraswati, in August 2008, provoked the second, more destructive round of violence.[2]

While the Kandhamal riots became international news, the attention they received drew attention away from the less widely known fact that since the late 1990s in India, the frequency of what I call "everyday" acts of anti-Christian violence has increased dramatically. I use the term "everyday" not to diminish the gravity of the attacks, but rather to convey something of their nature. First, they are "everyday" in a kind of literal sense. In the years for which I have the most reliable data, 2007 and 2008, there were around 250 annual attacks on Christians in India reported in various media outlets (most of them Christian). Yet from my ethnographic research I know of many attacks during this period that did not reach the attention of journalists, or even that of activists engaged in trying to

---

[1] See, for example, Chad Bauman, "Identity, Conversion and Violence: Dalits, Adivasis and the 2007–08 Riots in Orissa," in *Margins of Faith: Dalit and Tribal Christianity in India*, ed. Rowena Robinson and Joseph Marianus Kujur (Washington, DC: Sage, 2010); PUCL (Bhubaneswar) and Kashipur Solidarity Group, *Crossed and Crucified: Parivar's War against Minorities in Orissa* (Delhi: PUCL, 2009); Vrinda Grover, *Kandhamal: The Law Must Change its Course* (New Delhi: Multiple Action Research Group, 2010); Human Rights Organisations, "From Kandhamal to Karavali: The Ugly Face of the Sangh Parivar" (Nine Human Rights Organisations, 2009); Justice on Trial, *Kandhamal: Root Causes* (Ahmedabad: Justice on Trial, 2008); and Angana Chatterji, *Violent Gods: Hindu Nationalism in India's Present; Narratives from Orissa* (Gurgaon: Three Essays Collective, 2009).

[2] The identity of those who attacked the swami remains uncertain. Naxalites claimed responsibility for the assassination, but many of those engaged in the violence against Christians that resulted continue to believe that Christians had a direct or at least indirect hand in it. Ongoing court cases considering the guilt of several Christians accused of taking part in the assassination will likely not definitively settle the matter. For more, see Bauman, "Identity." The Naxalites are a Far Left radical Maoist/Communist revolutionary group active in large swaths of Indian territory, and particularly in states along India's eastern coast. The rebels draw strength from and build upon popular dissatisfaction with social stratification and economic disparity, and work primarily in rural areas, among tribal and lower-caste peoples. Due to their violent attacks on Indian police and governmental officials and institutions, the Naxalites were officially branded "terrorists" almost from the very moment of their origin, in the late 1960s. The Naxalites do not have a history of collaborating with Christians, but they do seem, in recent years and at least in some locations, to have championed low-caste causes. See Sudeep Chakravarti, *Red Sun: Travels in Naxalite Country* (New Delhi: Penguin, 2008).

reduce the violence. Moreover, the regularity of such attacks on Christians appears to have increased in the years since then, such that today there are probably, on average, about 300 to 400 attacks on Christians every year, or, about one every day.

Second, the attacks are "everyday" in the sense that they do not seem to merit much attention in India. Aside from occasional local reporting, many of the incidents of violence experienced by Christians in India—like more minor hate crimes in the United States—receive very little attention. And most receive none at the national level. They are "everyday," then, in the sense that they are, to many of those who produce and consume Indian media, relatively unremarkable. And the fact that they garner little attention suggests to me that to many Indians they are unsurprising, even expected, or perceived as "normal" and not particularly troubling.

But the attacks are "everyday" in a third sense, and that is that they have become routine, even *routinized*.[3] The everyday violence against Christians that this book examines is entrenched as one relatively regular form—albeit an obviously uncivil one—of communication between Hindus and Christians. The violence also tends to conform to a relatively small number of configurations. There are, for example, patterns in the style of violence deployed in the attacks, and in the presumed goals and identity of the attackers.

For example, those who perpetrate the attacks are more often than not associated with the Sangh Parivar, or the "Family of the Sangh," that is the Rashtriya Swayamsevak Sangh ("National Volunteer Organization," hereinafter RSS), which was founded in 1925 to promote and preserve *Hindutva*, the notion that "Hinduness" (the literal meaning of *Hindutva*) was an essential aspect of Indian identity and the vessel of its "traditional" values. These values, according to the RSS, were under threat from colonial, missionary, and other culturally non-Hindu intrusions. Naturally, then, members of the RSS and other Hindu cultural nationalists considered the growth of Christianity (and other "foreign" religions like Islam) problematic. Before independence, the growth and presence of these religions were viewed as an impediment to the construction of the unity required to successfully repel the British. Afterwards, they were deemed, by Hindu nationalists, a threat to the integrity and survival of the Indian nation itself.

[3.] On the notion of "routine" violence, see Gyanendra Pandey, *Routine Violence: Nations, Fragments, Histories* (Delhi: Permanent Black, 2006).

Over time, the RSS spawned a variety of social, cultural, political, and religious organizations that together comprise the "Sangh Parivar," or "the Sangh," for short. The most important of these, in terms of conflict between Hindus and Christians, are the Akhil Bharatiya Vanvasi Kalyan Ashram, or ABVKA ("All-India Forest-Dweller's Welfare Center," founded in 1952), the Vishwa Hindu Parishad, or VHP ("World Hindu Council," founded in 1964), the VHP's militant youth wing, the Bajrang Dal, or ("Bajrang[4] Party," founded in 1984), and the political party that became, in 1980, the Bharatiya Janata Party, or BJP ("Indian People's Party").[5] The BJP remains one of the two major political parties in India's parliamentary system and is a perennial rival of the more secular Congress Party. As this book went to press, in the spring of 2014, the BJP had just achieved its most impressive national electoral victory ever and was busy forming a new government. Together, individuals associated with all of these groups (or other groups within the Sangh) are named as the perpetrators in nearly every single media report of violence against Christians.

Some caution is necessary, however. As I note below, the media reports of violence against Christians have become as routinized as the violence itself and tend to follow a master narrative, the default assumption of which is that the Sangh is behind every incident. Moreover, in at least some incidents of which I have more intimate knowledge, the victims were aware that those who attacked them were associated at least vaguely with groups espousing a *Hindutva* ideology. But very often they were less certain about with which groups their attackers were specifically affiliated and how formally. So victim and eyewitness testimonies, and the media reports that publicize them, may at times implicate groups which are not

---

[4.] Bajrang is another name for the God, Hanuman, who is portrayed in the *Ramayana* as an ape-like human who assists the young prince, Rama, in his endeavor to rescue his wife from the demon-king, Ravana. By dint of having assisted and protected the God Rama, Hanuman is associated with the defense of Hinduism itself.

[5.] On these groups, see chapter 1, and Christophe Jaffrelot, "Militant Hindus and the Conversion Issue (1885–1990): From Shuddhi to Dharm Parivartan: The Politicization and Diffusion of an 'Invention of Tradition'," in *The Resources of History: Tradition and Narration in South Asia*, ed. J. Assayag (Paris: EFEO, 1990); Christopher Jaffrelot, *The Hindu Nationalist Movement in India* (New York: Columbia University Press, 1996); Christophe Jaffrelot, "The Vishva Hindu Parishad: A Nationalist but Mimetic Attempt at Federating the Hindu Sects," in *Charisma and Canon: Essay on the Religious History of the Indian Subcontinent*, ed. Vasudha Dalmia, Angelika Malinar, and Martin Christof (Delhi: Oxford University Press, 2001); Christopher Jaffrelot, ed., *Hindu Nationalism: A Reader* (Princeton: Princeton University Press, 2007); and Peter van der Veer, *Religious Nationalism: Hindus and Muslims in India* (Berkeley: University of California Press, 1994).

directly involved in the specific incidents of violence they are accused of masterminding.

In addition to patterns in the perpetrators of these attacks, there are clear patterns, as well, in the kinds of Christians targeted. One particularly intriguing pattern in the violence, and that which lies at the center of this book, is that the mainstream[6] Protestant, Catholic, and Orthodox groups that comprise the majority of the Indian Christian community are almost never targeted in the everyday acts of violence against Christians. Rather, the primary victims of the attacks are associated with the missions and churches of Evangelical and especially Pentecostal[7] groups.

Riot violence is not always rational in its methods and targeting. For example, in the interreligious (or "communal"[8]) riot in India, according to

---

[6.] Even though "mainstream" (or "mainline") Protestant is a term more familiar to western Christians than Indian Christians, many Indians do now use it, in part to distinguish "mainstream" Christians from Evangelicals and Pentecostals. When Indians use the term, and when I use it in this book, it refers to groups including (but not limited to) the Methodists, Lutherans, Disciples of Christ, American/British Baptists, Presbyterians, Reformed Churches, and Anglicans/Episcopalians. Outside of the United States, these groups are also often called "ecumenicals," because of their involvement in the global ecumenical movement. And in India, the terms "ecumenical," "mainstream," and "mainline" are used more or less interchangeably to refer in particular to those denominations which came together to create the ecumenical Church of South India (CSI, established in 1947) and Church of North India (or CNI, established in 1970).

[7.] While the reality is much more complicated, of course, scholars of Pentecostal or "Renewalist" movements have found it heuristically useful, to think of three primary "waves" of development. The first, beginning in the early twentieth century, witnessed the rise of Pentecostal denominations like the Assemblies of God and the Church of God in Christ. These groups are often referred to as the "Classical Pentecostals." In the second wave, beginning in the late 1960s and early 1970s, the Pentecostal emphasis on the activity of the Holy Spirit, manifest in expressive worship (including speaking in tongues) made its way into long-established Christian denominations like Roman Catholicism, the Anglican Church, and mainline Protestant denominations, in what is referred to as the Charismatic movement. In the "third wave," which began to build strength in the 1970s, and is perhaps still cresting today, many independent, sectarian congregations (or small groups of congregations) formed, inspired by, but with no strong denominational connection to the Classical Pentecostals or the Charismatics of the first and second wave. These independent congregations are generally referred to as "neo-Charismatic" or "neo-Pentecostal" (though, confusingly, the latter term is sometimes also applied to the second wave Charismatic churches). In this book, when I refer to the disproportionate targeting of "Pentecostals," I use the term to refer primarily to first wave Classical Pentecostals and third wave neo-Charismatics/neo-Pentecostals. For reasons discussed in chapter 2, second wave Charismatic groups are not as frequently targeted in the violence. For a nuanced discussion of the various forms of "renewalist" Christianity (a term which includes all of these groups and a few more) that gets beyond the three main "waves," see Allan Anderson, "Varieties, Taxonomies, and Definitions," in *Studying Global Pentecostalism: Theories and Methods*, ed. Allan Anderson et al. (Berkeley: University of California Press, 2010).

[8.] "Communal," in South Asian usage, points to the emphasizing, exaggeration, or exploitation of differences among (linguistic, caste, religious, etc.) communities for political gain. "Communalism," then, refers to the tensions, conflict, and violence that sometimes results. For a discussion of the putative proclivity of South Asians for "communalism," see the Conclusion.

Paul Brass "there are active, knowing subjects and organizations at work engaged in a continuous tending of the fires of communal divisions and animosities, who exercise . . . a form of control over the incidence and timing of riots. *But their control is not total.*"[9] Riots are, in this sense—to use Donald Horowitz's phrase, "a pickup game."[10] And the more generalized the violence, the evidence suggests to me, the more arbitrary the targeting often turns out to be.

Not surprisingly, then, in the context of the anti-Christian riots in Kandhamal, which involved a large number of non-local participants, the targeting of various Christian denominations appears to have been more balanced and may have even disproportionately affected mainstream Protestant and Catholic groups. Likely, this was due to the fact that the Kandhamal riots, once they began, were not a response to grievances held against particular individuals, but against Christians in general (though surely some of the attackers exploited the cover of generalized violence to carry out vendettas against their neighbors). Large, roving mobs containing a mix of local people and out-of-towners, often unfamiliar with the territory, and working out a generalized grievance against Christians might naturally be expected to look for obvious targets. And the obvious targets in Kandhamal were largely associated with mainstream Protestant and Catholic Christian communities, because of their more established and wealthier institutional presence. (None of this should suggest, however, that there was no targeted violence in Kandhamal, or that there was no trace of what Brass calls an "institutionalized riot system"[11] involving, among other things, organized gangs, apathy and/or cover from sympathetic politicians, and the assumption, on the part of the rioters, of legal impunity. The point is that relative to more isolated attacks on individuals or small groups, the targeting in riot situations, particularly those that spread like the riots in Kandhamal, is less precise.)

In the everyday acts of violence against Christians, however, Pentecostals and *Pentecostalized*[12] Evangelicals are disproportionately targeted. The question that animates this book, then, is, Why? In the 223 incidents of such violence reported in the media in 2007, press reports mentioned the

9. Paul R. Brass, *The Production of Hindu–Muslim Violence in Contemporary India* (New Delhi: Oxford University Press, 2003), 31. Emphasis added.
10. Donald Horowitz, *The Deadly Ethnic Riot* (Berkeley: University of California Press, 2001), 266.
11. Paul R. Brass, *Theft of an Idol: Text and Context in the Representation of Collective Violence* (Princeton: Princeton University Press, 1997), 16.
12. Although the term is a neologism, I do not, hereinafter, italicize it or other forms of it (e.g., "Pentecostalization").

name of a church, mission, or denomination in 147 cases. In those 147 incidents, Catholics were definitely involved in only 13 (9%); mainstream Protestant groups (CNI, CSI, Baptist, etc.), St. Thomas Christians, and the Orthodox were targeted only in 6 (4%). Altogether, then, mainstream Catholic, Protestant, and Orthodox groups were the victims in only 19 (13%) of the attacks. The proportions were similar in 2008.

There may be some irregularity in terms of how consistently different denominations report attacks against their members. Moreover, there is admittedly some uncertainty involved in discerning the denomination of a group by the name of its church or mission. But in most cases, particularly those involving mainstream groups, the denomination was clear even when it was not explicitly given. And even allowing for a relatively large margin of error, it is certain that attacks on mainstream Protestant, Catholic, and Orthodox denominations do not begin to approach proportionality with their demographic presence among Indian Christians, a presence the best statistics estimate at around 50%.[13]

The vast majority of the remaining cases involved violence against independent Evangelicals, Pentecostals, and Charismatics missions and churches. Except in cases that explicitly mention terms like "Pentecostal," the names of these remaining victimized groups or churches alone do not allow us to determine with any certainty their denominational affiliation or self-understanding, and no amount of additional inquiry would succeed in clearly and consistently distinguishing Indian Evangelicals and Pentecostals (defined in the broadest sense) one from another. Yet by process of elimination, as outlined above, it becomes clear that these two groups, taken together, are disproportionately targeted—87% of the time in 2007—in the incidents of everyday violence against Christians. Anecdotal evidence supports the statistical data; though there was some disagreement among my interlocutors, the overwhelming majority identified these groups as the primary targets of violence.[14]

---

[13] See David B. Barrett, George T. Kurian, and Todd M. Johnson, *World Christian Encyclopedia: A Comparative Survey of Churches and Religions in the Modern World*, 2nd ed. (New York: Oxford University Press, 2001), 360. In 2008, the proportion of attacks on Catholics (14%) and total mainstream Protestant, Catholic, and Orthodox (21%) rose significantly, but this reflects the large number of attacks in that year that took place in the context of the Odisha riots (in which, as I've argued, specific targeting declined as mobs in unfamiliar territory targeted clearly recognizable Christian institutions, of which the majority belonged to the older, mainstream Christian denominations).

[14] One reason for disagreement may have been related to the fact, as I've indicated, that mainstream Protestant and Catholic groups were regularly targeted in the Kandhamal violence. So those thinking of violence primarily in that context would have been more inclined to deny the disproportionate targeting of Pentecostals in the "everyday" acts of violence. But among those

The disproportionate targeting of these groups appears somewhat less disproportionate when one considers the distribution of churches rather than members across denominational divides. For example, the General Secretary of the most expansive and statistically inclined missions association in India estimates that there are around 300,000 churches in India, of which approximately 22% are mainline, 36% are Evangelical, 32% are Pentecostal or Charismatic, and the rest (10%) "emerging" independent churches without any clear denominational or institutional structure. These figures align better with the statistics on anti-Christian violence. But we must still answer the question of why the targeting of independent Evangelical, Pentecostal, and Charismatic groups is radically disproportionate to the number of Indians that adhere to them, particularly since, in the incidents of everyday violence (as opposed to large-scale riot violence), individuals rather than institutions tend to be targeted. Much of this book is dedicated to unraveling that particularly knotted question.

Although Pentecostals, like all Christians, frequently experience violence even from non-Christian family members when they first convert, the everyday incidents of violence on which this book focuses are more public and usually involve larger groups of attackers. Most of the attacks take place in the context of either evangelization or worship. And in what follows, I provide several examples of each.

Evangelists who preach in the open air are frequently physically threatened, attacked, beaten, and robbed of their evangelistic literature, Bibles, or other possessions. One Pentecostal pastor I interviewed in Dehradun, for example, was preaching in Rishikesh on the occasion of the Kumbh Mela[15] with several students from a Pentecostal bible college. As he and one of the students began crossing a bridge over the Ganges River, some RSS people saw them and their bag containing around thirty gospels and proverb collections. "They grabbed me," he said:

> and they pushed me to the net [of the suspension bridge]. And because I was a servant of God I was very young and healthy. So I was quite strong. I could do some beatings also, but because I was a servant of God I [couldn't fight

___
thinking primarily in the latter terms, there was widespread agreement about the disproportionate targeting of Pentecostals.

[15.] The Kumbh Mela, largest of all Hindu pilgrimages, is held every three years, rotating among four cities. The *Ardha* (half) Kumbh Mela is held every six years, alternating between Haridwar and Allahabad. It is possible that the pastor telling this story meant to say he was in Haridwar, since Rishikesh is not one of the Kumbh Mela towns. That said, Rishikesh is very close to Haridwar and is visited by a large number of pilgrims on their way to the latter. And so he may have merely been signaling that he was in Rishikesh during this time of heightened pilgrimage traffic.

back]. So they were pulling [out] one book [at a time] and throwing it [into the river] and saying *'Hara, hara Ganga.'* And they threw [away] all the books that way.

"Hara, hara Ganga" is an invocation of the Goddess Ganga, or the river Ganges, over which the altercation was taking place, and the act of jettisoning the gospels one by one while repeating this mantra mimics a central and widespread element of Hindu worship, that is, the throwing of offerings (e.g., flowers) toward an image or symbol of the divine while intoning mantras of praise. Whatever the intended meaning of this symbolic action, the pastor and the student perceived in it a threat to their health and well-being. The student ran for help, and soon a number of police officers arrived. The assailants ran away, but the police caught the leader of the gang. No arrests were made, largely because the pastor refused to press charges. But the police told the RSS leader that they would arrest him if it happened again.

The next day, the pastor was at it again, and was again assailed on one of the bridges crossing the Ganges, this time by two young boys. As they plundered his pack of evangelistic tracts, they challenged him, saying, "What are you doing?"

The pastor replied, defiantly, "I am standing here in my country that allows me to proclaim the word of God anywhere." Again, the pastor was able to escape real harm. "Twice I was caught," he told me, "But I was not beaten. I was about to be beaten, but God's grace saved me."

A non-Pentecostal CNI leader, an old friend of mine, had accompanied me to the pastor's house, and interjected at this point in the interview, "Does [the Pentecostal Bible College with which you are associated] allow Hindus to distribute literature on its campus during conferences?"

"No," the pastor replied.

"But since Christians give tracts at Hindu *melas*, why can't Hindus distribute at Christian conferences?" asked my friend.

"Because they don't really have anything to give to anybody, in the real sense," the pastor returned. "They don't have any good news by which they can attract people."

"But we don't allow the distribution of tracts inside our Christian campus," my friend said. "And Rishikesh is the Hindu 'campus.' Why should they allow if we can't allow?"

This telling exchange reflects disagreements among India's Christians about the desirability and appropriate forms and contexts of Christian evangelism. As might be expected, many Christians associated with the mainstream Catholic and Protestant denominations in India believe, like my friend, that those who are attacked in the context of evangelism bring the attacks upon themselves, by being insensitive (or intentionally provocative) in their choice of timing and location, or in the way they speak about Hindu practices and beliefs. The tension that these disagreements create among India's various Christian communities is one of the topics of chapter 3.

This particular incident was a mild one. Although he may have been slightly roughed up, the pastor was not, as he said, beaten. Moreover, the police in this case were helpful and cooperative. As the forthcoming narratives make clear, however, in the violence against India's Christians, police officers often collude with attackers to enable or prolong the ordeal, or to append legal harassment to the initial physical violence.

Many churches and missions in India currently invest in vacation Bible schools (VBS), hoping, as is the case even with VBS programs in the United States, that parents otherwise uninterested in or opposed to their children receiving Christian education might become less so in exchange for the free or subsidized childcare that VBS provides. Such programs are an increasingly popular form of evangelism, particularly among missionary groups, like those who strategically target the "4/14 window," that is, children between the ages of 4 or 14, who are theorized by some mission groups to be the most receptive to evangelization. Given the success of this implicit compact (i.e., free or cheap childcare in exchange for evangelical access) in getting Christian education to non-Christian children, and the influence VBS programs have over impressionable youth, it should come as no particular surprise that Hindu cultural nationalists find them objectionable. And they have recently become, it seems, something of a target for attacks.

Just before interviewing the pastor roughed up in Rishikesh, I spoke with an evangelist who ran VBS programs in and around Dehradun. He described his faith as Pentecostal, though his church did not formally use the name in order to avoid confining "the Spirit" to a denominational label. In the late 1990s, having just graduated from seminary, he started a VBS program in a rented government school and enrolled around 350 children, all of them Hindu. One morning, he said, soon after the program began:

> some anti elements, they came, got together in a mob. They had chains in their hands, iron rods in their hands, and . . . all sorts of [weapons] in their hands. [They had] one three wheeler with a microphone and loud-speaker. About two–three thousand people got together in a mob and they attacked

the VBS. There were twenty Sunday school teachers. They started beating kids. Beating school teachers. They asked, "Who organized this?"

The evangelist admitted to the attackers that he had organized the VBS and pleaded with them to stop beating the children. Members of the mob then approached two children (who the evangelist believes had been trained to say they had been pressured to convert to Christianity) and made a tape recording of their statements. The police came, took him to the police station, and held him for some time before releasing him. Local reporters picked up the story, and many of their reports appeared to support or at least justify the actions of the attackers.

A week later, during a second week of VBS organized by the same evangelist, the same people came. Again they abused him and his staff physically and verbally. Again the police came and took him away. This time, though, the police officers dealt more roughly with him, and the evangelist believes they were bribed to do so. A reporter who had written negatively about him after the first incident saw him at the police station, and the two began to have a conversation during which the reporter expressed regret for what he had written the previous week. Then a police officer told the reporter that the evangelist would be in jail for three years if he didn't pay a bribe. "These people have a lot of money and they are converting people," the policeman said. By this time, however, the reporter was feeling sorry for having exacerbated the situation; he came to the evangelist's defense, persuaded the police to release him, and took him home, where he and the evangelist found members of the latter's church praying for his release.

If Christian work among children is a flashpoint for violence, Christian work among young adults sometimes also provokes a backlash, as experienced by an independent Pentecostal pastor I met in the villages outside of Hyderabad. As part of his ministry, he used to regularly hold fasting prayer services under a *pandal* (a large tent) with around 150 Christians, mostly youth. According to his testimony, in the middle of one such service, a group of villagers associated with the BJP came, began beating people up, tore down the *pandal*, and overturned the food that had been prepared for the breaking of the fast. While this was going on, members of the mob abused the pastor with "filthy language" and accused him of "deviating the youth." Clearly, then, opponents of Christianity in India are as aware of the impressionability of children and youth as the Christian missionaries who target them, and are, because of this, particularly offended by what seems to them an especially effective way, on the part of Christian missionaries, of exploiting that impressionability for evangelistic gain.

When working with both children and adults, Christian evangelists in India, including Pentecostal evangelists, frequently show films about Jesus to inspire devotion to Christ. Sometimes these films are produced outside of India, but often evangelists show an originally Telugu film, *Karunamayudu* (in English as *Ocean of Mercy*; Tamil as *Karunamoorthy*; Hindi as *Daya Sagar*, etc.) that has been dubbed into many other languages, and that was produced in India, in 1978. The film is, according to many Christians, one of the most effective evangelistic tools they have, and many who view it come away positively impressed with the figure of Jesus. Not surprisingly, then, screenings of the film often draw the attention of those opposed to the spread of Christianity.

While conducting research in a small village outside of Hyderabad, I sat in a small, white-washed church that had been built, I was told, with funds from Joyce Meyer Ministries, across the table from a Pentecostal evangelist who worked in the region. Lowering his voice when he said "the BJP," and thereafter avoiding the acronym altogether because he feared he might be overheard, the pastor told me how, in the middle of a screening of *Karunamayudu* at a government hostel for students, members of "that particular sect" came, beat him up, damaged his projector, and threatened his life.

Similarly, an associate of the pastor who worked in another village, and who was also there for our conversation, told me about his mother, who was transporting some children from the VBS she ran to another town to watch a film about Jesus. Having caught wind of and objecting to her plan, some people associated with the Bajrang Dal—again, the interviewee whispered the name—stopped the vehicle in which she was traveling, dragged her out onto the village's main road, removed her sari, and beat her in front of a crowd of people who did nothing to protect her. In the assault, he said, she fractured several bones and had to be hospitalized for a month, incurring health expenses of over 40,000 rupees (around $800).

Earlier I indicated that most of the everyday attacks on Christians happened in the context of evangelism or worship. The line between the two is, of course, not absolutely clear in all cases. Nevertheless, while evangelism for relatively obvious reasons occasionally provokes a negative response, the provocation involved when worshipping congregations are attacked in their churches or prayer halls is somewhat more difficult to discern.

For example, according to the *Christian Post*, on Independence Day (August 15) of 2007, around twenty anti-Christian activists stormed into a hotel where Christians associated with the Full Gospel Church in Nanjangud, Karnataka, were conducting prayers for the nation. The attackers dragged two pastors and two church members out of the church hall, while abusing them and their fellow congregants. Then they forcibly took the four men to the police station. The police seemed sympathetic to the Christians, but held them under pressure from the attackers, telling them—though it was not true—that prayers could not be held on Independence Day without police permission, and that the Christians would need to return and appear before the police three days later.[16]

Just a few days afterwards, in a suburb of Bangalore (also in Karnataka), a group of fifty attackers disrupted an Indian Pentecostal Church of God congregation's Sunday worship service. Locking all the doors, they began beating church members. And then, after injuring a few of the congregants, the assailants opened up the doors, and chased them out while threatening to burn down the building. As they fled, the Pentecostals reassembled in another home. But to their dismay, the attackers followed and descended upon them there as well.

Similarly, twenty attackers raided a Pentecostal church in Karnataka's Hassan District in November 2007. After chasing away most of the worshippers, the assailants tied two pastors and another male member of the church to a pole, where they were kicked, punched, and otherwise beaten for four hours. Finally, the police came and freed the three men. But instead of detaining the attackers, they allowed them to go free while arresting the pastors and charging them with forced conversion. The pastors were released only later, on bail.[17]

Through extremely common narratives such as these, the outline of a "typical" attack can be roughly delineated. The violence ranges from vandalism to murder,[18] though the vast majority involve mild to severe physical beatings, often accompanied by vandalism. The attacks also frequently result in at least a few of the victims being taken to a police station, where they are further harassed, falsely accused of crimes, or held until they manage, through bribe or bail, to gain their freedom.

Two primary kinds of attack are common. In the first, pastors or evangelists are targeted for their evangelical work, while actually engaged in evangelism or later, in public spaces or their homes. In the second, entire

16. Bei Chatlai Beita, "Independence Day Prayers for India Disrupted, Barred," *Christian Post (Online)*, 16 August 2007, http://www.christianpost.com/news/independence-day-prayers-for-india-disrupted-barred-28915/.

17. Christian Solidarity Worldwide, *India: Religious Violence and Discrimination against Christians in 2007* (Surrey: Christian Solidarity Worldwide, 2008), 42.

18. Whereas in the Kandhamal riots dozens of Christians were killed, murders are relatively rare in the "everyday" incidents of violence against India's Christians. And while several instances of murder occurred during 2007 and 2008, the years for which I have the most complete data, none of the victims were clearly Pentecostal.

congregations become the victims of violence. Generally speaking, attacks of the first variety appear to involve responses to a specific provocation, or to the work of a specific person. Such attacks are frequently more spontaneous, while attacks of the second variety often seem somewhat more organized, and pre-planned. But these are generalizations, of course, and not every incident accords neatly to one or the other of these models.

At one level, the disproportionate targeting of Pentecostals and Pentecostalized Evangelicals in everyday anti-Christian violence makes a certain sense, not only to outside observers but also to Indian Christians and non-Christians. Concerns about the scope and style of Christian evangelism in India have a long history. And still today, many Indians object to the entire evangelistic endeavor, considering the attempt to convert another person to one's faith a betrayal of "real" religion, a socially disruptive, vulgar, and inconsiderate act. A smaller but more energetic subset of Indians seeks, on these grounds, to have proselytization legally banned, and in the absence of progress toward that legal goal, occasionally takes matters into its own hands and tries to make proselytization undesirable or impossible through the harassment of, or by committing outright violence against those who engage in it. (Although there is no clear distinction or obvious line of demarcation between the terms, in this book I tend to use "evangelism" in a more general sense to denote the act of Christians sharing their faith with others, no matter what the goal, method, or style, and "proselytization" in a more specific sense to denote evangelism which is more aggressive, or which has as its chief aim converting others to Christianity.)

If the provocation to which anti-Christian violence is a response is proselytization, then, it would make sense that the groups most regularly attacked in contemporary India would be those most regularly and openly engaged in it. And nearly everyone in India agrees that Pentecostals and Pentecostalized Evangelicals in India are not only the most actively engaged in evangelism but also the most likely to utilize adversarial and antagonistic methods toward their evangelistic ends. The Pentecostals, as one Christian observer I interviewed put it, are more "in your face," on average, than other Indian Christians. And so, at one level, the answer to the question of why such groups are disproportionately targeted appears a rather simple one.

At another level, however, it is clear that this simple answer obscures and masks a more complex reality, and also reflects and derives its prima facie plausibility from certain mainstream Protestant and Catholic prejudices against Pentecostal Christianity. I must admit, despite having no particular allegiance to any of these Christian communities, to sharing many of the same prejudices against Pentecostals as mainstream Protestant and

Catholic Indian Christians. Like them, if I am being honest, I instinctually find Pentecostals' expressiveness and enthusiasm a bit overwhelming, their attention to the spiritual world of spirits and demons irrational and unnerving, and their evangelistic fervor intrusive and uncouth. It was at first easy for me, then, to accept the common and simplest explanation for the disproportionate targeting of Pentecostal Christians at face value, and to unconsciously blame them for the violence against Christians, as many other Indian Christians do.

The assertion that Pentecostal beliefs and practices, and particularly their evangelistic ardency and style, help account for the disproportionate targeting is at least partially correct. But as I investigated the matter further, I came to realize that the very prejudices of mainstream Indian Protestant, Catholic, and Orthodox Christians against Pentecostals were another important part of the story. Intra-Christian and inter-caste dynamics—both of them conspiring to marginalize and make Pentecostals more vulnerable to violence—play an important role in their disproportionate targeting. Interreligious disputes about the propriety of proselytization are one aspect in the disproportionate targeting, then, but do not fully account for it. It was my discovery of this more complicated story that led to the writing of this book.

Recognizing the way that biases against Pentecostal Christians, some of which I myself unconsciously harbored, contributed to the targeting of Pentecostals in contemporary India also demonstrated to me that I would need to develop a greater degree of sympathy for Indian Pentecostal Christians if I wanted to be able to provide a thoughtful account of their disproportionate targeting. And here my own religious biography was of some utility.

Although I grew up Mennonite, socialized in a denomination that in the United States at least has traditionally been about as un-charismatic as any could be, there were church leaders within my family's religious community who, inspired by the influence of Evangelicalism in the 1980s, spoke of engaging in spiritual warfare against demonic forces. Their beliefs and dramatic stories captured my imagination, and for a brief period in my early youth I fancied myself a combatant in this war against the forces of evil, as part of which I occasionally prayed, for example, against the "evil spirits" of social-religious movements and phenomena (e.g., rock music and Wicca!) that I now consider to be utterly fascinating and positive elements of our sociocultural landscape. And then later, during college, I briefly attended a nondenominational church well within the Charismatic-Pentecostal spectrum. Pastors there taught that speaking in tongues was the birthright of all Christians, and I tried for some time, rather unsuccessfully, to claim it.

In the end, I came to believe—and the word seems especially appropriate here—that my convictions regarding spiritual realities and speaking in tongues were largely the result of socialization, suggestion, and social pressure. Nevertheless, I cannot disdain those who still maintain such convictions, because I recognize their allure. There is something deeply appealing about the assertion that spiritual agents are intimately involved in our lives (and those of others), and that by controlling them we might manage to gain some modicum of control over our social and physical environment, and even over our ultimate fate. And this is particularly true in the context of physical and psychological health. There is, moreover, something intoxicating about the collective effervescence of expressive communal worship experiences of Pentecostalism, and something cathartic about ecstatic experiences such as praying in tongues. For this reason, although I am today religiously unmoved by Pentecostal practices, beliefs, and experiences, I understand something of their seductiveness, and of their meaning and value for those who embrace them.

I have therefore tried to retrieve, remember, and draw upon these long abandoned aspects of my own religious biography in order to give to the Pentecostals featured in this book a more sympathetic treatment than they are often granted by western scholars, or even by other Christians. My commitment to looking beyond the simple explanations for why Pentecostals are disproportionately targeted in the violence against India's Christians is the first but not only demonstration of that sympathy. I have also tried to postpone judgment about whether Pentecostals are *to blame* for anti-Christian violence. It is clear enough that the style and fervor of Pentecostal evangelism provokes a backlash, and in some circles, even a violent one. However, accusing Pentecostals of being pugnacious, or even antagonistic, is not the same thing as suggesting that they are *responsible* for anti-Christian violence. To what extent we should hold Indian Pentecostals responsible for the violence they experience is a question that lurks around the edges of this entire monograph, but one that I do not directly consider until the Conclusion.

Data and Methods

Information in this book on the extent and nature of violence against Christians comes from a database I developed for incidents of anti-Christian violence in the years 2007 and 2008. In 2007, there were 223 such incidents; in 2008 the number grew to 279 (for a total of 502). "Violence," as I defined it for the purpose of developing the database, included: (1) any form of physical assault or coercion (e.g., murder, kidnappings, rape, beatings), and/or (2) any act that could intentionally or inadvertently harm an individual or group (e.g., throwing rocks through windows, arson, etc.). The vast majority of the incidents recorded in the database fall into the first category.[19]

The data was drawn primarily from media reports of violence. To gather this data, I paired keyword Internet searches with information from the more systematic incident lists maintained and publicized by three organizations, all of which are Christian: Compass Direct News (http://www.compassdirect.org/), the Global Council of Indian Christians (http://www.persecution.in), and Christian Solidarity Worldwide (http://www.csw.org.uk). It would have been desirable to use government data, or to pair (and compare) government data with that derived from media reports. But the Government of India does not collect—or at least does not publish—data on violence against Christians qua Christians. My database therefore contains the most thorough available catalog of anti-Christian violence for these years.

Christian activist and media narrations of anti-Christian violence tend to adhere to a rather well-rehearsed master narrative that frames "persecution" of Christians in simple terms as the unprovoked work of Hindus opposed to religious freedom and secular governance, and necessitating/justifying intervention not only from India's government but also from foreign powers, the United Nations, NGOs, and Christians worldwide. This master narrative plasters over a variety of more complicated facts that are investigated in later chapters of this book.

We must be wise to the possibility that in order to bolster the plausibility of this "master narrative," Christian media sources have consciously or unconsciously inflated the severity of incidents they chronicle. Nevertheless, I am relatively confident that the number of incidents has not been inflated, because in the course of my own ethnographic research I have been told many stories of attacks that occurred in 2007 and 2008, but which were not registered by these Christian media outlets, and which therefore do not appear in the database.

[19.] While reports of groping and molestation of women occasionally appeared in the media, reports of rape almost never did. It may be the case that there were very few incidents of rape, though the low number of reported cases may result from the fact that rape often goes unreported in India (as elsewhere) because of the social shame involved in being victimized by it.

While the numbers, therefore, are probably not *inflated*, they might still be *distorted* somewhat by the fact that certain denominations have more fully developed marketing and communications capabilities, and would therefore be more able to bring attention to incidents affecting their members. But for a variety of reasons, I doubt that this possible source of distortion would have had more than a very minimal effect on the data.[20] And if there is any bias of this kind at all, it would likely favor the larger, mainstream Indian Christian denominations. Given their institutional size and stability, one would expect them to be better positioned than Pentecostal groups to publicize acts of violence experienced by their members.

The database of incidents provides evidence of the disproportionate targeting of Pentecostals, but is, of course, of no utility in accounting for it. For that, qualitative methods of investigation were necessary. For the most part, though I have occasionally drawn upon data gathered during earlier periods of fieldwork in India, the analyses that follow in this book derive from interviews and ethnographic work conducted over the course of several months and two trips to India in 2011. This work took place almost entirely around the cities of Delhi, Dehradun (Uttarakhand), Pune (Maharashtra), Varanasi (Uttar Pradesh), Raipur (Chhattisgarh), Bangalore (Karnataka), Hyderabad (Andhra Pradesh), and Chennai (Tamil Nadu). But the majority of the interviews were conducted in villages outside of these major urban centers, because violence against Christians in contemporary India is primarily a rural and small-town affair, and happens primarily in the northern and southern states of India (i.e., not in the heavily Christianized northeastern states).

It should be clear from this list, but bears mentioning nonetheless, that I did not conduct research in any of the northeastern Indian states of Assam, Arunachal Pradesh, Meghalaya, Tripura, Nagaland, Manipur, and Mizoram. These states have a unique ethnic and religious identity, and Christianity is far more prevalent there than elsewhere in India, even predominating in many areas. And so while not entirely dissimilar from the rest of India, the region operates according to its own, distinctive dynamics that are not in any thorough way discussed in this book. Therefore, though I speak frequently of "India" in the pages that follow, the reader should keep in mind that the intended referent of the term is not the entirety of the

---

[20.] For a more thorough, state-by-state statistical analysis of the incidents of violence in 2007 and 2008, see Chad Bauman and Tamara Leech, "Political Competition, Relative Deprivation, and Perceived Threat: A Research Note on anti-Christian Violence in India," *Ethnic and Racial Studies* 35, no. 12 (2011): 2195–216.

republic, but rather only its central and southern peninsular parts, or what are more commonly referred to as "North" and "South" India.

I have chosen to obscure the identity of nearly every individual and organization in this book, and have even withheld the names of villages in which certain incidents occurred when I thought conveying these details alone might expose those who had been victimized in them to further violence. Remarkably, despite the regularity of incidents of violence against them, most Indian Christians, even most Indian Pentecostals (at least those outside of Kandhamal) do not seem to live in a constant, chronic state of fear. Rather, theirs is a more acute anxiety, arising only episodically, in the context of the kinds of incidents described in this book. Yet the Christians I interviewed were discreet, particularly in the smaller villages where complete privacy is hard to come by, where citizen's rights and freedoms are more difficult to claim, and where police protection is more regularly unreliable, compromised, capricious, or even colluding. During many of the interviews, including some of those described above, my interlocutors lowered their voices when speaking about those who had attacked them, even when the interviews were conducted indoors. I take a cue from their discretion, metaphorically lowering my voice by not mentioning the names of victims and others whom I consulted in the course of my research, particularly when they told me things that might be controversial.

The only individual exceptions are very public figures, who are by dint of their positions accustomed to being accountable to, and bearing the consequences of their public statements. And the only institutional exception is Gospel for Asia (GFA). Much of what I say about GFA is drawn from the organization's own website, and from the published reflections of its founder, K. P. Yohannan. Moreover, GFA is already very much on the radar of those opposed to the spread of Christianity in India, and I do not in this book reveal anything about the organization that is not already widely known.

Plan of the Book

In chapter 1, I provide some context for the analysis of Indian Pentecostalism by situating it historically within the global Pentecostal movement. India can claim pride of place in this history; though many scholars continue to privilege the revival in 1906, on Azusa Street, in Los Angeles, as Pentecostalism's founding moment, Pentecostal-like renewal movements surfaced in India as early as 1860 and continued right up through the beginning of the twentieth century. Chapter 1 also briefly describes the growth of Pentecostalism in India, which has been particularly spectacular since the 1970s, before dealing with some of the definitional issues that plague the study of Pentecostalism in India, as elsewhere.

Chapter 2 provides information on the context in which anti-Christian violence occurs, a kind of bare bones primer for those not terribly familiar with Indian Christian history or contemporary Indian debates about conversion, the putative "foreignness" of Christianity, and the appropriateness of proselytization. In the first half of the chapter, I sketch a history of Hindu–Christian conflict, from India's earliest Christians, the famous St. Thomas Christians of what is today Kerala and Tamil Nadu, through the colonial era and the rise of Hindu nationalism, to the present day. Through this history I show that violent encounters between Christians and Hindus qua Christians and Hindus are the result of contingent contextual factors (including most importantly, colonialism) and are not necessarily inherent or inevitable in the interaction of adherents of these two faiths. In the second half of the chapter, I consider the criticisms of those opposed to Indian Christianity, or at least to Christian proselytization, from Mohandas Gandhi to more contemporary figures like Arun Shourie, paying particular attention to the ways that Pentecostals are, or are not, implicated in their critiques.

Drawing upon interviews with Indian Christians and Hindus, and providing illustrative narrative examples of violence against Pentecostals, chapter 3 deals directly with the central question at hand, that is: How are we to account for the disproportionate targeting of Indian Pentecostal Christians in contemporary anti-Christian violence? As adumbrated earlier, the superficially obvious answer is evangelism, and there is no doubt that the evangelistic enthusiasm of many Pentecostals (indeed, their enthusiasm in general), and their tendency to speak in the idiom of spiritual warfare, offends and creates tensions with many non-Christian Indians. But the obviousness of this factor has often impeded the development of more nuanced, complicated, and accurate explanations for the disproportionate targeting of Pentecostal Christians, and chapter 3 attempts to get rather quickly beyond it by focusing on two less obvious factors: (1) the greater social marginalization and vulnerability of Pentecostals and Pentecostal churches, and (2) their consistently countercultural posture, which leads some Pentecostals to intentionally adopt antagonistic modes of communication with non-Christians in order to provoke reactions, even violent ones, as confirmation of their commitment to the evangelistic cause. As the enumeration of these additional factors suggests, while superficial explanations of the disproportionate targeting of Pentecostal Christians tend to exclusively emphasize interreligious (i.e., Hindu–Christian) dynamics, the more thorough analyses provided in chapter 3 point to the equal importance of intra-Christian dynamics in the marginalization, vulnerability, and disproportionate targeting of Pentecostal Christians.

Drawing upon fieldwork in both North and South India, chapter 4 describes the nature of Christian, and particularly Pentecostal supernatural healing in India; the way it functions in Indian Christian society to confirm faith, provoke conversions, and activate ministry; and its growing centrality to Christian mission on the subcontinent. While the relevance of Pentecostal faith healing to questions of violence may not be immediately clear, I argue that the emergence of Pentecostal faith healing as a (if not the) primary factor in conversions to Christianity in India today alters contemporary debates about conversion in significant ways. Unlike massive missionary medical institutions, faith healers cannot be accused of luring impecunious Hindus to the Christian faith through potent demonstrations of medical prowess enabled by foreign funding. Similarly, Pentecostal faith healers, whose practices draw upon and in many ways resemble those of Hindu and other non-Christian Indian healers, cannot be accused of having an obviously westernizing influence. Pentecostal faith healing therefore undermines two of the most common complaints about Indian Christianity: (1) that it succeeds by exploiting its greater access to western wealth and power, and (2) that it leads in every situation to westernized ways of thinking and acting.

If there is some correlation between the presence and activity of Pentecostal Christians and incidents of anti-Christian violence, then it is logical to hypothesize that significant variation in the former may affect the nature and frequency of the latter. With this in mind, chapter 5 investigates a number of important recent trends in the global missionary movement and concludes that they favor the growth of Pentecostalism and the increasing Pentecostalization of all Indian Christianity. As might be inferred from this, one of the central arguments of this chapter is that the future of Pentecostal Christians in India, and of the violence against India's Christians, will not merely be a function of internal Indian dynamics, but, rather, will be affected in appreciable ways by transnational flows of Christian money, missionary methods, and theology. Along the way, the chapter looks closely at the complications of foreign funding, and the effects of anti-Christian violence on the nature and scope of missionary work in India (with special reference to Pentecostal Christianity).

In the Conclusion, then, I take the various components of this volume's analyses into account in order to make the argument that the disproportionate targeting of Pentecostals and Pentecostalized Evangelicals in contemporary anti-Christian violence is not just a matter of current social, cultural, political, and interreligious dynamics internal to India, but is rather related to identifiable historical trends, as well as to historical and contemporary transnational flows of people, power, and ideas. The conclusion also highlights and interrogates the presumed "naturalness" of violence as a reaction to the provocation of proselytization, and then, in the final pages, takes up the question of whether and in what context it makes sense to hold provocative proselytizers responsible for the violence they (and others) suffer, what kinds of assumptions or prejudices the question itself might cloak, and even whether the question is appropriate to ask in a scholarly work.

This book deals with complicated and controversial subjects. Among the ways I have tried to simplify things is to remain obsessively focused on the central puzzle of the disproportionate targeting of Indian Pentecostals in contemporary anti-Christian violence. Many scholarly texts on what in India is generally called "communal" violence succumb quickly and frequently to the temptation to demonize the perpetrators of the violence, and do so with peremptory judgment and a kind of dramatic rhetorical flourish that seems almost demanded by the blatant bigotry and tragic violence being described. While there is reason to censure acts of violence as the condemnable acts they are, and while nothing in these pages should be taken to absolve those that engage in criminal assaults, the victims, not the perpetrators, are the focus of the book. I have therefore tried to avoid ad hominem castigations of the Sangh Parivar, and have also tried to find mediating ground, in my depictions of the violence, between overly bland descriptions that would not adequately honor the damage done to victims' bodies, minds, and souls, and overly sensational or lurid accounts that might risk appearing to exploit that damage to hasten judgment upon its perpetrators, or even for my own scholarly or fiduciary advantage (e.g., in the sale of a few more books).

I have, for the same reason, generally chosen the blander "low-caste" over the more politicized "*dalit*," and the less loaded "tribal," or the Indian bureaucratic "scheduled tribe" (ST) over the competing alternatives of "*adivasi*" and "*vanvasi*."[21] The politics that are signaled by one's choices

---

[21.] "*Vanvasi*" (forest-dweller) is the preferred term of the Sangh Parivar, because it does not grant to the tribals the status of "original inhabitant," which is the literal meaning of "*adivasi*," the term preferred by those that seek to shelter the tribals from Sangh (and other outsiders') influence. On the politics involved, see Nandini Sundar, "Adivasi vs. Vanvasi: The Politics of Conversion and Re-conversion in Central India," in *Assertive Religious Identities,* ed. Satish Saberwal and Mushirul Hasan (New Delhi: Manohar, 2006).

in these terminological matters are related, of course, to the subject of this book. And no term is neutral or value-free. But I have chosen to narrow the range of the controversies in which I engage, and I hope that by so doing, I will increase the likelihood that readers from across the political spectrum will be able to engage the many intricacies of this difficult subject with an open mind.

Where, then, does the "spirit" of anti-Christian violence lead? Clearly, for a variety of reasons, to India's Pentecostals. And like the evil spirits of Pentecostal demonology, the spirit of anti-Christian violence is hell-bent on wreaking havoc in the hearts, minds, and bodies of India's Christians. India's Pentecostals are not fully responsible for the violence they and other Christians experience, for just as the Pentecostal belief in malignant spirits and demons shifts some of the responsibility for evil behavior away from the agency of humans, so too does the fact that the spirit of anti-Christian violence has a mind and agency of its own shift blame away from Pentecostals. There are certainly factors in the targeting of Pentecostals in anti-Christian violence over which they have no control, including the fact that their social location makes them particularly vulnerable to attack. But just as Pentecostals believe that their faith, or lack thereof, affects the extent to which they are vulnerable to spiritual attack, so it is with the spirit of anti-Christian violence. For while Pentecostals may not be directly responsible for the violence they experience, they do, in a variety of ways, make themselves more vulnerable to it by provoking, and even, occasionally, celebrating it.

CHAPTER 1 | Who Are India's Pentecostals?
History, Definitions, Deliberations

THE MINISTERIAL CAREER OF one Chhattisgarhi pastor I interviewed serves as a demonstration of the difficulty inherent in trying to reify and define Indian Pentecostalism. Born a Mennonite (a denomination whose Indian adherents identify more easily and clearly with Evangelicalism than their North American counterparts), he began moving to more and more Charismatic Mennonite congregations, and then to a nondenominational church established by the famous, personally charismatic Indian evangelist, Bakht Singh. Later he joined an Assemblies of God Church, which he left to become a wandering evangelist. Eventually he became a pastor, and moved to Dehradun, where he became associated with the Pentecostal Doon Bible College (DBC). He continues to self-identify as Evangelical, but pastors a Pentecostal church attended by many DBC students, who are, as I indicate below, in many ways themselves indistinguishable from Evangelicals.

There is much debate in scholarly circles about how to define Pentecostals and differentiate them from other groups. In this chapter, I therefore take up the question of definition, with special attention to the Indian context, and to the history of Pentecostalism in the subcontinent. Defining Pentecostalism, and determining the central characteristics of Indian Pentecostalism, is important in the context of this book precisely because many of the factors in the disproportionate targeting of Pentecostals are related to their distinctive characteristics. Moreover, for similar reasons, it is important that we attempt to clearly delineate what makes Pentecostals different from other kinds of Indian Christians.

In no case is this more difficult than when one tries to differentiate Indian Pentecostals from Indian Evangelicals. It is common for scholars (with differing degrees of self-consciousness) to conceive of Evangelicalism and Pentecostalism, respectively, as genus and species, implying that Pentecostalism can be relatively easily distinguished from other, non-Pentecostal species of Evangelicalism. In the Indian context, however, it may be more appropriate to think of Evangelicalism and Pentecostalism as two similar species of Christianity that have produced both novel surviving hybrid species—*Lonicera* flies of the religious realm—and a hybrid swarm of interbreeding, backcrossing, intraspecific hybrids. To signal this complexity, and to refer to these hybrids, which are not always clearly identifiable as belonging to one or the other of the two "species," I frequently resort to the imprecise but heuristically useful term, "Pentecostalized Evangelicals." While certain kinds of Evangelicals in India are not targeted terribly frequently in the violence, those that fall into the category of "Pentecostalized Evangelicals" are targeted as frequently (or almost as frequently) as Pentecostals themselves.

Indian Pentecostals and Charismatics in the Global Context

While acknowledging antecedents in the Evangelical awakenings of the late nineteenth century, many early histories of Pentecostalism tended to focus on the Azusa Street revival that took place in Los Angeles, beginning in 1906, as the origin and ancestor of all forms of Pentecostalism today. While Azusa Street was undeniably a catalytic moment in the history of the movement, the centering of the United States in early Pentecostal historiography surely also reflected certain American prejudices about the centrality of America (and the West more generally) in the development and global expansion of Christianity.

More recently, scholars have begun to stress the "polycentric"[1] origins of Pentecostalism, recognizing not only antecedents in Western awakenings and the holiness movement but also a number of Pentecostal precursors elsewhere. When the story is told in this way, India figures prominently because of a series of Indian Christian revivals in the late nineteenth and early twentieth centuries that featured phenomena like those manifest in Azusa's spirit-oriented movement (among them, significantly, speaking

---

[1] Allan Anderson, "Varieties, Taxonomies, and Definitions," in *Studying Global Pentecostalism: Theories and Methods,* ed. Allan Anderson et al. (Berkeley: University of California Press, 2010), 25.

in tongues). Indian revivals displaying Pentecostal spiritual experiences occurred as early as 1860 among Indian Christians influenced by the Plymouth Brethren, continued through 1873, in Indian Anglican (Church Missionary Society) circles, and then spread to the Khasi Hills in 1905, among Presbyterian missions inspired by the Welsh revival.[2]

The most important Indian revival, however, took place at the Mukti Mission of Pandita Ramabai, where, beginning in 1905, hundreds of young women, many of them poor orphans, child widows, or famine victims, experienced healings, prophecies, and the gift of tongues. Immediately, the mission began sending out "praying bands" to spread the revival, and even more significantly, perhaps, for the future development and growth of Pentecostalism, was the fact that the Mukti Mission hosted a large number of international missionaries (including, eventually, missionaries from Azusa Street) who became important figures in the dispersion of Pentecostalism around the globe.[3]

Michael Bergunder argues that it was the development of a large and active global Pentecostal missionary network (more than the influence of any particular revival) that accounts for the rapid growth of Pentecostalism at the beginning of the twentieth century.[4] Over time, both the experiences of the Azusa Street revivalists and their distinctive interpretations of their experiences (e.g., of tongues as the initial and only sure evidence of baptism by the Holy Spirit) came to dominate the thinking of this missionary network, and therefore the nascent Pentecostal movement. In this sense, then, Azusa Street remains important.

Nevertheless, early non-Western sources of Pentecostalism must be given their due, and, as Allan Anderson argues, "this is especially true of the Mukti revival, because the Pentecostal phenomena of healings, tongues, and prophecy also occurred there, and it was a must-see place

[2] Arun Jones, "Faces of Pentecostalism in North India Today," *Society* 46, no. 6 (2009); Wonsuk Ma, "Asian (Classical) Pentecostal Theology in Context," in *Asian and Pentecostal: The Charismatic Face of Christianity in Asia*, ed. Allan Anderson and Edmond Tang (Costa Mesa, CA: Regnum, 2005); Allan Anderson, "Revising Pentecostal History in Global Perspective," in *Asian and Pentecostal: The Charismatic Face of Christianity in Asia*, ed. Allan Anderson and Edmond Tang (Costa Mesa, CA: Regnum, 2005); and Roger Hedlund, "Indigenous Pentecostalism in India," in *Asian and Pentecostal: The Charismatic Face of Christianity in Asia*, ed. Allan Anderson and Edmond Tang (Costa Mesa, CA: Regnum, 2005).
[3] Ramabai had attended a Keswick convention in 1898. Todd Johnson and Kenneth Ross, *Atlas of Global Christianity 1910–2010* (Edinburgh: Edinburgh University Press, 2009), 100; Jones, "Faces"; and Michael Bergunder, *The South Indian Pentecostal Movement in the Twentieth Century* (Grand Rapids, MI: Eerdmans Publishers, 2008), chapter 1.
[4] Michael Bergunder, "The Cultural Turn," in *Studying Global Pentecostalism: Theories and Methods*, ed. Allan Anderson et al. (Berkeley: University of California Press, 2010), 60–63.

of pilgrimage for international travelers."[5] Fanning out from the Mukti Mission, or arriving directly from abroad, foreign Pentecostal missionaries began establishing churches, and, over time, what have come to be known as the "classical" Pentecostal denominations (e.g., the Assemblies of God) in various parts of India. In nearly every case, they were assisted by Indian missionaries, some of whom became instrumental in the inauguration and/or growth of distinctively South Asian Pentecostal denominations, like the Ceylon Pentecostal Mission (1923) and the Indian Pentecostal Church (1933).

Pentecostalism grew steadily but not remarkably in India until after independence in 1947. In the 1960s and early 1970s, Pentecostalized faith and worship began to make inroads into the Catholic Church and the older, established Protestant denominations in the form of the Charismatic movement, while over the next few decades independent "neo-Pentecostal" or "neo-Charismatic"[6] denominations and churches emerged from (or beside) the older, more established Pentecostal denominations and proliferated rapidly. The growth of Pentecostal and Charismatic Christianity accelerated dramatically after this period, in India and around the world.

The expansion of neo-Pentecostalism also contributed to the progressive fracturing and diffusion of the Pentecostal movement. In India, this fracturing allowed space for the emergence of lower caste Pentecostal leaders, who had chafed under the leadership of upper caste Christians and therefore established their own independent churches and denominations, some of which drew members exclusively from the lower castes. Though discernible all over India, the shift was particularly conspicuous in Kerala and other areas of the South, where leadership of the Pentecostal movement had previously been dominated by higher caste Christians.[7] The emergence of lower caste Pentecostal leadership has had important consequences for Pentecostals in India and may be one factor in their disproportionate targeting.

Today, the most commonly adduced estimate suggests that there are around 500 million Pentecostal and Charismatic Christians worldwide,

---

[5.] Anderson, "Varieties," 25.
[6.] Churches manifesting theologies and ritual practices similar to that of earlier Pentecostals and Charismatics, but outside of the traditional denominational space those earlier groups inhabited.
[7.] Jones, "Faces"; V. V. Thomas, *Dalit Pentecostalism: Spirituality of the Empowered Poor* (Bangalore: Asian Trading Corporation, 2008); and Allan Anderson, "Introduction: The Charismatic Face of Christianity in Asia," in *Asian and Pentecostal: The Charismatic Face of Christianity in Asia*, ed. Allan Anderson and Edmond Tang (Costa Mesa, CA: Regnum Books, 2005).

representing a quarter of the global Christian population and two-thirds of all Protestants. In Asia, Pentecostal and Charismatic Christians now comprise approximately one-third of all Christians.[8] Official Indian estimates, based on census reporting, generally assert that Christians constitute 2.3% of the population, a percentage that would mean there were today around 27 million Christians (based on a total Indian population of 1.2 billion, as of 2011). However, statisticians working with alternative sources of data estimate the number of Indian Christians to be much higher. According to them, if one includes in one's statistics marginal Christian groups that deviate from some of the more common Christian orthodoxies, secret Christians who are devoted to Christ but who do not publicly declare their allegiance (or their exclusive allegiance) to Christ, and those who might more publicly profess their Christianity but who, in order to preserve their access to lower caste reservations, do not officially declare themselves Christian in response to census questionnaires, then the number of Indian Christians is probably actually closer to 58 million (i.e., 4.8% of the total Indian population).[9]

How many of those Indian Christians are Pentecostal or Charismatic is not entirely certain. The *Atlas of Global Christianity* estimates that there are roughly 30 million "Renewalist" Christians in India. "Renewalist" is a widely inclusive term the editors of the *Atlas* employ to refer to nearly everything that could be considered Pentecostal or Charismatic (e.g., the Roman Catholic Charismatic renewal, classical Pentecostal denominations, neo-Pentecostals/neo-Charismatics, and denominationally independent Protestants who might be Pentecostalized in theology and worship, but who are not affiliated with any classical Pentecostal denomination). If the *Atlas* is correct, then around 50% of India's Christians are Renewalist Christians, and these communities are growing quickly (compared to other Christians), at a rate of around 5% a year.[10] At first glance, these percentages seem entirely too high. Yet the degree of Pentecostalization in India is so stunning, and the *Atlas*'s definition so inclusive, that its figures are quite likely an accurate rough estimate both of the size and of the proportion of

---

[8] David B. Barrett, George T. Kurian, and Todd M. Johnson, *World Christian Encyclopedia: A Comparative Survey of Churches and Religions in the Modern World*, 2nd ed. (New York: Oxford University Press, 2001); Allan Anderson et al., "Introduction," in *Studying Global Pentecostalism: Theories and Methods*, ed. Allan Anderson et al. (Berkeley: University of California Press, 2010), 2; and Anderson, "Charismatic Face."

[9] Barrett, Kurian, and Johnson, *Encyclopedia*; and Johnson and Ross, *Atlas*.

[10] "Renewalist" Christianity is growing at a rate of 5.02% in South Asia, more than in any other UN region by a significant margin. Johnson and Ross, *Atlas*, 102–3.

Charismatic, Pentecostal, and Pentecostalized Christianity in India. For reasons I note in the next chapter, however, Charismatic Catholics are quite infrequently targeted in acts of violence. And so, when I speak of the "disproportionate targeting of Pentecostals," I refer primarily to the Protestant elements of this larger realm of "Renewalist" Christianity.

Defining the Field

As a discerning reader will have already intuited, estimates regarding the presence and growth of Pentecostalism worldwide depend significantly on the definitions one deploys. One of the defining features of contemporary Pentecostal Christianity is its sectarian and fissiparous nature, and the growth of neo-Pentecostalism, and its legions of independent and semi-independent churches, the "hybrid swarm" previously mentioned, has complicated issues of definition and identification exponentially. Moreover, the Pentecostal emphasis on freedom in the spirit, and freedom to follow the spirit where it leads, creates a scenario in which Pentecostalism is always in a state of becoming, always emergent and yet-to-be-determined. Every Pentecostal generation is, as Everett Wilson points out, "the first generation."[11] James Clifford famously quipped that cultures do not stand still for their portraits,[12] and in portraits of the Christian family, Pentecostalism is the rutchy, restless, unruly child, always appearing blurred and out of focus. (Thankfully, like Hindu devotees of Krishna the toddler/butter thief, I have a certain fondness for mischievous children.)

Most scholars of Pentecostalism agree that there are several broad movements of the last century that bear a "family resemblance" and should therefore be understood as related to one another, part of an expansive (and expanding) Pentecostal family tree.[13] There is general consensus about the core branches of this tree, which Walter Hollenweger identified as: (1) the

---

[11] Everett Wilson, "They Crossed the Red Sea, Didn't They? Critical History and Pentecostal Beginnings," in *The Globalization of Pentecostalism,* ed. Marray Dempster, Byron Klaus, and Douglas Petersen (Irvine, CA: Regnum, 1999), 106.

[12] James Clifford, "Introduction: Partial Truths," in *Writing Culture: The Poetics and Politics of Ethnography,* ed. James Clifford and George E. Marcus (Berkeley: University of California Press, 1986), 10. Also quoted in Sushil Aaron, "Emulating Azariah: Evangelicals and Social Change in the Dangs," in *Evangelical Christianity and Democracy in Asia,* ed. David H. Lumsdaine (New York: Oxford University Press, 2009), 90.

[13] The term "family resemblance" is, of course, Wittgenstein's. For an application of the notion to the study of Pentecostalism, see Anderson, "Varieties," 15.

"classical" Pentecostal denominations (e.g., Assemblies of God, Church of God [Cleveland, Tennessee], Church of God in Christ) that emerged or became Pentecostal in the first decades of the twentieth century; (2) the Charismatic renewal that began among Anglican, Catholic, and the mainline Protestant churches in the 1960s and 1970s; and (3) Pentecostal-like independent churches (i.e., what others have called neo-Charismatic or neo-Pentecostal churches), the growth of which became particularly discernible in the 1970s.[14] These three are also frequently referred to, respectively, as the first, second, and third waves of the global Pentecostal movement, and each wave has grown in strength, so to speak. The *Atlas of Global Christianity* estimates their numbers worldwide—again, respectively—at 94 million, 206 million, and 313 million.[15]

Scholars such as Allan Anderson,[16] Peter Wagner,[17] and others have attempted to add additional categories, but beyond the three core branches of the Pentecostal family tree, scholarly consensus molders. And though Barrett's inclusive definition of "Renewalists," which would include each of the three waves and many more, dominates current scholarly work on Pentecostalism, its expansiveness makes it difficult to deploy with any precision and impedes attempts to clearly differentiate Pentecostals from other Christians.[18]

Those who attempt to secern Pentecostals from other Christians with reference to their ostensibly distinctive theology focus, usually, on the common Pentecostal understanding of glossolalia as "initial evidence" of Holy Spirit baptism. Such definitions are seductively simple, but also fatally so, because there are Pentecostals all over the world (including in India) who do not embrace this understanding, and many now only rarely (if at all) feature tongues in their worship services. Bergunder reports that among the South Indian Pentecostals he analyzed, and even among neo-Pentecostals, belief in tongues as "initial evidence" was nearly universal.[19] But my own fieldwork suggests greater variability. Many neo-Pentecostal pastors I interviewed conceived of tongues as a sign of commitment, piety, and belief, but

---

[14.] Walter J. Hollenweger, *Pentecostalism: Origins and Developments Worldwide* (Peabody, MA: Hendrickson, 1997), 1.

[15.] Johnson and Ross, *Atlas*, 102.

[16.] Allan Anderson, "Pentecostal and Charismatic Movements," in *Encyclopedia of Mission and Missionaries*, ed. Jonathan J. Bonk (New York: Routledge, 2007), 332; and Anderson, "Varieties," 17–20.

[17.] Anderson, "Varieties," 22–23; and C. Peter Wagner, *Churchquake: How the New Apostolic Reformation is Shaking up the Church as We Know It* (Ventura, CA: Regal Books, 1999).

[18.] Bergunder, "Cultural Turn," 52–53.

[19.] Bergunder, *South Indian*, 141–43.

not necessarily the sole indicator of Holy Spirit baptism, and this conception is consistent with global neo-Pentecostal trends.[20] The wide range of Pentecostal opinions on tongues also undermines the once common assertion that Pentecostalism is "Evangelicalism + tongues,"[21] as does the fact that many self-identified Evangelicals in India believe in and/or have experienced the gift of tongues.

Other theological definitions suggest that Pentecostals share a common theological emphasis on the Holy Spirit. Apart from being rather vague, such definitions fail to recognize that common experiences and a common desire for certain kinds of experiences unite Pentecostals far more than theology or doctrine. Robert M. Anderson therefore usefully situates Pentecostalism within a broad movement of churches "concerned primarily with the *experience* of the working of the Holy Spirit and the *practice* of spiritual gifts."[22]

Anderson's position suggests that there may be virtue in adopting a phenomenological approach to defining Pentecostalism. Jacobsen concurs, averring succinctly that "in a general sense, being Pentecostal means that one is committed to a Spirit-centred, miracle-affirming, praise-oriented version of the Christian faith."[23] And André Drooger's sociological definition of Pentecostalism notes a "central emphasis on the experience of the Spirit, accompanied by ecstatic manifestations such as speaking in tongues."[24]

All of these definitions mention Pentecostal worship, the expressiveness of which is also, of course, related to belief in the pervasive presence and activity of the spirit that is discussed below. But the distinctiveness of Pentecostal worship also has theoretical ramifications. Drawing upon her research on Ghanaian Pentecostals, Birgit Meyer stresses the "materiality" of Pentecostal worship, and the centrality of "sensational forms," which "address people by appealing to the senses and the body in distinct ways and by forming specific religious subjects."[25] This element of

---

[20.] On this, see Henri Gooren, "Conversion Narratives," in *Studying Global Pentecostalism: Theories and Methods,* ed. Allan Anderson et al. (Berkeley: University of California Press, 2010), 100.

[21.] Bergunder, *South Indian*, 2.

[22.] The quotation is Allan Anderson's paraphrase of Robert M. Anderson's argument. The paraphrase appears in Allan Anderson, *An Introduction to Pentecostalism: Global Charismatic Christianity* (New York: Cambridge University Press, 2004), 14. See also Anderson, "Varieties," 16–17. The original argument appears in Robert Mapes Anderson, *Vision of the Disinherited: The Making of American Pentecostalism* (New York: Oxford University Press, 1979), 4.

[23.] Quoted in Anderson, "Varieties," 26.

[24.] As paraphrased by Anderson, "Varieties," 21.

[25.] Birgit Meyer, "Pentecostalism and Globalization," in *Studying Global Pentecostalism: Theories and Methods*, ed. Allan Anderson et al. (Berkeley: University of California Press, 2010), 122.

Pentecostalism is quite frequently neglected by scholars, but the palpable and relatively greater importance of feeling, of expression, of suggestion, and even of what Émile Durkheim called "collective effervescence" in the production of Pentecostal worship and Pentecostal subjects leads Meyer, and me along with her, to conceive of Pentecostal religion more along Durkheimian than (William) Jamesian lines. James's insistence on placing the "genesis of religious experience in private feelings," Meyer correctly contends, neglects "the importance of religious forms in generating religious experience as well as the role of authorized structures of repetition in shaping and affirming specific religious subjectivities."[26]

Not surprisingly, the Holy Spirit, and manifestations of it, features prominently in the phenomenological descriptions of Pentecostalism given above. Among Indian Pentecostals, the presence and activity of the Holy Spirit is not merely an abstract, hypothetical reality, as it is for many mainstream Protestant, Catholic, and Orthodox Christians. It is, rather, a constant and tangible presence, one which transforms both the experience and interpretation of all Christian ritual and dogma. For example, while praying over the Eucharist before distributing the bread and grape juice, a Pentecostal pastor in a Bangalore church I visited petitioned, in an idiom one would never hear among mainstream Protestants or Catholics, "With this bread and cup, Lord, *bring something supernatural.*"

Pentecostals in India (and elsewhere) generally agree that there are nine spiritual gifts available to the church. These gifts are mentioned in 1 Corinthians 12:8–10, and include (1) the "word of knowledge"; (2) the "word of wisdom";[27] (3) the ability to discern, identify, and thwart the presence and workings of evil spirits; (4) faith; (5) the ability to heal and experience healing through the power of God; (6) the ability to work miracles; (7) to prophecy; (8) to speak in tongues; and (9) to interpret the tongues of others. Bergunder suggests that among the South Indian Pentecostals he studied, tongues, the interpretation of tongues, healing, prophecy, and the word of knowledge receive special emphasis.[28] My own fieldwork confirms Bergunder's assertion, though with the caveat that the discernment of spirits be considered an integral element of healing. Belief in the ability of God (and faith in God) to miraculously heal and preserve health is one thing that clearly differentiates most Pentecostals from

---

[26.] Meyer, "Pentecostalism," 123.

[27.] Both the "words" of knowledge and wisdom involve becoming a temporary conduit for a supernatural revelation from the Holy Spirit.

[28.] Bergunder, *South Indian*, 146.

mainstream Protestants, Catholics, and the Orthodox, for whom God's ability to heal generally manifests in far less supernatural ways, and most regularly through the hands of a trained, allopathic doctor. But even this distinction breaks down in rural India, where belief in healing through direct divine intervention is found among almost all Christian communities. Chapter 4 is devoted to an analysis of the gift of healing, exorcism, and the discernment of spirits in India. Here, however, I will devote a few paragraphs to each of the other five gifts that Bergunder identifies as having special importance among Indian Pentecostals.

The general nature of glossolalia, as a phenomenon, is relatively widely understood. Gone are the days that Pentecostals believed the spirit gave them the ability to speak in foreign tongues (xenoglossolalia) as early, soon-to-be-disillusioned Pentecostal missionaries[29] believed, based on their reading of Acts 2:11. Rather, glossolalia today sounds to outsiders rather like gibberish or a made-up language. Many practice the gift of tongues only in private prayer, and some Pentecostal pastors insist that is where it belongs. As one Indian Pentecostal pastor put it, while defending his church's prohibition against the expression of tongues in church services: "God is silent." But in other Pentecostal contexts, glossolalia frequently occurs during worship services, usually in the context of moments of collective prayer or praise. Among English-speaking Indian Pentecostals, such prayers often begin with the quiet repetition of "Jesus," "yes, Jesus," or "praise Jesus," the sibilants in these phrases blending together into what sounds like a chorus of whispers, or the rising and falling hiss of breaking waves heard from a distance. Sometimes, but not always, these phrases give way to glossolalia, at least among some members of the congregation. And then usually, toward the end of the time of prayer or praise, the language switches—to use the words of 1 Corinthians 13:1—back again from the tongues of angels to that of humans. Those who are able to interpret tongues are expected to do so, and many Indian Pentecostals believe that one should not speak in tongues unless an interpreter is available.

Prophecy is also held in high regard among Indian Pentecostals and Charismatics, and generally takes place in the context of worship services (though prophecies can be given privately as well). Women and the laity frequently prophesy in some Indian Pentecostal churches;[30] in other Pentecostal contexts (such as an Assemblies of God church I visited

---

[29.] Ibid., 5.
[30.] Ibid., 171.

in Bangalore) only the senior pastor (a male) regularly prophesies. The content of prophecy ranges from the very general, where it is sometimes indistinguishable from a "prophetic" sermon encouraging or demanding renewal, transformation, and reform, to the specific (e.g., "naming" a particular individual for whom God has a specific message and then relaying that message to the person named). And while prophecies sometimes involve actual predictions of things that will happen to individuals, they can also involve predictions of future social, geopolitical, or environmental events. In some cases, Pentecostal prophecies involve a word of encouragement (often to ministry) aimed at particular people; such prophecies are known as a "word of knowledge."

Closely related to, and sometimes indistinguishable from the prophetic "word of knowledge" is the "word of wisdom" that involves the supernatural revelation of God's will, or an interpretation of mundane events from a supernatural perspective. While conducting fieldwork on the outskirts of Dehradun, in northern India, I received my very own word of wisdom. After Sunday worship in a thatched-roof, Pentecostal church located near a shockingly polluted and parched creek bed desperately craving the cleansing monsoon, a man approached me with some urgency. Without introduction, and standing somewhat closer than I might have liked, he soberly unleashed an unwavering, prolix concatenation of words.

The "word of wisdom" was about Muammar Gaddafi and the chaos in Libya, which the United States was at that time, in the fall of 2011 (indirectly) invading. Not immediately aware what was happening, and, frankly, trying to exorcise the spirits of my own discomfort, I quipped that he could blame the chaos in Libya on Americans. He didn't even acknowledge my clumsy interjection, intent, instead on delivering the revelation the Holy Spirit had laid upon him, which turned out not to be a condemnation of American bellicosity—I should have known better than to expect censure of American interventions in Muslim lands from a lay Pentecostal in rural India—but rather about the slow wrath of God that takes its time but always arrives eventually to punish the unrighteous, this time, for Gaddafi, in the form of a foreign military force.

While evangelism is not, strictly speaking, a gift of the Spirit, in the worldview of many Indian Pentecostals, it is certainly part of life in the Spirit, such that active evangelism may represent another distinctively Pentecostal phenomenon. In fact, for many Pentecostals involved in evangelism or missionary work, it is the Spirit that empowers mission. Many neo-Pentecostal pastors in India understood the primary purpose of spiritual gifts like prophecy, healing, and the discernment of spirits to be for mission, not for the life of the church. "The gifts," one neo-Pentecostal mission leader working in rural Karnataka insisted, "are *for evangelism, not for use in the church* . . . the prophetical must be used for evangelism." According to Kirsteen Kim, the distinctive evangelistic theology of Pentecostals is derived from their reading of the story of Pentecost (Acts 2) in which the gift of tongues is understood to enable the international expansion of the fledgling Christian church.[31]

It is clear, then, that there are distinct Pentecostal ways of thinking about mission and evangelism. What is less certain is whether Pentecostals actually engage in evangelism more than Christians in other denominations. Premillennial eschatological assumptions about the imminent return of Jesus give many of them a certain evangelistic urgency.[32] Additionally, reliance upon Spirit guidance (rather than education, for example) as the primary credential for all manner of ministerial positions contributes to a broad diffusion of agency, activity, and leadership within Pentecostal (and especially neo-Pentecostal) churches, which means that lay and female Pentecostals are more involved in evangelism than is the case in many other forms of Christianity.[33] For example, in several instances when I asked Pentecostal pastors why their churches were growing, they made references to their wives, who were out working among (usually poor and usually female) non-Christians, showing compassion and praying for their needs. In one survey, 72% of converts to neo-Pentecostalism (the vast majority of whom had converted from other forms of Christianity) said that they had become "more committed to witnessing to their faith."[34] This may help explain why Barrett's statistics suggest that Pentecostal and Charismatic Christians provide 38% of evangelistic "harvesters" (Barrett's term), even though they represent, according to his statistics, only 26% of Christians worldwide.[35]

But on the ground, in India, many Indian Christians perceived self-identified non-Pentecostal Evangelicals to be more engaged in mission than Pentecostals. For them, Pentecostals were focused inward, on achieving the experience of God, whereas Evangelicals looked outward and emphasized spreading the message of God (or, as one critical South Indian

---

[31] Kirsteen Kim, "Theology," in *Encyclopedia of Mission and Missionaries,* ed. Jonathan J. Bonk (New York: Routledge, 2007), 439.
[32] Gooren, "Conversion Narratives," 100; and Anderson, "Movements," 334.
[33] Anderson, "Movements," 334.
[34] Paul Parathazham, "Neo-Pentecostalism in India: Preliminary Report of a National Survey," *Word and Worship* 29 (1996): 96.
[35] Barrett, Kurian, and Johnson, *Encyclopedia,* vol. 1:20.

Christian observer put it, "soul-winning, soul-winning, soul-winning"). For others, however, the perception was exactly reversed (that is, that Pentecostals were more engaged in mission than Evangelicals who do not self-identify as Pentecostal). This suggests, then, that no broad generalizations can be made about whether Indian Pentecostals or Evangelicals are the more evangelistic. Rather, they are similar enough in this regard that local variations matter more than general denominational differences. Moreover, as I discuss below, complicating the issue is the fact that in the Indian context, it is incredibly difficult to differentiate Evangelicals and Pentecostals in the first place. But the relatively high average involvement of Indian Pentecostals in evangelistic activities is undeniable.

Though the phenomenological approach to defining Pentecostalism represents an advance over theological approaches, it remains imperfect. As Chan contends, "A phenomenological definition of Pentecostalism will tend to end up becoming too inclusive and overloaded. For instance, on the basis of a phenomenological definition, it would be difficult to see how the holiness movement and the Pentecostal movement could be distinguished from each other."[36] Additionally, as indicated just above and discussed more fully below, phenomenological approaches even have difficulty clearly differentiating Pentecostals from Evangelicals, many of whom are now, in India and elsewhere, significantly Pentecostalized.

The uncertainty involved in theological and phenomenological approach, and the unwieldiness of inclusive definitions of Pentecostalism have led some scholars to adopt other approaches. Among these, the historical method pioneered by Michael Bergunder deserves special mention.[37] But if the point of the exercise, in the context of this book, is to delineate the distinctive beliefs and practices of Indian Pentecostals and demonstrate how these distinctive characteristics relate to the disproportionate targeting of Pentecostals in acts of anti-Christian violence, then theological and phenomenological approaches will serve us better. Nevertheless, to avoid the pitfalls inherent in these approaches—that is, that one assumes, in an a priori fashion the characteristics that define the field—I would advocate pairing them, as implied at certain points above, with close attention to self-identification.

---

[36] Simon Chan, "Whither Pentecostalism?" in *Asian and Pentecostal: The Charismatic Face of Christianity in Asia*, ed. Allan Anderson and Edmond Tang (Costa Mesa, CA: Regnum Books, 2005), 579.
[37] See Bergunder, *South Indian*; and Bergunder, "Cultural Turn."

How then, are we to identify our field? Any satisfactory approach to identifying Indian Pentecostalism will need to deal with what I consider the considerable challenge of differentiating it from Indian Evangelicalism. The differentiation is made more difficult by two corresponding trends in India, the Pentecostalization of Evangelicalism, and the Evangelicalization of Pentecostalism. Because Pentecostals have so effectively utilized mass media in India, appearing regularly on Indian television shows watched by tens of millions,[38] and projecting their music, through tapes, CDs, and mp3s, into the homes of nearly all Indian Christian families that listen to "Christian" music (as Bergunder attests[39]), most Indian Christians in India, are related to Pentecostalism, like all actors to Kevin Bacon, by at most a few degrees of separation, and many have been influenced in significant ways by Pentecostalism without having any conscious or demonstrable connections to it. These forces have produced millions of self-identifying Evangelicals who display marks generally considered uniquely Pentecostal (e.g., tongues). Richard Howell, head of the Evangelical Fellowship of India (a massive interdenominational alliance) told me bluntly, "Millions of [Indian] Evangelicals speak in tongues every day," and maintained that the belief in supernatural and miraculous healing through prayer had become nearly universal among Indian Evangelicals in the last ten to fifteen years.

But among Pentecostals, too, particularly urban, well-established, well-educated, and "respectable" Pentecostals, the importance of this and other "unique" Pentecostal traits is diminishing, such that many are more or less indistinguishable in worship and theology from the average Indian Evangelical. Following Miller and Yamamori, we might call these Pentecostals "routinized Pentecostals."[40]

The line between Evangelical and Pentecostal is never very clear, and it is widely acknowledged that except, perhaps, for its accentuation of the charismatic gifts Pentecostal theology is otherwise quite similar to that

---

[38.] On this, see Jonathan D. James, *McDonaldisation, Masala McGospel and Om Economics* (Washington, DC: Sage, 2010). Though flawed in various ways—on which, see Chad Bauman, "Review of *McDonaldisation, Masala McGospel, and Om Economics*, by Jonathan K. James," *Journal of Hindu-Christian Studies* 24, no. 1 (2011)—James's analysis does succeed in demonstrating the vast influence of contemporary Christian programming in India, in which, over the last ten to fifteen years, Pentecostal and Charismatic programming has become dominant. One of James's central and most convincing arguments is that the rise of Charismatic televangelism has contributed to a substantial Charismaticization even of non-Charismatic Christians and churches.
[39.] Bergunder, *South Indian*, 221.
[40.] Donald E. Miller and Tetsunao Yamamori, *Global Pentecostalism: The New Face of Christian Social Engagement* (Berkeley: University of California Press, 2007), 30.

of Evangelicalism in its emphasis on literal readings of the Bible, personal salvation (and powerful experiences thereof), moral, prudent, and chaste living, and personal evangelism.[41] In India, the blurry lines separating these two movements are made yet more gauzy by the reality, as Arun Jones describes it, that "ecstatic worship is not an uncommon phenomenon in the religious milieu of the subcontinent, and various Christian groups, borrowing from their surroundings, have engaged in ecstatic worship and other religious activities such as healing and divination that are typically associated with Pentecostalism."[42] Moreover, as Richard Howell put it, "we are living in a time of multiple Christian identities" involving the eclectic assimilation of practices and beliefs. "In India," he said, "denomination walls are very fluid, and always have been." And this is particularly true in North India, where the smaller numbers and proportion of Christians encourages the crossing of denominational boundaries.[43]

Some of the blurring of denominational lines is intentional, as in groups that intentionally position themselves between Evangelicalism and Pentecostalism, and see the charismatic gifts as empowerment for mission. For example, Blessing Youth Ministry (BYM) and groups like it resist calling themselves Pentecostal because of what they consider the recessive and introverted nature of Pentecostalism. The middle ground staked out by BYM and other indigenous missions reflects global trends. For example, one North Indian pastor associated with the Vineyard movement that has grown from its California roots into a global denomination, fluently described his approach as "empowered Evangelicalism," a self-identification Vineyard has promoted to demarcate a third space between Pentecostal and Evangelical Christianity. The nondenominational movement, which is intimately related to the emergence of neo-Pentecostalism, has also been influential in India and exacerbates the blurring of religious boundaries by encouraging independent Christians to eschew specific sectarian identities so that they will not be hobbled by the routinized obsessions of particular denominations while on their quest to follow the spirit where it leads.

Earlier I spoke of the Evangelicalization of Indian Pentecostalism. But the Pentecostalization of Indian Evangelicalism is clearly the stronger process today, such that while earlier scholars spoke of Pentecostalism as "Evangelicalism plus tongues," we may now profitably consider defining

---

[41.] Anderson, "Charismatic Face," 2.
[42.] Jones, "Faces," 504.
[43.] Jones, "Faces," 507.

Indian Evangelicalism as "extroverted Pentecostalism," "Pentecostalism plus an *insistence* on evangelism," or even—since so many Indian Evangelicals speak in tongues—as "Pentecostalism *minus* the *insistence* on tongues" (as a universal and necessary Christian experience).

It is in this context that paying attention to self-identification provides some assistance. In the broadest sense, then, the Pentecostals of India, as I used the term in this book, are those who identify with either "Pentecostal" or "Charismatic," though this basic definition must be complicated by one caveat. The caveat is that those who identify with the term "Charismatic" must do so in more than the restricted sense denoting merely a shift from hymns to "praise and worship" songs (as the term is occasionally used both in India and North America), that is, they must identify with the term in the broader sense of expecting tangible manifestations of the Holy Spirit and the charismatic gifts.

Once we look at all of those who self-identify as Pentecostal or Charismatic, we can begin to enumerate the characteristics they have most in common, and those which distinguish them from groups that self-identify in other ways. Inevitably, most of these common, distinguishing marks will refer to phenomena related to manifestations of the Spirit, and particularly tongues (or at least a belief in the possibility and desirability of tongues). There is much in my approach that is similar to the phenomenological method, except that often in the phenomenological approach—though it is not acknowledged—the field is first delimited by identifying those communities that manifest certain presupposed characteristics, whereas in my approach, the field is delimited first by self-identification.

Only after establishing the field in this way should we begin to look for common characteristics. Groups that do not self-identify as Pentecostal or Charismatic should not be included in this exercise. However, after establishing the core, distinguishing marks, we can begin to describe a related field of groups that are, to various degrees, Pentecostalized (or Pentecostal-like). Among these groups in India are those Miller and Yamamori call "proto-Charismatic" because, while resisting denominational identification as part of their post-denominational orientation, they "affirm most, if not all, of the experiences that Pentecostal and charismatic Christians believe are central to their lives."[44]

In addition, as I have argued, we must include many self-identifying Evangelicals within this category. The complicated self-identity of

---

[44] Miller and Yamamori, *Global*, 28.

one of my interviewees is typical of this kind of Evangelical: "You can relate my experience and my theology somewhat to Pentecostalism or Charismatic [Christianity]. But I am more often Evangelical . . . I do support the Pentecostal experience, but I don't emphasize . . . that [everyone] needs to have the gift of tongues or only tongues as the initial evidence of being baptized in the Holy Spirit." Clearly, then, there are some similarities between Pentecostals and Pentecostalized Evangelicals like this. And there are significant numbers of Pentecostalized Evangelicals both in India and elsewhere. "Mass Protestantism of Latin American and Asia," argues Paul Freston, is "largely a pentecostalized evangelicalism."[45]

Within this field of Pentecostal Christianity, as I have defined it, the focus of the analysis that follows is on certain subgroups. Groups associated with the Catholic Charismatic Renewal are rarely targeted in anti-Christian violence, for reasons I will discuss later, and the same can be said for self-identifying Charismatic groups within mainstream Protestant denominations. Classical Pentecostal denominations like the Assemblies of God are well-established and "respectable," and work more in urban areas where there is less everyday anti-Christian violence. So while they experience some violence, and while their experiences are considered in what follows, the primary focus of the ensuing analysis is on independent Pentecostals and neo-Pentecostals, highly Pentecostalized Evangelicals or "proto-Charismatics," and the workers of Pentecostalized Evangelical mission agencies. These are the groups, within the larger Pentecostal category, that seem to be targeted the most in anti-Christian violence.

Having now made more explicit what we meant when we say "Pentecostals," we move on, in the next chapter, to an examination of the various factors that conspire to produce their disproportionate targeting in contemporary anti-Christian violence. And these two exercises are of course related; many of the traits that typify Pentecostalism—e.g., their enthusiastic (raucous?) worship, their zealous (obnoxious?) evangelistic tendencies, and their rhetoric of "rupture"—help account for the fact that Pentecostal more regularly than other Christian groups are the victims of violence. Nevertheless, these theological and liturgical tendencies cannot fully account for the disproportionate targeting of Pentecostals. Rather, at play are also certain other non-theological factors having to do primarily with the social location of Indian Pentecostals vis-à-vis Hindus and other Christians.

---

[45] Paul Freston, "Evangelical Protestantism and Democratization in Contemporary Latin America and Asia," *Democratization* 11, no. 4 (2004): 21.

Before we can turn to these social and cultural factors, however, we must develop a clearer sense of the underlying grievances that animate the Hindu nationalists' critique of Indian Christianity. In many cases, these grievances have a rather long history, and many of them emerged in the context of and are still related to the legacy of European colonialism in India. The next chapter, therefore, sketches a history of Hindu–Christian conflict and then considers Pentecostal Christianity from the perspective of certain relatively contemporary critics of Christianity.

CHAPTER 2 | Pentecostalism in the Context
of Indian History and Politics

HISTORICALLY SPEAKING, HINDU–CHRISTIAN relations in India have been relatively cordial.[1] In fact, more than a thousand years of mostly peaceful coexistence between India's Hindus and Christians preceded the first incidents of what we might call interreligious violence between them. There were, of course, acts of violence committed by Hindus and Christians against one another during these thousand years. But these incidents appear to have taken place primarily in the context of contestations over group status, and to have been no more frequent than incidents of violence committed by Hindu groups against other Hindu groups during the same period. Such is clearly not the case in our contemporary context, however, and so the first part of this chapter traces the history of Hindu–Christian conflict, attempting, along the way, to account for its emergence.

Not all Hindu–Christian conflict is violent, and since the latter half of the twentieth century a relatively standardized intellectual critique of Indian Christianity has emerged, focusing on its proselytization, its putatively inappropriate use of wealth and "foreign funding," and its ostensibly denationalizing effects. In the second part of the chapter, then, I outline and analyze this critique. In its aggressive evangelism, and in other, obvious ways, Pentecostalism is implicated by the critique of Indian Christianity. But, in other respects, the story is more complex, and it is this kind of complexity that the present chapter seeks to elucidate.

---

[1] Sections of this chapter appeared first in Chad Bauman, "Hindu–Christian Conflict in India: Globalization, Conversion, and the Coterminal Castes and Tribes," *Journal of Asian Studies* 72, no. 3 (2013): 633–53. Reprinted with Permission. Copyright 2013, Cambridge University Press.

Part One: A Short History of Hindu–Christian Relations

India's first substantial community of Christians, the Malayalam-speaking St. Thomas or "Syrian" Christians, had achieved a relatively high status within South Indian society already by the sixth century.[2] And in the medieval period, these Syrian Christians rose to even greater prominence as a respected, high-ranking warrior and trading community within the petty kingdoms of the Malabar coast, competing for, and receiving, "honors" and patronage in exchange for loyalty and service.[3]

Their religious apparatus, which focused on the shrines of powerful, miracle-working saints (many of them from Syria), was one among many such cults—similar to, and intertwined with, Hindu and Muslim cults. And the "honors" the Christian community received would have involved being given the privilege of making certain sacred offerings during Hindu ceremonies and festivals. For these reasons, the Syrians were in fact during this period perceived to be a ritually pure community, and neither they nor their shrines were considered polluting to upper-caste Hindus.[4]

When the Portuguese arrived in 1498, they quickly established an alliance with the Syrian Christians, though relations between the two communities would later become complicated, particularly after 1560, when the Inquisition (which considered Syrian Christianity inadequately orthodox) was established in Goa. Over the next centuries, European Catholics repeatedly attempted to detach the Syrians from their beloved Eastern patriarchs and bring them under the ecclesiastical authority of the *Padroado Real*, to which a substantial number of Syrian Christians agreed at the Synod of Diamper in 1599.[5] Apart from providing a powerful and enduring symbol of Christian imperialism and excess (i.e., the Inquisition), the Portuguese also initiated a process whereby the cult of Syrian Christianity was progressively Europeanized and at least temporarily disentangled from those

---

[2] Susan Bayly, *Saints, Goddesses and Kings: Muslims and Christians in South Indian Society 1700–1900* (Cambridge: Cambridge University Press, 1989), 8. The St. Thomas/Syrian Christians are so-called because of their claims to have been founded by St. Thomas in 52 C.E. and because of their historical connections with the West Asian Church of the East and use of a Syriac liturgy. Although many scholars doubt the community's claim that St. Thomas arrived in the region in 52 C.E., the community came into existence no later than the third or fourth century.

[3] Ibid., 35, 247–48, 73–74, 460.

[4] Ibid., 27, 35, 69–70, 275.

[5] Robert Eric Frykenberg, *Christianity in India: From Beginnings to the Present*, ed. Henry Chadwick and Owen Chadwick, Oxford History of the Christian Church (Oxford: Oxford University Press, 2008), 131–36; and M. N. Pearson, *The Portuguese in India*, vol. I.1 *of The New Cambridge History of India*, ed. Gordon Johnson, C. A. Bayly, and John F. Richards (New York: Cambridge University Press, [1987] 2006), 119.

of other South Indian religions. Additionally, through the work of Francis Xavier and other missionaries, they oversaw the first mass infusion of lower-caste Hindus into the Christian fold.

These trends accelerated after 1795, when the Hindu states of Malabar (Travancore and Cochin) became tributary states of the British East India Company (BEIC), which promptly demilitarized its new clients, putting warrior communities like the Syrian Christians, who were already reeling from disruptions in their land and sea trade, out of work. Less necessary, wealthy, and powerful within this altered economic and political landscape, the Syrians began to lose the patronage of local rulers, and the status and honors that patronage had in the earlier era secured.[6]

Soon thereafter, evangelical BEIC residents began to take an active interest in Syrian Christianity. Considering it unacceptably syncretistic, they set about reforming it, with the help of British missionaries, in the direction of "orthodox" Protestant Christianity. They also sought to "protect" Syrian Christians from what they assumed was their forced participation in temple ceremonies. What the British did not realize, of course (or did not care to condone) was that it was the Syrians' "syncretistic" practices and participation in these ceremonies that had previously safeguarded their integration at a high level within the local hierarchy of purity and pollution.[7] Then, when missionaries began to assert publicly that newly converted, low-caste Christians were to be considered of the same status as Syrian Christians, the effect was to further erode the latter's social standing. By midway through the nineteenth century, upper-caste Hindus in Cochin and Travancore were treating Syrian Christians like a ritually polluting caste; by the 1880s they were routinely denied honors in local Hindu festivals, and Hindu–Christian rioting as a result of honors contestations became a regular feature of town centers with large Syrian and upper-caste Hindu populations.[8]

It bears mentioning that since the late nineteenth century Syrian Christians have been largely successful in recapturing their high-caste standing. They have done this, in part—whether consciously or unconsciously—by standing against the pressures of Europeanization in their religious life, and by cultivating ritual connections with their Hindu neighbors through the adoption of high-caste Hindu practices involving, among

---

[6.] Bayly, *Saints*, 281–84, 460; and Ajantha Subramanian, *Shorelines: Space and Rights in South India* (Stanford, CA: Stanford University Press, 2009), 73.

[7.] Bayly, *Saints*, 252, 82–85, 88, 96–98; and Subramanian, *Shorelines*, 74.

[8.] Bayly, *Saints*, 292–93, 300–302, 13; and Subramanian, *Shorelines*, 75.

other things, temple festivals and life-cycle rituals. This adoption is paired, significantly, with the official rejection of syncretic practices not associated with high-caste standing (e.g., menstrual taboos and astrological inquiries).[9] The fact that Syrian Christians have managed to reclaim their higher-caste status may help explain why Syrian Christians are very rarely targeted in acts of anti-Christian violence today. But, of course, lower-caste Christians had no originally high status to "reclaim," and Protestant aversions to anything that might be considered "syncretistic" make it particularly difficult for lower-caste Protestant (and especially Pentecostal) Christians to generate and sustain meaningful ritual connections with their Hindu neighbors.

Elsewhere in the nineteenth century, the work of European missionaries, whose numbers surged after pro-missionary changes to the Company's charter in 1813, provoked controversy and resistance, not only for their evangelical activities but also for their role in colonial education and their successful advocacy of social reforms (e.g., the banning of *sati* in 1829), and policy changes that favored lower castes, peasants, and Christians.[10] These reforms undermined traditional social arrangements and the authority of the landholding classes, while demonstrating the widening reach and influence of missionaries in British India.[11] While missionaries were occasionally targeted in the anti-Christian harassment and violence that ensued, native Christians bore the brunt of it, and often found themselves driven out of their homes, beaten up, or even killed, usually by mobs supported by their landlords.[12]

Already by mid-century, then, convert Christians in India, like Syrian Christians, were beginning to be perceived as a religious community distinct from other Indian religious communities, and one with suspect loyalties to British rule. The Great Rebellion of 1857 substantiates this latter claim. In the Rebellion, which had been provoked primarily by Indian concerns about British intrusions into their social and religious lives, native Christians were regularly the focus of rebel attacks.[13] The

---

[9] Corinne Dempsey, "Selective Indigenization and the Problem of Superstition in Kerala," *Vidyajyoti: Journal of Theological Reflection* 69, no. 6 (2005): 404–14.

[10] On *sati*, see John Stratton Hawley, ed., *Sati, the Blessing and the Curse: The Burning of Wives in India* (New York: Oxford University Press, 1994).

[11] Ian Copland, "Christianity as an Arm of Empire: The Ambiguous Case of India under the Company, c. 1813–1858," *Historical Journal* 49, no. 4 (2006): 1025–54.

[12] Muhammad Mohar Ali, *The Bengali Reaction to Christian Missionary Activities 1833–1957* (Chittagong: Mehrub Publications, 1965).

[13] Kim Wagner, *The Great Fear of 1857: Rumours, Conspiracies and the Making of the Indian Uprising* (Oxford: Peter Lang, 2010).

perception of Indian Christian "difference" and disloyalty only strengthened in the second half of the century, as did the reactionary conservatism of India's increasingly apprehensive elites, who felt threatened by what they considered the mounting pervasiveness and power of evangelical Christianity. Anti-missionary rhetoric became the hallmark of the resulting, late nineteenth-century Hindu revivalism, while scattered attacks on missionaries and native Christians continued.[14]

British colonial strategy and policy also contributed to the greater differentiation of religious communities in India. Throughout the nineteenth century, British officials had attempted to manage affairs on the ground in India in part by managing the relationship of India's religions. From the beginning of the nineteenth century, for example, colonial authorities carefully balanced the proportion of "Hindus" and "Muslims" in city police forces, and relied upon those they considered India's "natural leaders" (frequently either religious or caste officials) to mediate their rule to the masses.[15] Toward the end of the century, the British also began conducting decennial censuses, and at the beginning of the twentieth century they began granting separate electorates for India's religious minorities. The censuses force-fit the many complicated (and often plural and syncretic) religious identities of India's people onto the Procrustean frame of "world" religions, while separate electorates apportioned political representation based on religious demographics, further politicizing religious identity. Individually, the colonial policies described in this paragraph "frequently buttressed the supposedly primordial corporate identity and structures of leadership of castes and religious sects . . . thereby rendering rigid what had hitherto been more negotiable entities."[16] In combination, their effects were even more dramatic.

Even in the colony's tributary states, where representational politics were generally slower to emerge, colonial-era tendencies toward enumeration had profound effects. The princely state of Travancore, for example, began conducting its own censuses in this same era. The growth of the Christian community, evidence for which was provided by the censuses, caused concern among the rulers of the state and contributed to the creation of policies—such as the granting of rights and benefits only

---

14. Tanika Sarkar, *Hindu Wife, Hindu Nation: Community, Religion, and Cultural Nationalism* (Bloomington: Indiana University Press, 2001).

15. Sandria B. Freitag, *Collective Action and Community: Public Arenas and the Emergence of Communalism in North India* (Berkeley: University of California Press, 1989), 16, 19, 57–78.

16. Prashant Kidambi, *The Making of an Indian Metropolis: Colonial Governance and Public Culture in Bombay, 1890–1920* (Hampshire: Ashgate, 2007), 159.

to non-Christian lower-caste communities—that both bolstered the state's Hindu character and sought to defend and support Hindus and "Hindu" social patterns and authority from challenges mounted by the un-Hindu Other. This process signaled a shift that would be replicated elsewhere in India "away from a commitment to overlapping sovereignties that allows for mutuality between Hindu kingship and a variety of other religious affiliations to a defensive posture on Hinduism that requires the incorporation of non-Hindus into an exclusive sovereignty."[17]

Beginning toward the end of the nineteenth century, rapid urbanization in India helped spur the development of associational life, while the progressive British abandonment of interventions in the public arena after the Rebellion made that space a politicized one.[18] In this hotly contested public arena, urban groups sought to mobilize their local constituencies, and often did so by defining themselves over and against other competing groups. Constituencies thus mobilized could (and, increasingly after the turn of the century, did) join with others elsewhere in pursuit of larger, regional or even national projects. In moving back and forth between the small-scale, relational identities at the local level and broader, more ideologically oriented identities invoked by common pursuit of regional or national goals, local religious groups came to have a greater sense of being part of a larger religious community ("Hindu" or "Muslim," for example). Groups turned against a local "Other" were thus increasingly turned against more regionally or nationally defined "Others."[19]

Another important and related feature of the developing North Indian urban spaces of the late nineteenth and early twentieth centuries was the growing importance of the middle class. As Sanjay Joshi has shown with reference to Lucknow, the urban middle classes that rose to public prominence under colonial rule produced a "fractured modernity" informed by liberal tendencies but limited by tradition and their own self-interest, and therefore espousing often contradictory positions on social, cultural, religious, and political matters. For example, concerns about preserving their privilege in the face of lower-caste challenges prevented them from enthusiastically supporting efforts to undermine caste. (The middle class emerged primarily from middle- and upper-caste communities.) Challenges from religious minorities often produced similarly conservative reactions. The

---

[17] Subramanian, *Shorelines*, 93.

[18] Sanjay Joshi, *Fractured Modernity: Making of a Middle Class in Colonial North India* (New Delhi: Oxford University Press, 2001), 103–4.

[19] Freitag, *Collective Action*, 53–56, 80, 94–96, 125, 46, 284.

middle class in Lucknow not only was capable of producing sharp divisions between "Hindu" and "Muslim" but also contributed to the homogenization of "Hindu" belief and practice in order to expand its political influence to a progressively broader cross-section of society.[20] Similar processes were underway elsewhere in urban India.[21]

Perhaps the most important association to emerge at this time was the Arya Samaj. Founded in Bombay in 1875 by Swami Dayananda Saraswati (1824–83), the Arya Samaj was one of the earliest Hindu associations to deal openly and directly (not just rhetorically) with the challenge of Christian proselytizing. Fueled by concerns over what appeared, in the decennial censuses, to be declining Hindu numbers and a massive rise in conversions to Islam and Christianity, the Samaj developed campaigns of mass "purification" (*shuddhi*) in order both to reconvert converts to Christianity and Islam, and to "purify" members of the traditionally "impure" lower castes, marking them as integral members of the Hindu community in order to decrease the possibility that they would convert to minority religions to seek social advance.[22]

Nevertheless, Christianity continued to gain converts in significant numbers, due in part at least to a series of devastating famines throughout India during the last two decades of the nineteenth century. During the famines, mission organizations often managed massive feeding programs (sometimes at the behest of the British and with colonial funds and backing) provoking at least a few grateful recipients to convert. More significantly, perhaps, the famines also created an orphan crisis, to which missionary groups responded by establishing orphanages around the country, and in them, raising children born Hindus as Christians.[23]

As a result of these political and demographic changes, many advocates of Hinduism began to assert that the growth of Christianity represented a serious threat to the Hindu faith, as in U. N. Mukherji's 1909 series of periodical articles appearing in *The Bengalee*, "Hindus—A Dying Race." Christian conversions and antagonistic colonial policies also spurred the

---

[20] Ronald Inden, *Imagining India* (Oxford: Blackwell, 1990); and Joshi, *Fractured*, 2–12, 162; and Peter van der Veer, *Gods on Earth: Religious Experience and Identity in Ayodhya* (New York: Oxford University Press, [1988] 1997).

[21] On Bombay, for example, see Kidambi, *Making*, 12–13, 161–66.

[22] Kidambi, *Making*, 174–76; and Iris Vandevelde, "Reconversion to Hinduism: A Hindu Nationalist Reaction against Conversion to Christianity and Islam," *South Asia: Journal of South Asian Studies* 34, no. 1 (2011): 34–39.

[23] Chad Bauman, *Christian Identity and Dalit Religion in Hindu India, 1868–1947* (Grand Rapids, MI: Eerdmans Publishers, 2008), 76–79; and John Zavos, "Conversion and the Assertive Margins," *South Asia: Journal of South Asian Studies* 24, no. 2 (2001): 82.

development of regional Hindu Sabhas ("Societies"), beginning in 1907, and then the All-India Hindu Sabha (or Mahasabha, "Great Society") in 1915. Although the Mahasabhites remained largely focused on Muslims throughout the 1920s, many continued to harbor misgivings about missionaries and the growth of Christianity, which they lumped together with Islam as a "foreign" faith promoting foreign loyalties. Similar concerns, as well as apprehensions about a potential loss of unity in the struggle for independence, led prominent Indian intellectuals to seek some fundamental, stable essence of Indian identity that could be used to galvanize Indians and motivate them to fight for their liberation. V. D. Savarkar's 1923 tract, *Hindutva: Who is a Hindu?*, posited an essential Indian identity based on *Hindutva*, or Hinduness. When Savarkar became president of the Hindu Mahasabha in 1937, his more radical views became the norm within that body.

Inspired by Savarkar's views, the Maharashtrian Keshav Baliram Hedgewar (1889–1940) founded the RSS in 1925. Hedgewar's objective was to propagate the ideology of *Hindutva* while infusing "new physical strength into the majority community."[24] The RSS grew dramatically in the next decades and spawned several other important organizations, including, eventually, what became the BJP. Of the many organizations associated with the Sangh Parivar, the ABVKA (founded in 1952), and the VHP (founded in 1964) are particularly pertinent to the history of Hindu–Christian conflict because they were created for the precise purpose of neutralizing the influence and reversing the successes of Christian missionaries.[25] To do so, both have at times revived the Arya Samaj's practice of *shuddhi*, though under names like *paravartan* ("return," "turning back") or *ghar vapasi* ("homecoming"). Despite this, missionaries continued to successfully convert large numbers of Hindus (and adherents of other religions) to Christianity and continued to receive a disproportionate number of converts from among the lower castes and tribes.

Even Gandhi, whose more irenic conception of Indian nationhood contrasted significantly with that of Savarkar and Golwalkar, became, in the 1930s and 1940s, increasingly opposed to the work of Christian missionaries, whose success among lower-caste Hindus threatened to dilute the

---

[24] Christopher Jaffrelot, ed., *Hindu Nationalism: A Reader* (Princeton: Princeton University Press, 2007), 16.

[25] Sumit Sarkar, "Conversion and Politics of Hindu Right," *Economic and Political Weekly*, 26 June 1999, 1697; and Zavos, "Conversion," 84.

Hindu voice and vote.[26] Although he spoke approvingly of Christ and of Christian scriptures, Gandhi publicly and repeatedly accused Indian converts of being denationalized and decried Christian missionaries' targeting of lower-caste Hindus, whom he considered, somewhat controversially, inadequately intelligent to make their own religious decisions.[27] Gandhi mainstreamed criticism of Christian evangelical efforts and also called the appropriateness of conversion itself into question. Gandhi's views on the topic reflect an ambivalence about Christianity in India that was (and remains) typical of many even moderate Hindus.[28]

At Independence in 1947, British India was divided into predominantly Muslim Pakistan and predominately Hindu India, setting off a massive migration (of Pakistani Hindus and Sikhs to India, and Indian Muslims to Pakistan), and provoking interreligious riots that resulted in hundreds of thousands of deaths. Aside from this fierce internecine violence, the Partition had a more general deleterious effect on interreligious interactions in India. As Zamindar argues in *The Long Partition*, in order to address the multitude of questions about citizenship, passports, and evacuee property that Partition generated, India had to develop a range of bureaucratic guidelines, distinctions, and definitions, all of which served to determine (and concretize) the nation and its limits. Such determinations very often revolved around religion, contributing to processes begun in the late nineteenth century that increasingly defined the Indian nation as a Hindu one, and rendered fluid and blurry religious definitions static and permanent through the force of a bureaucratic machinery.[29] The Partition was therefore "long" not only because it remains powerful as a rhetorical device— the Partition as perpetual grievance against Muslims, for example, or as a warning of what could happen if the Christian community grew large enough to demand a separate homeland—but also because it continues to shape how Indians think about religion and about the religious Other.

Despite the prominence, in public discourse, of the perceived Muslim threat to the integrity of India during and after Partition, traditionalist

---

[26] Robert Eric Frykenberg, "Introduction: Dealing with Contested Definitions and Controversial Perspectives," in *Christians and Missionaries in India: Cross-Cultural Communication since 1500*, ed. Robert Eric Frykenberg (Grand Rapids, MI: William B. Eerdmans, 2003), 7–8; and Susan Billington Harper, *In the Shadow of the Mahatma: Bishop V. S. Azariah and the Travails of Christianity in British India* (Grand Rapids, MI: William B. Eerdmans, 2000), 292–345.
[27] Sebastian C. H. Kim, *In Search of Identity: Debates on Religious Conversion in India* (Oxford: Oxford University Press, 2003), 33.
[28] A longer discussion of Gandhi's views appears below.
[29] Vazira Fazil-Yacoobali Zamindar, *The Long Partition and the Making of Modern South Asia: Refugees, Boundaries, Histories* (New York: Columbia University Press, 2007), 229, 38.

Hindu organizations continued to voice concern about Christian mission work among lower-caste Hindus and tribal peoples during the Constituent Assembly debates of 1946–50, in the course of which a constitutional ban on conversion was unsuccessfully proposed. And conversion remained a live issue in the next decades, in which a number of state-sponsored reports on Christian mission work appeared, the most famous of which was the *Christian Missionary Activities Inquiry Committee Report* (1956), or the Niyogi Report (so named after the judge who led the inquiry) that was sponsored by the Madhya Pradesh state government.

The *Report* confirmed the fears of opponents of Christianity by alleging that the Christian population was growing by leaps and bounds, that the Hindu population was declining rapidly, and that Christian missionaries sought not only converts but also the establishment of an independent Christian state along the lines of Pakistan. Witnesses appearing before the committee frequently complained that missionaries used their orphanages, schools, and hospitals to lure non-Christians to the fold. Although the provision of social services to indigent Indians with foreign funds was therefore preferable to their being used to support evangelism alone, even missionary social service was, in the view of committee members, problematic.

The *Report* recommended that foreign missionaries focused on evangelism be sent home and laws be drafted that would prohibit conversion by "force," "fraud," "inducement," and "allurement." This latter recommendation inspired a series of such laws (euphemistically called "Freedom of Religion" laws) in Odisha (1967), Madhya Pradesh (1968), Arunachal Pradesh (1978), and elsewhere.[30] Similar laws were proposed at the national level at least three times (in 1954, 1960, and 1978), but failed each time to gain acceptance.[31]

Although the putative Muslim menace remained the primary concern of most Hindu nationalists in the twentieth century, it is clear, then, that apprehensions about Christianity never faded completely from view. And

---

[30.] Chad Bauman, "Postcolonial Anxiety and Anti-Conversion Sentiment in the Report of *the Christian Missionary Activities Enquiry Committee*," *International Journal of Hindu Studies* 12, no. 2 (2008): 192. Many of these laws were also modeled on laws promulgated by princely states, such as Rajgarh, Patna, Sarguja, Udaipur, etc. These states were quasi-autonomous political entities under the British but became part of the Indian union at Independence (with several prominent exceptions, e.g., Kashmir). As part of that process the princely state laws were officially superseded by those of India and the states of which they became part (in which there were at the time no anti-conversion laws), and were thereby abrogated.
[31.] Faizan Mustafa and Anurag Sharma, *Conversion: Constitutional and Legal Implications* (New Delhi: Kanishka Publishers, 2003), 109–11.

then for reasons discussed below, the late 1990s brought increased attention to India's Christians and the work of Christian missionaries, such that by the end of the century, VHP General Secretary Giriraj Kishore could declare that Christians constituted "a greater threat [to India] than the collective threat from separatist Muslim elements."[32]

The late 1990s brought a sharp surge in acts of violence against Christians, and the year 1998 appears to mark a turning point. The United Christian Forum for Human Rights (UCFHR) estimates that there were only thirty-two registered cases of communal violence against Christians between 1964 and 1996.[33] In 1997 the rate of violence grew dramatically, to fifteen, and then in 1998 the number jumped drastically to ninety.[34] There had in independent India occasionally been riots involving Christians, such as those in 1982, in and around Mandaikadu village, Kanyakumari District, Tamil Nadu.[35] But these riots, and others like them, seemed an aberration to many, and also were not perceived, as incidents in the late 1990s were, to mark a rising tide of more generalized anti-Christian sentiment. The first large-scale, anti-Christian riot that did occurred in 1998, in the Dangs, Gujarat, a region dominated by tribal peoples, many of whom had become Christian. No Christians were killed in these riots, which began on Christmas Day. But over the course of a few days, rioters vandalized or destroyed dozens of Christian houses and places of worship.

Between 1998 and 2007, the number of documented attacks on Christians continued to climb, reaching present levels of over (at least) 250 annually. And then, on the day before Christmas in 2007, Hindu–Christian

---

[32.] Sushil Aaron, *Christianity and Political Conflict in India: The Case of Gujarat* (Colombo: Regional Centre for Strategic Studies, 2002), 31.

[33.] While there is no doubt in my mind that acts of violence against Christians qua Christians increased significantly after 1998, anecdotal evidence suggests that the UCFHR data significantly undercounts incidents prior to that date. What seems likely to me is that incidents of anti-Christian violence were rare enough in the pre-1998 period that they did not seem to merit recording and are therefore underdocumented.

[34.] Aaron, *Christianity*, 47.

[35.] The Kanyakumari riots began when rumors spread during a popular Hindu festival that some Hindu women taking ritual baths had been molested by Christian men. A confrontation between Hindus and Christians ensued, and police firings intended to disperse the crowds instead killed at least six Christians. Violence between Hindus and Christians spread to surrounding villages in the days and weeks afterwards. According to official estimates, by the time the riots ended, nine Christians had lost their lives, and several hundred villagers saw their homes destroyed. But many locals believe the official death toll was too low and failed to register the deaths of several Hindus killed in the violence. Many churches, temples, and convents were also destroyed, desecrated, or otherwise vandalized as well. See A Maria David, *Beyond Boundaries: Hindu–Christian Relationship and Basic Christian Communities* (Delhi: Indian Society for Promoting Christian Knowledge, 2009), 70–72.

riots broke out in Kandhamal, Odisha. These riots lasted for a few days, subsided, and then broke out again in August 2008. In the two rounds of Kandhamal riots,[36] there were, all told, more than fifty deaths, dozens of cases of sexual assault and rape, the destruction of thousands of homes, and the temporary or permanent displacement of over five thousand refugees.

Most but not all of the victims were Christian. Christians occasionally retaliated, and one Christian attack alone destroyed 120 Hindu homes. Additionally, a significant factor in the first round of violence was a December 24, 2007, altercation between Christians and the aging Swami Lakshmanananda Saraswati, a popular but controversial local Hindu spiritual leader and anti-conversion activist, in which the swami claimed to have been injured. Many rioters framed their violence against Christians as a response to that altercation. Similarly, the second round of riots was touched off by the brutal assassination of the swami and several others as they participated in a celebration of Krishna's birth (Krishna Janmashtami) at the swami's ashram. Naxalites claimed responsibility for the killing, describing it as a response to his "anti-minority" activities. But many of those who attacked Christians afterwards believed that the Naxalites either were Christian or were supported financially and logistically by Christians. Subsequent police investigations and court cases have yet to definitively settle the matter.[37]

The sharp increase in Hindu–Christian violence leads logically to questions about why the violence should increase at this particular historical moment. Superficially, the obvious answer is politics. In the year 1998, the BJP came to power at the center, the last time it had done so before its 2014 rout of the Congress Party. The BJP and other institutions of the Sangh Parivar have historically been more likely to implicitly and explicitly condone anti-minority violence than their Congress Party rivals (though it should be kept in mind that the anti-Sikh bloodletting after the assassination of Indira Gandhi in 1984 occurred under Congress rule). Yet the anti-Christian violence continued long after the BJP was swept out of power in 2004, and though many of India's Christians draw upon anecdotal evidence to assert a connection, my own statistical analyses of anti-Christian violence (conducted with Tamara Leech) do not suggest a strong correlation between anti-Christian violence and BJP rule,

---

[36] Despite the fact that the "riot" was a largely one-sided, anti-Christian affair, I use the term here to preserve some semblance of neutrality and to recognize that there was some retaliation by Christians, as noted below.

[37] Chad Bauman, "Identity, Conversion and Violence: Dalits, Adivasis and the 2007–08 Riots in Orissa," in *Margins of Faith: Dalit and Tribal Christianity in India*, ed. Rowena Robinson and Joseph Marianus Kujur (Washington, DC: Sage, 2010).

at least at the state level.[38] Moreover, explanations based on BJP power do not account for why the BJP should have come to power in the first place, or why Christians should displace Muslims as the primary target of Sangh-affiliated anti-minority activities, as Sarkar claims, perhaps with some exaggeration, they did in 1998.[39]

Some have speculated that the turning of the Sangh Parivar's attention toward India's Christians was a result of the public backlash it suffered after the 1992 destruction of the Babri Masjid[40] in Ayodhya, which it had at least indirectly encouraged, and the deadly Hindu–Muslim riots that subsequently ensued. This backlash may have created a situation in which anti-Muslim activities offered diminishing electoral returns.[41] Others have pointed out that 1998 was the year that Sonia Gandhi, whose Italian and Christian origins are a perennial political issue, became president of the Congress Party. It is not surprising, therefore, that anti-Christian rhetoric might have gained political traction at about the same time. Still others have suggested that the increase of anti-Christian rhetoric and violence in the late 1990s was a response to well-publicized—and to many, offensively strategic—Western, Christian evangelical efforts, such as AD2000 and Beyond, or the Joshua Project, which set ambitious goals to reach the whole world with the Christian message by the end of the millennium.[42]

While there is no doubt some merit and truth in all of these explanations, another likely factor, as I have argued elsewhere,[43] is that the uptick in anti-Christian violence is linked to the increasingly powerful and tangible impact of globalization[44] in India after the early 1990s, and with the way that Indian Christianity has come to stand, symbolically, as a proxy for it. In the eyes of its many critics, Indian Christianity represents the shift to

---

[38.] Chad Bauman and Tamara Leech, "Political Competition, Relative Deprivation, and Perceived Threat: A Research Note on anti-Christian Violence in India," *Ethnic and Racial Studies* 35, no. 12 (2011): 2195–216.

[39.] Sarkar, "Conversion," 1691.

[40.] The Babri Masjid ("Babar's Mosque"), allegedly built over the ruins of a Rama temple, had been a bone of contention between India's Muslims and Hindus for many years, and restoring the temple had been a central plank of Sangh Parivar politics in the 1980s and 1990s. After months of agitation, and in the midst of a Sangh demonstration at the scene, Hindu nationalists entered the disputed site and destroyed the mosque brick by brick. Afterwards, Hindu–Muslim riots killed at least 2,000, most of them Muslim. For more, see van der Veer, *Gods on Earth: Religious Experience and Identity in Ayodhya*.

[41.] Aaron, *Christianity*, 44.

[42.] Zavos, "Conversion," 75.

[43.] Bauman, "Hindu–Christian Conflict."

[44.] Globalization, as I understand it here, refers to the increasingly sophisticated and far-reaching interconnectedness of national and regional economies, peoples, and cultures through faster and more regular transportation and trade, and the speedier exchange of ideas and lifestyles.

merit and skill-based (as opposed to ascriptive) status systems because of its penchant for establishing (and using to its advantage) educational institutions, training facilities, and co-ops. Similarly, Christianity symbolizes the challenge of foreign meaning-making systems because of its literacy programs (particularly those operating in English). Christianity represents the unwieldy and uncontrollable flow of foreign capital and investment because of the Christian community's ostensibly greater access to foreign wealth and power (which is perceived to reproduce the inequities of globalization). And then, of course, Christianity comes to be associated with the socially disruptive effects of globalization through its development work among lower-caste and tribal peoples, which inverts traditional caste and class hierarchies, both in terms of the relationship of those communities with higher-caste Hindus and in terms of their relationship with local, non-Christian groups of similar status. In addition, the Christian community comes to be associated with the secularist critique of Hindu nationalism because it demands the right to live and practice its religion freely, and because it demands the right to propagate its message through conversion. In so many ways, then, Christianity represents all that threatens the "traditional" order as imagined by Hindu nationalists, and the latter have done well to forge the rhetorical link between the challenge posed by globalization and that posed by the existence of a minority Christian community.

Whatever the reason that violence against Christians increased after 1998, the increase occurred in the context of a broader social debate about the appropriateness of evangelism in India's secular society, and about the extent to which the Hindu majority could or should accommodate India's religious minorities, particularly those with foreign origins—without risking the disintegration of the nation. While nothing I say below should suggest that those who advance a reasoned critique of Christianity, or of Christian evangelism, are directly responsible for violence against Christians, it is impossible to understand contemporary tensions between Hindus and Christians, or why Pentecostals might be disproportionately targeted in the anti-Christian violence that sometimes results, without knowing something of this critique. It is for this reason, then, that we turn in the next section to that critique.

Pentecostalism and the Contemporary Critique of Conversion

Rising anti-Christian violence in the 1990s was accompanied by the increasing prominence and sophistication of Indian public intellectuals critical of Christianity, and in particular of Christian evangelical efforts. It is important to emphasize that I am not positing a causal connection here. With few exceptions, those engaged in an intellectual critique of Christianity and Christian conversion efforts did so without advocating violence, even indirectly. And even if a significant correlation between their critique and anti-Christian violence could be clearly established, it would remain difficult to determine whether the critique was the cause or a reflection of the violence, or whether the two drew independently from similar sources of civil discontent. Moreover, the fact that some of those engaged in anti-Christian violence have justified their attacks as a response to the provocation of evangelism does not necessarily implicate those who articulate an intellectual critique of missionary practices in that violence.

Nevertheless, public criticism of Christian efforts to convert others to their faith, and of the way they go about doing it, does provide some cover and ready justifications for those engaged in violence against Christians. This public critique in many ways merely gives voice to widespread Hindu ambivalence about Christian evangelizing. One of the reasons why violence against Christians continues then is that a relatively significant number of Hindus who would not themselves engage in it find Christian proselytization inappropriate and offensive, and therefore also find it somewhat difficult to loudly or forcefully condemn those who respond to it with violence.

Arun Shourie's *Missionaries in India* (1994) marks, perhaps, the apex of a genre of literature dedicated to this critique of Christian missionizing, both in terms of its quality and in terms of its popularity and impact. Shourie's ideas will be discussed below, but first we must deal briefly with a few of his predecessors. Although the early nationalists had often condemned Christian conversion efforts, Gandhi, as indicated above, was the first to popularize, and to make popularly palatable, a principled critique of conversion, or at least of conversion as most Christians understood it. And since Gandhi is frequently quoted by other critics of Christian conversion efforts, his influence over the discourse of conversion in India is rivaled only by that of the Niyogi Committee, and the phrase it popularized, "force, fraud, and allurement/inducement" (along with all of its assumptions and implied assertions).

"I believe that there is no such thing as conversion from one faith to another in the accepted sense of the term," Gandhi asserted, "It is a highly personal matter for the individual and his God."[45] Conversion, for Gandhi,

---

[45] Quoted in Robert Ellsberg, ed., *Gandhi on Christianity* (Maryknoll, NY: Orbis Books, 1991), 48.

was about inner transformation, moral advance, and self-purification, an ultimately individual act that could take place within any religious tradition. His understanding of conversion was informed by his conception of religions as primarily (and most importantly) repositories of spiritual practices rather than salvifically efficacious doctrinal assertions. No one religious tradition could claim a monopoly over truth or salvation, and therefore it was better to remain within one's own tradition, the spiritual practices of which were particularly suited for those in a particular cultural context, than to seek salvation or spiritual advance elsewhere.

Nevertheless, there was for Gandhi nothing particularly wrong in acknowledging that many religious traditions contained within them spiritual wisdom and effective spiritual practices. But because adherence to a particular religious tradition did not determine one's ultimate spiritual fate, finding truth in another tradition did not require that one begin affiliating with that tradition formally, and certainly not to the exclusion of affiliation with one's natal religious community (as many Christians believe true conversion demands). In fact, a change of affiliation without a subsequent "moral rise" was meaningless and potentially counterproductive, according to Gandhi. "The form of worship in a particular manner in a church, a mosque or a temple is an empty formula," he said, and "it may even be a hindrance to individual or social growth, and insistence on a particular form or repetition of a credo may be a potent cause of violent quarrels leading to bloodshed and ending in utter disbelief in Religion."[46] Conversion as a change of affiliation from one religious community to another was therefore useless and disruptive, and for this reason to be avoided. "If a person wants to believe in the Bible, let him say so," Gandhi insisted, "But why should he disregard his own religion? This proselytization will mean no peace in the world."[47]

Gandhi was critical not only of Christian efforts to convert others to their faith but also to the methods they employed. In particular, he frequently criticized what he viewed as the illegitimate mingling of evangelism and Christian educational or medical service. In his view, true "service" was only service if it was free from the ulterior motive (or, in his words, the "mental reservation"[48]) of conversion. Foreshadowing an argument the

---

[46.] Clifford Manshardt, ed., *The Mahatma and the Missionary: Selected Writings of Mohandas K. Gandhi* (Chicago: Henry Regnery Company, 1949), 72.
[47.] Manshardt, *Mahatma*, 73. See also K. L. Seshagiri Rao, "Conversion: A Hindu/Gandhian Perspective," in *Religious Conversion: Contemporary Practices and Controversies*, ed. M. Darrol Bryan and Christopher Lamb (London: Continuum, 1999), 144–46.
[48.] Ellsberg, *Gandhi*, 45.

Niyogi Committee would amplify, Gandhi viewed the combination of evangelism and service as an illegitimate form of allurement to the faith, and accused it of giving rise to "suspicion if not even secret hostility."[49]

Finally, Gandhi was among the first of many critics of Christian evangelizing to contemplate the possibility of a ban on conversions in independent India. Due to his untimely death within months of independence, of course, Gandhi had very little direct influence on the development of India's constitution. And, as indicated above, though several states have passed laws regulating or circumscribing conversion, efforts to have such a law implemented at the national level have so far consistently failed. Nevertheless, Gandhi aggravated his missionary interlocutors by replying ambiguously, and often somewhat contradictorily, to questions about whether he would advocate the banning of conversion in an independent India. In a strong statement from which he later backed away, at least to some extent, he said, "If I had power and could legislate I should certainly stop all proselytizing. It is the cause of much avoidable conflict between classes and unnecessary heart-burning among missionaries."[50]

If Gandhi established the logical grounds for a reasoned critique of Christian conversion, it was Ram Swarup (1920–1998) who is most responsible for reviving and re-popularizing that critique in the 1980s. In 1982, Swarup established a publishing house, the Voice of India, which he used to promote a plethora of works defending Hinduism and its centrality to Indian culture. Although he borrowed many of his arguments about Christian conversion from Gandhi, he added to them an element of acidity and presented them with a biting, sarcastic wit that Gandhi's writings typically lacked. While the basic arguments of the anti-conversion critique in contemporary India are mostly Gandhi's, then, the vitriol is more properly traced to Swarup.

Swarup agreed with Gandhi's argument that religion should be about interior things and moral improvement and that no religion could claim a monopoly on salvation, truth, or efficacious spiritual practices. "[D]ifferent peoples and different races have their own presiding genius, their own talents and their own *svadharma* [personal *dharma*, or spiritual practice/duty]," he maintained. "They worship the best when they worship through their *svadharma*."[51] And he also shared with Gandhi a

---

[49] Ibid., 45.

[50] Ibid., 47.

[51] Ram Swarup, *Hinduism vis-à-vis Christianity and Islam* (New Delhi: Voice of India, [1982] 1992), 6.

great deal of discomfort regarding the methods employed by Christian missionaries.

But far more than Gandhi, Swarup impugned the nature of Christianity itself, in the context of a more general critique of ethical, revelation-based, exclusivistic monotheisms. Such religions, for him naturally, inexorably, and irreversibly nurtured among their adherents a lack of respect for other religions. Swarup insisted, "The fact is that intolerance is inbuilt into the basic Semitic approach and cursing comes naturally to it. The Bible is full of curses invoked on rival-gods, prophets, apostles, doctrines. For example, Paul told his Galatian followers that 'should anyone preach to you a gospel contrary to that which we preached to you, let him be accursed.' "[52] Even "inclusive" Christian theologies, according to Swarup, failed to overcome this basic intolerance, because they refused to relinquish the insistence that there was something unique and superior about Christianity.

Sita Ram Goel (1921–2003), a close associate of Swarup's and even more so the iconoclast and satirist, placed Swarup's arguments about the intolerant and expansionistic tendencies of Christianity within a more general critique of western colonialism and neo-colonialism, from which, in Goel's view, Christianity could not be disentangled. In fact, because it concerned itself with expansion, and not merely internal things, Christianity proved itself a political rather than a religious tradition. In a line he repeated often, including in his introduction to a reprint of the Niyogi Committee Report, Goel argued that "Christianity has never been a religion; it has always been a predatory imperialism par excellence."[53]

Goel traced Christianity's imperialistic urge to the Bible as Swarup had also done, and particularly to the history of the Israelites, who in Goel's view colonized the lands of others with God's approval. "The problem with the Biblical tradition," he suggested, is that unlike the "Vedic tradition [which] advises people to be busy with themselves, that is, their own moral and spiritual improvement. . . . The Biblical tradition . . . teaches people to be busy with others."[54] Whereas Gandhi viewed the Christian obsession with numbers and conversions to be a perversion of Christianity, then, Swarup and Goel believed it to be the natural and even inevitable efflorescence of basic Christian beliefs.

[52.] Ibid., 32.

[53.] Sita Ram Goel, *Vindicated by Time: The Niyogi Committee Report on Christian Missionary Activities* (New Delhi: Voice of India, 1998), 3.

[54.] Sita Ram Goel, *History of Hindu–Christian Encounters AD 304 to 1996* (New Delhi: Voice of India, [1986] 2010), v–vi.

From the colonial period forward, many foreign missionaries and Indian Christians responded to the accusation that Christianization necessarily entailed denationalization and deculturation by promoting efforts at "indigenization," that is, the use of (usually Sanskritic) Hindu concepts, terms, and rituals in the articulation and ritual expression of Indian Christianity. Such efforts were particularly common in Roman Catholic circles, where they were aided by the notion of natural theology, and more recently by Vatican II's relatively positive (if not uncontested) valuation of non-Christian cultures and religions.[55] To Goel, however, efforts to indigenize Indian Christianity were not an indication of Christian respect for Indian culture and Hindu religion, but rather a cynical ploy, born from frustration at the ineffectiveness of more direct methods, to downplay the significant differences between Christianity and Hinduism and trick Hindus into conversion.[56]

It was on this tradition of polemic and critique that Arun Shourie (b. 1941) drew in his widely read and cited *Missionaries of India: Continuities, Changes, Dilemmas*. Even before writing the book, Shourie was a well-known public intellectual and journalist with a reputation for taking bold and controversial stances on the issues of the day, but also for being a tireless defender of the freedom of the press. From 1998 to 2004, he was, in addition, a minister in the BJP government. The kernel of *Missionaries in India* originated as a presentation to the Catholic Bishops Conference of India consultation in 1994, to which Shourie had been invited. But, in the book, and much to the consternation of the bishops, Shourie quoted liberally from reports produced for the consultation (which were not intended to become public) to build a case that Christian evangelistic methods were boorish, cynically calculating, and materialistic. To him, missionary strategizing sounded "more like the Planning Commission, if not the Pentagon, than like Jesus."[57]

Like Gandhi and Swarup, Shourie therefore subtly differentiated between appropriate religion (which was interior, non-expansionist, and

---

[55] Attempts to indigenize Indian Christianity by using the symbols and rituals of Sanskritic Hinduism have in more recent years been called into question by the rise of *dalit* theology and its well-developed critique of what it views as the upper-caste hegemony that undergirds and benefits from Sanskritic (that is, more national, all-Indian forms of) Hinduism. On this, see Xavier Gravend-Tirole, "From Christian Ashrams to Dalit Theology—or Beyond: An Examination of the Indigenisation/Inculturation Trend within the Indian Catholic Church," in *Constructing Indian Christianities: Caste, Culture, and Conversion*, ed. Chad Bauman and Richard Fox Young (Delhi: Routledge, 2014).

[56] Sita Ram Goel, *Catholic Ashrams: Sannyasins or Swindlers?* (New Delhi: Voice of India, [1988] 2009), 26.

[57] Arun Shourie, *Missionaries in India: Continuities, Changes, Dilemmas* (New Delhi: Rupa & Co., 1994), 15. The "Planning Commission" is responsible for formulating India's five-year strategic plans.

non-strategizing) and Christianity. Like Swarup and Goel, Shourie traced the ostensibly inherently expansionist nature of Christianity to what he considered its ineluctable doctrinal exclusivism.[58] And like Goel, Shourie linked Christian evangelism to western imperialism, arguing that missionaries had colluded with colonial officials and western scholars (and still collude with their contemporary equivalents) in a common effort to colonize the consciousness of Indians and thereby make of them collaborators in the maintenance and expansion of western hegemony.[59]

Only a united India, in Shourie's view, would be able to resist this neocolonial threat. But Christians know this as well, which is why, in Shourie's view, they target the marginalized members of Indian society (lower-caste and tribal peoples) for conversion. Christian missionizing is therefore doubly sinister, because it not only represents a threat to the survival of Indian cultures and religions but also prevents an effective, unified response.

Gandhi, Swarup, Goel, and Shourie all seem rather assiduously to avoid what might be perceived as incitement to violence. Their primary response to what they consider the provocations of Christian evangelists is critique and polemic. Nevertheless, while few critics of Christian evangelism would encourage violence openly in published documents (as opposed to in political speeches), there are some who do provide an explicit justification (or at least an excuse) for it. Among them is Ashok Chowgule (b. 1948), who has for a long time been involved in the leadership of the VHP, at both state and national levels. Chowgule agrees with many of the views of the others that have been discussed in this chapter, but more than them suggests that there is a limit to Hindu tolerance, and that Hindus must more aggressively stand up to what he perceives to be the intolerance of evangelism.[60] There are also in Chowgule's writings mildly menacing passages, such as when he approvingly quotes Shripaty Sastry, who suggests that attacks on Christians are an inevitable consequence of their evangelical work, and that foreign missionaries should leave the country now, "with sweet memories of India," and "while the going is good."[61]

Of all the contemporary critics of Indian Christianity, Pravin Togadia is perhaps the best-known of those whose public rhetoric verges over into what we might with little ambivalence call hate speech. When he was the

---

[58.] Ibid., 12.
[59.] Ibid., 109, 32.
[60.] Ashok V. Chowgule, *Christianity in India: The Hindutva Perspective* (Mumbai: Hindu Vivek Kendra, 1999), 13.
[61.] Ibid., 95.

International General Secretary of the VHP in 2011, Togadia was quoted calling for a new Indian constitution that would allow "anyone who converts Hindus to be beheaded."[62] Earlier, Togadia had visited Kandhamal and delivered speeches many believed inflamed communal tensions in the period after Lakshmanananda Saraswati's assassination in 2008. In these speeches, he reportedly suggested that there was no place for Christians in Odisha and recommended that Christians be treated like "the cows they ate."[63] For his part in the riots, he was forbidden to re-enter Kandhamal in 2010, though he entered anyway and was arrested by the authorities.

Statements like Togadia's, and even Sastry's, require us to consider the relationship between provocative or threatening rhetoric and actual physical violence. It is tempting to distinguish the two, including in the category of "violence," only actual or threatened physical action intended to injure, maim, kill, or coerce another person to do something against their will (as in kidnapping or forcing someone to undergo a conversion ceremony). And the working definition of an "act of violence" that I employ in this book is restricted primarily to these kinds of physical violence, though I do also include vandalism within my definition because of the possibility that it might result in physical harm. Nevertheless, intolerant, hateful, or menacing rhetoric is related closely to physical violence because it encourages the development of prejudice, and provides ready justification among social actors more inclined to employ physical violence.

For this reason, John Corrigan and Lynn Neal—drawing on the work of Simon Wiesenthal, J. Gordon Melton, David Bromley, and others—encourage us to envision acts of rhetorical intolerance, along with other acts of intolerance as a point along a continuum that includes physical violence. Doing so, they argue, "helps us attend to the ways hateful ideas, words, and acts are related to violent practices. It illuminates the variety of ways violence is disseminated and enacted. No one would dispute that lynchings, murders, and bombings are violent acts and that in certain historical contexts they have been motivated by religion."[64] However, thinking in terms of a continuum rather than a binary "helps us see how cross burning, vandalism, hate speech,

[62] Express News Service, "Behead Those Who Convert Hindus: Togadia," *The Indian Express* 2011, http://archive.indianexpress.com/news/behead-those-who-convert-hindus-togadia/872403/.
[63] Harsh Mander, "Barefoot: Remembering Kandhamal," *The Hindu (Online)*, 17 December 2011, http://www.thehindu.com/opinion/columns/Harsh_Mander/barefoot-remembering-kandhamal/article2723257.ece; and Vrinda Grover, *Kandhamal: The Law Must Change its Course* (New Delhi: Multiple Action Research Group, 2010).
[64] John Corrigan and Lynn S. Neal, eds., *Religious Intolerance in America: A Documentary History* (Chapel Hill: University of North Carolina Press, 2010), 14.

public protests, threatening notes, written treatises, and the propagation of false allegations can also be viewed as religiously violent acts."[65] While I retain the more restrictive use of "violence" in this volume for the sake of referential clarity, then, it is important to keep in mind, as Corrigan and Neal suggest, that physical violence lies on continuum with what we might call rhetorical violence and should not be assumed to have no relationship with it.

Interestingly, one of the most prominent contemporary critics of Christian missionary practices, Swami Dayananda Saraswati (b. 1930), applies similar reasoning to his analysis of proselytization. Dayananda is founder and convenor of the important Hindu Dharma Acharya Sabha and has developed his own, distinctive approach to the issue. For Dayananda, the effort to convert another person is itself an act of violence, in fact a worse form of violence than physical violence because "the religious person is the deepest, the most basic in any individual. When that person is disturbed, a hurt is sustained which is very deep."[66] Physical violence is therefore, as I read the implications of Dayananda's statements, a natural and inevitable result of evangelical activities: "Religious conversion destroys centuries-old communities and incites communal violence. It is violence and it breeds violence."[67]

Although Dayananda states the opinion more clearly and aggressively than others, perhaps, the sentiment is widely shared, even among many committed secularists. And, of course, it is nearly universal among those associated with the Sangh Parivar. It is for this reason, then, that Sangh activists and politicians commonly respond to acts of violence against Christians with accusations that they are caused by Christian evangelical activities, and that the root problem is not therefore the violence but the provocation of proselytization. For example, in the wake of the anti-Christian riots in the Dangs, Gujarat, in 1998, the then BJP Prime Minister, Atal Behari Vajpayee, who was visiting the affected areas, implied his own interpretation of events, and indirectly blamed the Christian victims by calling for a "national debate" about religious conversions. And, of course, in the very regular targeting of Christian evangelists in the everyday acts of violence against Christians, there is implied the argument that evangelists deserve to be attacked, that violence is an appropriate response to the act of proselytization.

---

[65] Ibid., 14.
[66] Swami Dayananda Saraswati, "Conversion is an Act of Violence," *Hinduism Today (Web Edition)*, November 1999, http://www.hinduismtoday.com/modules/smartsection/item.php?itemid=4308.
[67] Saraswati, "Act of Violence."

Three primary grievances, then, are articulated in the intellectual work of the figures profiled here. And these grievances continue to surface in contemporary public debates, in the recent writings of figures like Radha Rajan and Sandhya Jain,[68] and even abroad, in, for example, the work of Rajiv Malhotra[69] and the Hindu American Foundation.[70] Rhetorically, the grievances tend to be expressed against Christians in general, and so, in the section that follows, I consider each of the grievances with special regard to Pentecostal Christianity.

The first of these grievances is that evangelism, and the attempt to convert another person to one's faith, is crassly cynical, a perversion of what religion is and should be about, and ultimately a socially disruptive endeavor. It is not my intent, at this point, to evaluate the legitimacy of these claims, but rather to think about the extent to which they are relevant to Pentecostalism and Pentecostalized Evangelicalism. For many of India's mainstream Orthodox, Protestant, and (non-Charismatic) Catholic Christians, evangelism is no longer a priority. While these Christians certainly preach within their own spaces, and may even occasionally offer altar calls, they are not generally engaged in open-air evangelism, nor do they tend in aggressive terms to criticize Hinduism. There are exceptions, of course, but for the most part, these groups conceive of mission primarily in terms of social service and care for Christians already within their congregations.

Pentecostals, however, are, along with Evangelicals, among those most committed to evangelism in India, and often conduct it aggressively while deploying a hyper-critical idiom that devalues or even demonizes

---

[68.] See, for example, Radha Rajan, "A Question of Identity," *VigilOnline.com*, 31 July 2007, http://www.vigilonline.com/index.php?option=com_content&task=view&id=879&I; Radha Rajan, "PIO Hindus—Gateway to White Imperialism," *VigilOnline.com*, 31 July 2011, http://www.vigilonline.com/index.php?option=com_content&task=view&id=1473&Itemid=71; Radha Rajan, "Tamil Nadu Politics: Cancerous Church Eats into Dravidian Parties," *VigilOnline.com*, 30 March 2011, http://www.vigilonline.com/index.php?option=com_content&task=view&id=1510&Itemid=71; Sandhya Jain, "Is There Imperial Design behind Conversion Overdrive?" *The Organiser (Online)*, 20 May 2007, http://www.organiser.org/dynamic/modules.php?name=Content&pa=showpage&pid=184&page=5; Sandhya Jain, "So the Caste Is a Convert's Nightmare Still! Let the Prodigals Return Home," *The Organiser (Online)*, 8 April 2007, http://www.organiser.org/dynamic/modules.php?name=Content&pa=showpage&pid=178&page=7; and Sandhya Jain, *Evangelical Intrusions, Tripura: A Case Study* (New Delhi: Rupa & Co., 2010).

[69.] See Rajiv Malhotra, *Being Different: An Indian Challenge to Western Universalism* (New Delhi: HarperCollins Publishers India, 2011); and Rajiv Malhotra, *Breaking India: Western Interventions in Dravidian and Dalit Faultlines* (New Delhi: Amaryllis, 2011).

[70.] See Hindu American Foundation, "Hindu American Foundation Policy Brief: Predatory Proselytization and Pluralism," http://www.hafsite.org/sites/default/files/HAF_PolicyBrief_Predatory_Proselytization.pdf.

Hinduism and its gods and goddesses. The existence of Pentecostals and other aggressive evangelistic groups therefore contributes to the perpetuation of certain kinds of stereotypes about Christians and their obsession with conversion that might be otherwise more difficult to sustain.

Even though few critics of Christianity in India are thoroughly familiar with the subtleties of Christian denominational differentiation, many do have some understanding of the differences among them. For example, in a debate televised on CNN-IBN's Face the Nation after the first (December 2007) round of riot violence in Kandhamal, Ram Madhav, national spokesperson for the RSS, referred to a *Christian Science Monitor* article that he claimed suggested that "Christian missionaries' conversion zeal is responsible for all the violence."[71] The article, by Scott Baldauf, makes no such claims, at least not directly, but it does describe a "new breed" of sectarian, independent missionaries in India who placed "an emphasis on speed" and who are "returning to practices of proselytizing that were long ago abandoned by the mainline missionaries because they were seen as offensive."[72] Pentecostals and sectarian Evangelicals, of course, comprise a significant proportion of those Baldauf describes as the new breed of missionary, and by referencing the article, Madhav therefore evinces at least some ability to distinguish between various kinds of Indian Christianity.

There is a rough concurrency, of course, between the emergence and increasing prominence of this new breed of aggressively evangelistic Evangelicals and Pentecostals and the dramatic rise in everyday incidents of anti-Christian violence. The disproportionate targeting of these groups is complex and is influenced by a range of factors. Nevertheless, it would be illogical to ignore the correspondence between the growing strength of these groups and increasing violence against Christians, or to dismiss it as pure coincidence, particularly since it is these very groups that are especially targeted in the attacks.

The second grievance commonly leveled against evangelistic Christians in India is that they use their superior access to western wealth and technology to lure non-Christians to the fold. All denominations of Indian Christianity, even those (like the St. Thomas Christians) not established by European missionaries, have benefitted directly and indirectly, since

---

[71.] CNN-IBN, "QOTD: Violence and Conversion in the Name of God," *CNN-IBN (Online)*, 2 January 2008, http://www.ibnlive.com/news/qotd-violence-and-conversion-in-the-name-of-god/55440-3.html.

[72.] Scott Baldauf, "A New Breed of Missionary: A Drive for Conversions, Not Development, Is Stirring Violent Animosity in India," *Christian Science Monitor (Online)*, 1 April 2005, http://www.csmonitor.com/2005/0401/p01s04-wosc.html.

the colonial period, from the inflow of western Christian wealth intended to help build up the Indian Christian church. And those benefits still continue today, both in terms of the institutions, endowments, and buildings western missionaries left behind, and in terms of the continuing freight of foreign funds flowing into India, earmarked for Christian missions.

Although Pentecostalism has a relatively long history in India, it cannot boast the impressive institutional strength of the Indian Catholic Church, many of the St. Thomas Christian denominations, or the ecumenical Protestant denominations (e.g., CNI, CSI). Until more recently, then, these latter groups had an almost exclusive monopoly, among Christians, on the kinds of educational or medical institutions that critics suggest Christians have used to impress and induce non-Christians to their faith through the offering of free or subsidized services only to Christians or potential converts.[73]

Larger Pentecostal denominations like the Assemblies of God have in recent decades begun to catch up and also now boast some impressive social service and educational institutions.[74] But in part due to the sectarian nature of Pentecostalism, these remain the exception, rather than the norm. And they are particularly atypical of the smaller-scale, rural Pentecostal individuals and groups most regularly targeted in the violence against Christians. The criticism that Gandhi, the Niyogi Report's authors, and others have leveled against India's Christians, that is, that they used their medical, vocational, and educational institutions to lure impecunious Indians to Christianity, therefore pertains more clearly to non-Pentecostals than to Pentecostals.

Nevertheless, the Pentecostals are catching up, as indicated above. In addition, Pentecostals and Pentecostalized Evangelicals are today awash in foreign funding, a result, in part, of the shift in foreign (especially American) financial support from foreign to indigenous Indian missionaries, a shift that favors Pentecostal evangelists, as I explain more elaborately in chapter 5. Such evangelists are frequently not particularly shy about adorning themselves (in new western-style clothes, finer homes and vehicles, etc.) with the funds that support them. And though it is difficult to ascertain the extent to which it is true in reality, the belief persists among

---

[73.] On which, see Chad Bauman, "Does the Divine Physician Have an Unfair Advantage? The Politics of Conversion in Twentieth-Century India," in *Asia in the Making of Christianity: Agency, Conversion, and Indigeneity*, ed. Jonathan Seitz and Richard Fox Young (Leiden: Brill, 2013).

[74.] Donald E. Miller and Tetsunao Yamamori, *Global Pentecostalism: The New Face of Christian Social Engagement* (Berkeley: University of California Press, 2007).

many non-Christians, non-Pentecostal Christians, and even Pentecostal Christians in India that at least some of these Pentecostal evangelists are paid per capita by their foreign funders for the conversions they provoke. To the extent that it does exist, of course, this compensation scheme inevitably, and in actual practice, invites abuse, and promotes exactly the kind of crass, materialistic, and aggressive evangelism that the critics of Christianity in India most abhor. Combined with the gospel of health and wealth for which Pentecostalism is well-known (but which appears to be somewhat less widespread in India than elsewhere, for reasons I can't fully discern, and have not explored), the money that today flows through Pentecostal channels, and which is manifest particularly in the lives of Pentecostal leaders, might easily suggest to potential converts that conversion could provide some material benefit.

Nevertheless, Pentecostal Christianity in India actually undermines the rhetoric of conversion by inducement and allurement in another, equally important way. As I argue in chapter 4, Pentecostal faith healing practices are dependent neither on foreign funding nor on access to western technological power. Critics of these practices assert that they are no more effective than a placebo, and amount to a socially undesirable form of medical quackery. Accordingly, those who continue to view Christian medical practices as an allurement to the faith are slowly beginning to shift the focus of their remonstrances from missionary hospitals to the practice of faith healing and exorcisms. But the point remains that the force of the argument implied by the phrase, "force, fraud, and inducement," is, as it pertains to medicine at least, undermined considerably by the fact that Pentecostal healing functions largely without the assistance of foreign funders.

The final grievance that animates the critique of Christian conversion in India is that Christianization entails a process of denationalization. The accusation functions on at least two interrelated levels. On the first, what we might call the lower level, the assertion of Christianity's critics is that converts cease to think, act, and dress like Indians, or worse, that they become positively captious in relation to the traditions that they abandon. India's earliest Christians did not fall prey to this accusation, for reasons indicated earlier, but critics have since the early colonial period accused converts to Christianity of becoming cultural aliens in their own land. As the tentacles of European colonialism in India extended into further and further cultural and geographic domains, and as the growing presence of European missionaries made it progressively easier for them to control India's Christians and influence their belief and practice in the direction of

European orthodoxy, these accusations surfaced even more regularly. And then, in the late colonial period, the independence movement lent them a sharper political edge.

Early colonial-era converts wrestled with this dilemma, and some of them, particularly high-caste converts who had a greater stake in the maintenance of traditional Indian social structures (e.g., Nehemiah Goreh and Brahmabandhav Upadhyay)[75] tenaciously attempted to articulate a Christianity that was thoroughly Indian. And as already mentioned, "indigenization" efforts have often enjoyed institutional support from mainstream Orthodox, Catholic, and—to a lesser extent—Protestant denominations in India. This support is related, no doubt, and particularly in the post-missionary period, to the fact that leadership in these denominations remains dominated by higher-caste communities that seek to preserve their traditional social status, which requires of them a certain deference to broader Indian notions of appropriate high-caste decorum, and to Indian culture more generally.

In contradistinction to India's mainline Christians, who are perceived by all parties to be more thoroughly acculturated, India's Pentecostals, more than any other Christian community, have resisted adjusting themselves to Indian social norms and Hindu religious beliefs and practices, at least officially. In the Indian context, the global Pentecostal movement's tendency to position itself rhetorically outside of and against the cultures of the places where it resides may resonate with the leadership of Pentecostal denominations, and particularly with the smaller, more sectarian ones, where—relative to the mainline denominations—a far greater proportion of lower-caste leaders may be found. For such leaders, the fact that deference to "traditional" Indian social and cultural norms generally implies deference as well to vestigial notions of caste stratification makes "indigenization" a far less appealing project.

And yet, Pentecostalism is thoroughly Indian in at least one aspect. Pentecostals' focus on faith healing, and their willingness to do battle with troublesome spirits and demons with officially prescribed practices, brings them and their faith very much into conversation with popular Indian religion. In addition, it draws to Pentecostals many non-Christians in search of physical and spiritual healing, blurring what many outside

---

[75] On Goreh, see Richard Fox Young, *Resistant Hinduism: Sanskrit Sources on Anti-Christian Apologetics in Early Nineteenth Century India* (Vienna: Indological Institute, University of Vienna, 1981), 101 ff. On Upadhyay, see Julius Lipner, *Brahmabandhab Upadhyay: The Life and Thought of a Revolutionary* (Oxford: Oxford University Press, 1999).

observers presume to be a clear line of demarcation between Pentecostals and non-Christians.

The accusation that Christianization entails denationalization functions at a second, higher level as well. In the view of many of its critics, Christianization was, during the colonial period, little more than the handmaiden of colonization. And today, suggest critics like Radha Rajan and Sandhya Jain, it continues to further the western neocolonial project, that is, the globalization of western intellectual, artistic, sartorial, social, cultural, and political hegemony. Many of Indian Christianity's critics also suspect Indian Christians of divided loyalties, of being a fifth column in the Indian body politic. Of course, these suspicions must be understood in the context of Partition, which signifies to many Hindus what can happen when a religious minority grows too large and powerful, as well as in the light of ongoing secessionist movements in the Northeast of India, which draw strength and much of their leadership from the Christian communities that predominate there.

Here again, the Pentecostals' rhetoric of "rupture," their articulation of a Christian culture against culture, raises the hackles of those committed to the preservation of what they consider "traditional" Indian and Hindu culture. But so, too, does the fact that their theology, dress, and musical styles closely resemble those of the western Christians who support them, and who appear regularly in massive rallies and on Indian television stations. So while all Indian Christians are suspected by some of foreign loyalties, it may be the case that the self-presentation of Pentecostals as a community set apart (and yet curiously westernized) makes their presence and work in India more provocative than that of other Christian communities.

Chapter 1 located Indian Pentecostalism within the global Pentecostal movement and within the context of Indian Christianity more generally. In this chapter, then, I have attempted to provide some context for anti-Christian violence and for the relationship of Indian Pentecostalism to it. Together, these two chapters prepare the way for a more nuanced and thorough analysis of the disproportionate targeting of Pentecostals and Pentecostalized Evangelicals. It is to that, then, that we now turn.

CHAPTER 3 | Where the Spirit (of Violence) Leads

The Disproportionate Targeting of
Indian Pentecostals

MANY INDIAN OBSERVERS—CHRISTIAN, non-Christian, and even Pentecostal—account for the disproportionate targeting of Pentecostals in the violence against Christians today with reference to their supposedly more consistent commitment to, and more aggressive style of evangelism. There is certainly some truth to the assertion that Pentecostal proselytization is provocative, and that this provocation alone occasionally leads to violence. But this factor is only part of the story. Indeed, its superficial persuasiveness is related in part to certain prejudices about Pentecostalism that one finds consciously or unconsciously held by both more established, high-status Christians, and among higher-caste Hindus. This explanation is therefore convenient, but also incomplete.

The point of this chapter, therefore, is to provide a broader, more nuanced enumeration of the many factors that together conspire to make Pentecostals more vulnerable to anti-Christian violence. Some of the factors are related to the nature of Pentecostal faith and belief. These are, perhaps, the more obvious ones. Others, however, have more to do with the social location of Pentecostals, with the many subtle ways in which Pentecostals—not uniquely but certainly more so than most other Indian Christians—challenge or run afoul of hegemonic (if not uncontested) Indian cultural norms and mores. Over these, Pentecostals have less control. And yet their effects are no less real.

It is possible to adduce more than a dozen discrete factors involved in the disproportionate targeting of Indian Pentecostals, and I will discuss each of them in the analysis that follows. For heuristic purposes, however,

I will group them under three broad headings/sections focusing on certain general characteristics of Indian Pentecostalism: its (1) evangelical assertion and enthusiasm, (2) the greater presence and participation, within it, of marginalized and vulnerable peoples, and (3) its countercultural posture.

Evangelical Assertion and Enthusiasm

Evangelism alone does not distinguish Pentecostals from other Evangelicals, and it may even be the case that many independent, self-identifying mostly un-Pentecostalized Evangelicals[1] are, on average, more active in evangelism than Pentecostals. That said, many of those I interviewed in India, both Hindu and Christian, believed that Pentecostals were more "enthusiastic" and "zealous" (terms that can have positive or negative connotations, depending on one's perspective) than others in their evangelization and also more likely to cause offense.

The "enthusiasm" of Pentecostal evangelists is related, no doubt, to their general enthusiasm, a positive sign, for many Pentecostals, of life in the Spirit. This enthusiasm manifests most regularly in Pentecostal worship, which is often quite boisterous. This boisterousness itself may incline many Indians unfavorably toward Pentecostals. In general, Indians excel at and take pride in grace and self-discipline, avoiding over-action, avoiding getting dirty in their daily activities, like the proverbial lotus growing up from the mud. This is particularly true among female and upper-caste Indians, who are, as a mark of their respectability, expected to maintain a certain level of demure propriety. And though the convention is now regularly flaunted by contemporary urban women and the glitterati, and though there are significant regional differences, in many parts of India, especially rural India, women who let their hair down (literally and figuratively) are associated popularly with both prostitution and possession (the latter of which can be a blessing or an embarrassment, again, depending on one's perspective). It is perhaps already clear, then, that the three broad factors involved in the disproportionate targeting of Pentecostals, outlined just above, are interrelated, because the very freedom and enthusiasm that Pentecostals express in their worship and evangelization identifies them with lower-caste and disreputable people (a key element of the factors discussed in the second section) and with culturally inappropriate behavior (a central element in the third).

---

[1] That is, Evangelicals not associated with the larger, western Evangelical denominations that in India at least are less inclined toward evangelism.

But in this section we will focus on evangelical enthusiasm more specifically. For Pentecostals, mission is demanded, activated, and driven by the Holy Spirit. Pentecostals associated with EFI, Richard Howell suggested, are generally "extraordinarily motivated . . . and their faith is played out in [evangelism]." And, as the Indian leader of a Charismatic mission based in the United States averred, "Pentecostals are on the offensive . . . the mainlines are all status quoists." This latter point is one which many Indians repeated, particularly with reference to the CNI and CSI, which most perceived to be static in terms of growth and evangelism, in no small part because they were distracted by engagement in consolidation projects, usually involving the maintenance and protection of large and lucrative properties (or litigation involving the same). The enthusiasm with which Pentecostals engage in mission is therefore distinct and makes them more "visible," as another Indian Pentecostal put it, and vulnerable to attack.[2]

A brief excursus is necessary here to help explain why Charismatic Catholics, while similar to Pentecostals in this regard, are distinct in certain ways. While conducting research in Pune, I was invited to attend a Charismatic prayer group meeting. I arrived late, unaware that the group had decided to integrate me into their program and was awaiting my arrival. As soon as I entered the room, I was asked to come to the front and share something. Not knowing what was expected, and not being testimonially inclined, I talked a bit about my research, about why I was interested in Pentecostals and Charismatics, and then about my Mennonite upbringing. (I've found that Indians are almost universally interested in the Amish and Mennonites, once they come to know about them.) The group peppered me with questions for half an hour, those I had intended to interview becoming the interviewers.

Several things were striking about the exchange. The first was their genuine interest in what, it became clear, was not a very charismatic brand of Christianity (though some had heard of, and were impressed by, the Amish community's gracious response to a shooting spree that had taken place in a one-room Amish schoolhouse several years earlier). The other was the complete disinterest of the parish priest, who during the entire service sat in the back, checking and writing text messages on his mobile phone. This was predominantly a lay event, and a very feminine one at that; women in

<hr />

[2] On this as a pan-Asian phenomenon, see Wonsuk Ma, "Asian (Classical) Pentecostal Theology in Context," in *Asian and Pentecostal: The Charismatic Face of Christianity in Asia*, ed. Allan Anderson and Edmond Tang (Costa Mesa, CA: Regnum, 2005), 76.

the group asked more questions than men, and many of them were clearly recognized as leaders.

Eventually I was able to ask some questions. I asked about what distinguished Charismatics from other groups (like Pentecostals, etc.), and I asked about Charismatic ideas about evangelism and non-Christian religions. The answers were not as interesting as the fervor with which they were articulated. One lay member jumped out of his seat at the opportunity to speak about evangelism. He told a story in which he had shared the gospel with a Hindu and averred that in so doing he was "bold; not afraid of anything." And as he talked about the gospel's demand to speak of Jesus to non-Christians, he suddenly took on the aspect of an Evangelical televangelist. His bloodshot eyes darted and flared. His head seemed too tightly attached to his neck, jerking and jumping unnaturally when he wanted to emphasize his points. His jowls danced along to the rhythm.

At the end of the service, a woman leader of the group asked if the group could pray that I would receive the Holy Spirit. My feeble attempt to ward off this very scenario by talking about my Mennonite background had clearly failed. She asked me to bow my head and stand with my palms extended and turned upwards. Then she told me—suggested might be a better term—that I would indeed receive the Holy Spirit if I truly believed. And then she, and the rest of the group, broke into glossolalia as I listened, partly absorbed in the experience, partly humored by it, and partly attempting to register clinically to the variety of tongues being expressed around me.

Eventually, after about five minutes, the praying shifted to English, and then ended. I found myself somewhat relieved that I had not received the Holy Spirit or fallen to the floor in fits. Such was the power of suggestion throughout the meeting, and especially in this part of it, and such is the extent of my own suggestibility, that part of me was actually worried I might do so.[3] The group then broke into a song, the lyrics of which promised me the Holy Spirit was mine. Throughout the encounter, the parish priest continued his text messaging vigil.

After the service ended, I apologized profusely to a male leader of the group for having been so late. If I had known I was to be the featured speaker, I asserted, I would have been more prompt. In response, he said

---

[3.] For a critique of the imprecision of terms like "suggestion" and an attempt to explore more thoroughly the mechanisms which make Charismatic practices convincing and efficacious, see Thomas J. Csordas, *The Sacred Self: A Cultural Phenomenology of Charismatic Healing* (Berkeley: University of California Press, 1994), 3, 161.

that my lateness had been an answer to prayer. Other things were planned for the meeting, and when he heard I was coming he was worried that the other work on the agenda would not get done. So he had "placed it in God's hands" in prayer. My tardiness allowed the other work to get done. This kind of answer to prayer, he said, was part of a "pattern" he had discerned in his Charismatic life, that is, that answers to prayer came regularly, and often, as in this case, somewhat mysteriously.

There is much that could be said about this encounter, but I offer it here simply to make the point that Charismatic Catholics also conceive of themselves as an evangelical people. And they are at the forefront of direct *Catholic* evangelistic efforts. The journalist and Christian and *dalit* rights activist John Dayal, for example, himself a Catholic, suggested in conversations with me that there is a "large overlap" between the evangelistic "wing" of the Indian Catholic Church and the Charismatic renewal. Nevertheless, directly evangelical projects make up, Dayal estimated, only about 25% of what Catholics do in mission (the rest involving the running of service institutions, social activism, etc.). And despite the attestation of the enthusiastic evangelist described above, many Catholics, Charismatic of otherwise, consider evangelism something that priests, rather than the laity, should do.

The Catholic sociologist Paul Parathazham, on whose published work this book has already drawn considerably, told me that in general, Charismatic Catholics "don't have that conversion thing. They want to convert only within Catholicism. Within Catholicism they want to draw more people into their way of prayer and looking at things." And, of course, the response of the Catholic Charismatics just described to my non-Charismatic presence among them also suggests a focus on renewing and reforming other Christians (though my vague and evasive answers to questions about my own faith may have egged them on). Therefore, Charismatic Catholics, while evangelistic in a certain ways, are generally not evangelistic in the kinds of "visible" ways that increase one's vulnerability to attack. They also, as discussed below, have a supportive and protective institutional network that many Pentecostals and neo-Pentecostals lack.

It is clear, then, that Indian Pentecostals are not at all times, in all places, more missionary-minded than all other kinds of Christians in India. But they are active, in general, and they are perceived by both Indian Christians and non-Christians to be more assertive, aggressive, and critical in their evangelical approach than other Christians, including independent Evangelical pastors. The "countercultural posture" of Pentecostals, as I discuss below, has many aspects. But one of them seems to be a predilection for condemning the religion, and particularly the "idols" of Hinduism (or even of Catholicism!). Arun Jones writes, "A certain brand of Pentecostal preachers in India seem to relish the opportunity publicly to condemn other religions—and perhaps at times even other Christian groups—and thus gain some notoriety for themselves."[4] Mainstream Christian groups condemn such acts, in part because they know they are socially disruptive, and in part because they suspect they may suffer the consequences of them.

As if to prove the point, in a private interview with me, the Indian head of a large, international Pentecostal mission organization active mostly among OBCs in western India repeatedly referred to Vishnu as "the personification of the devil."

"Do you say that publicly in India?" I asked, shocked that a well-educated, highly placed, contemporary mission leader would do so.

"Yes, I do," he replied assuredly.

Similarly, if more subtly, a Brahman convert leading a Pentecostal worship service in Bangalore testified, "You know why I'm happy today? I'm happy because 20 years ago I was washing and worshipping the idols. I knew more than 75 slokas.[5] But I didn't know if my God was alive. But now I know my God is alive. I know my redeemer lives." There is much of interest in these six sentences. But the core message is that Brahman priests, custodians of India's high-caste cultural traditions, and the traditions embraced and promoted by the Sangh Parivar, worship inanimate objects ("idols" that are not "alive") through obsessive but ultimately ineffectual ritualism ("washing . . . the idols," and the repetition of slokas) that fails to produce any confidence about one's ultimate fate. (Interestingly, the testimony seemed designed to clearly highlight the upper-caste origins of the worship leader. Later, without prompting, the pastor of the congregation privately noted the same.) The worship leader's testimony was indirect, but indirectly deeply, deeply critical of common Hindu rituals and belief. Similarly, Pentecostals also seem to be somewhat more provocatively evangelical than most other Indian Christians in their interpersonal relations. One Assemblies of God convert in Bangalore, for example, oppugned his mother's Hindu faith for some time after his conversion by regularly walking into her puja room and knocking down the statues and

---

[4.] Arun Jones, "Faces of Pentecostalism in North India Today," *Society* 46, no. 6 (2009): 508.
[5.] "Slokas" are Sanskrit liturgical passages.

images of the gods in order to fight what he considered the "power of idolatry."

For many Pentecostals, such confrontations are part of a program of Bible-oriented Christian truth-telling designed to shake non-Christians out of their religious complacency. For others, they initiate an engagement with non-Christian "spiritual powers of darkness." Yet even some Pentecostals condemn evangelistic methods involving harsh criticism of others' beliefs and consider them an unnecessary provocation. As one put it, "sometimes when we are overzealous and we take some unnecessary steps in preaching the gospel, then we can invite trouble for ourselves."

Pentecostals may be targeted in part, then, because they are more assertive, more critical, and more visible in their evangelism. But another factor is their success. The best statistics suggest that Pentecostal Christian growth easily outpaces that of all other forms of Indian Christianity.[6] A significant proportion of that growth, perhaps as much as 72%, if Parathazham's research on Indian neo-Pentecostals can be taken as a general guide, is the result of Christians joining from other, mostly mainline denominations. Nevertheless, converts from non-Christian religions comprise the remaining 28% of growth, and in certain specific contexts, the proportion of non-Christian converts may be much higher. One Assemblies of God pastor, for example, claimed that his urban church had grown from 15 to 5,000 members in the last 33 years, and that 70% of the converts had been Hindu. Regardless of the source of Pentecostal and neo-Pentecostal growth, it is substantial; more than half of Parathazham's survey respondents had joined in the last five years.[7]

It is clear, then, that Pentecostals are more frequently than other Christian communities pushing into new, non-Christian territories, provoking conversions in towns and villages and among communities where there have never been conversions before. Nearly universally, Indian Christians involved in mission told me that the social backlash was far

---

[6.] The growth is particularly pronounced, Richard Howell maintains, among neo-Pentecostal churches led by first-generation converts. Interestingly, while the growth of Christianity in India is low for Asian countries (2.75%, i.e., not even in the top ten), the growth of "Renewalism" in South Asia (which includes Pakistan, Bangladesh, etc.) is higher than anywhere else in the world (about 5.21%). See Todd Johnson and Kenneth Ross, *Atlas of Global Christianity 1910–2010* (Edinburgh: Edinburgh University Press, 2009), esp. 101, 35, 43.

[7.] Paul Parathazham, "Neo-Pentecostalism in India: Preliminary Report of a National Survey," *Word and Worship* 29 (1996). It should be kept in mind, however, that this study is now more than a decade old.

greater, and far more likely to turn violent, in the early years of missionary work in new locations. As one Indian mission leader put it, where churches are emerging for the first time, local people say "these people were *our* people, and now they have converted."

Conversions can be socially disruptive, particularly when the conversions are brought about by groups like the Pentecostals who sometimes demand of converts, as described below, a rather visible and drastic disentanglement from their previous sociocultural and religious milieu. (Although for counter-examples, see the excellent ethnographic work of Nathaniel Roberts on religion and relatively nondisruptive "conversions" in the slums of Chennai.[8]) And when non-Christians in such places convert in large enough numbers to establish and begin building a church structure, a very visible symbol of their permanent presence, local resistance frequently coalesces into legal or physical behavior intended to impede construction, or even (but far less frequently) into violence.

One of the issues in Pentecostal growth, of course, is that Pentecostal preachers often create propaganda about growth disproportionate to the actual reality. For reasons related, perhaps, to the pressures of foreign funding, Indian Pentecostals are often accused, even by other Indian Pentecostals, of exaggerating their numbers or inflating them artificially by—as in one example I encountered—having a large number of dead people on their rolls. Although this may be related to the "cycle of blame" described below, many mainstream Indian Christians feel that Pentecostals are too hasty to baptize those that express interest in Christianity, and too little concerned with prior teaching, testing, and discipleship. As one Malayali Mar Thomite[9] priest working in rural Karnataka put it, the "mainlines follow some discipline," but the "independent churches are spoiling our name. . . . Some independent churches are doing [evangelism] for livelihood only. Nowadays it has become a very commercial thing. . . . Those people if they baptize one person and take [a] photo and send [it] to somebody, the local pastor gets five hundred rupees . . . still this thing is happening here."

---

[8] Nathaniel Roberts, "The Power of Conversion and the Foreignness of Belonging: Domination and Moral Community in a Paraiyar Slum" (PhD diss., Columbia University, 2008); and Nathaniel Roberts, "Anti-conversion Law in a Secular State: Religious Difference and the Threat to 'Public Order'" (paper presented at the Max Planck Institute for the Study of Religion and Ethnic Diversity, Göttingen, February 22, 2011).

[9] The Mar Thoma church is one contemporary form of St. Thomas Christianity.

Marginalization and the Participation of
Vulnerable Peoples

A second major factor in the targeting of Pentecostal and Charismatic Christians is their marginalization and vulnerability. There are three primary and interrelated factors in this marginalization: (1) their lack of a supportive and protective denominational network (particularly in the case of the independent or quasi-independent churches), (2) their more frequently rural location, and (3) the greater presence and participation, among them, of women and lower-caste/tribal Indians. The paragraphs below address each of these factors in turn.

Pentecostalism imbibes and accentuates the sectarian spirit of Protestant Christianity, and the Pentecostal emphasis on what Bergunder calls "experiential spirituality" and unmediated religious experience is frequently used to support claims of authority and the desire to establish new churches or ministries. As he puts it, "the stereotyped usage 'God has told me' is indeed a reflection of the desire to follow God's will in everything, but, semantically, it is often a synonym for 'I have made up my mind.'"[10] In reality, then, the Pentecostal desire to live life according to conscience and God's will, and the democratizing force latent in the assertion that the charismatic gifts are available to all, contributes to an independent spirit that encourages fission and schism and precludes or impedes the construction of larger denominational structures.[11] This is particularly true among the neo-Pentecostal and independent, Pentecostalized Evangelical churches in India. Because of this, when members of these congregations are harassed, attacked, or sued, they generally don't have access to the institutional support and resources that might help them respond effectively, or even prevent such situations from arising in the first place.

Another factor in the special vulnerability of Pentecostal churches to anti-Christian violence is their location. While many Pentecostals are located, and thrive in urban India, they maintain, by dint of being on the growing edge of Indian Christianity, a far more active presence in rural areas than other Indian Christians (with the exception, perhaps, of Catholics). So far, at least, anti-Christian violence appears to be primarily a rural and

---

[10] Michael Bergunder, *The South Indian Pentecostal Movement in the Twentieth Century* (Grand Rapids, MI: Eerdmans Publishers, 2008), 133.

[11] Thomas J. Csordas, *Language, Charisma, and Creativity: The Ritual Life of a Religious Movement* (Berkeley: University of California Press, 1997), 133; and Joel Robbins, "Anthropology of Religion," in *Studying Global Pentecostalism: Theories and Methods*, ed. Allan Anderson et al. (Berkeley: University of California Press, 2010), 162.

small town affair. Many urban Christian evangelists, for example, told me that they never had any problems in the cities, but only when they went out into the villages, a difference they attributed to rural traditionalism, suspicion of outsiders, intolerance of differences, and a lack of education. In fact, some, like the highly placed administrator of a large mission based in a suburb of Hyderabad, argued that anti-Christian violence was an opportunistic crime committed in areas, like Kandhamal, with maximal poverty and minimal police presence, and therefore dismissed the statistical evidence of greater Pentecostal targeting as nothing more than an adventitious effect of their greater rural presence. Many Christians in fact believed that the mainline Christians were not attacked primarily because they were not present in the rural areas where violence was more common. As John Dayal explained, in typically colorful language, "The episcopal, mainline churches have withdrawn from the countryside. . . . They're not there to be victimized. . . . You can't drown on a mountaintop."

There are denominational (or rather, non-denominational) and demographic reasons, then, for the greater vulnerability of Pentecostal churches to attack. These are exacerbated, however, by social, cultural, and inter-religious factors that lead mainline churches to distance themselves from Pentecostal Christians, even (or perhaps especially) during periods of violence. As indicated earlier, one of these factors is the perception, among mainstream Christians, that Pentecostal Christians are "undisciplined," aggressive, and overly adversarial in their evangelism (and therefore deserving, in some sense, of the violence to which they fall prey).[12] Aside from finding such aggressive evangelism distasteful or inappropriate, many mainline Christians, in order to avoid being attacked themselves, simply do not want to be associated with more aggressively evangelistic Christians.

Obvious in the use of terms like "undisciplined," however, is another, deeper layer of antipathy. Not only non-Christians (as noted above) but also many "respectable" mainstream Indian Christians consider Pentecostals a rather indecorous lot. To some extent, this has to do with universal tensions between "mainstream" and "popular" religion, and/or liturgical versus free or "ecstatic" religion. But it also reflects more specifically Indian issues, such as inter-caste competition and intra-Christian disagreements regarding how Christianity should relate to Hinduism. And, of course, many Pentecostals encourage mainline Christians to marginalize them

---

[12.] Jones, "Faces," 507–8.

by keeping to themselves (i.e., in the company of properly "born-again Christians"),[13] criticizing mainline Christians as "idol worshippers," or denouncing them as overly complacent, inadequately evangelistic, or unduly acculturated.

Many social activists in India understand anti-Christian violence primarily as anti-*dalit* violence, that is, as violence against members of low-caste communities by local elites (but using interreligious provocation as a convenient excuse and rallying cry). Not surprisingly, then, many also identify the greater participation of low-caste Christians in the leadership of Pentecostal churches as one of the reasons for their special targeting. Leadership of low-caste Christians in Pentecostal and Charismatic churches increased substantially after the 1970s, when the neo-Pentecostal movement took off and indigenous Christians displaced foreign missionaries as the dominant players in the Pentecostal movement.[14] These changes coincided with the increased visibility of the human rights movement in India. All of these processes favored the development of low-caste leadership, and, as indicated earlier, many members of marginalized castes established new churches as a way to free themselves from what they considered the upper-caste domination of leadership in mainstream Catholic, Protestant, and Orthodox churches, and in the older, larger Pentecostal denominations. The net result of these social forces is that in general[15] the leadership of Pentecostal (but especially neo-Pentecostal) Indian Christianity today is far more *dalitized*—to use the term that social activists and church leaders often use—than that in the mainstream Protestant and Catholic churches.

In addition, low-caste lay Christians themselves participate in the life of these churches more than they do (or are allowed to do) in the mainstream churches. The presence of charismatic gifts pluralizes leadership, leaving space for evangelists, prophets, healers, and those with the gift of tongues to flourish and express themselves alongside the primary pastor/s. "The strength of the Dalit Pentecostal Churches," contends Thomas approvingly, "is that they allow full participation of almost all the members."[16] In the

---

[13.] On this, see Parathazham, "Survey," 93.

[14.] V. V. Thomas, *Dalit Pentecostalism: Spirituality of the Empowered Poor* (Bangalore: Asian Trading Corporation, 2008), 319–23.

[15.] I must emphasize the general nature of this statement. Regional differences exist. For example, Hedlund indicates that Pentecostalism in Andhra Pradesh is drawn far more evenly from various sectors of society. See Roger Hedlund, "Indigenous Pentecostalism in India," in *Asian and Pentecostal: The Charismatic Face of Christianity in Asia*, ed. Allan Anderson and Edmond Tang (Costa Mesa, CA: Regnum, 2005), 221.

[16.] Thomas, *Dalit Pentecostalism*, 376.

mainline churches, Fr. Selvaraj Arulnathan of the Indian Social Institute added in an interview, the "dalits have no role," but in the Pentecostal churches, "Instantly they can raise their voice, instantly they can give their testimony, become pastors, etc."

This puts the interests of Pentecostals at odds with those of mainstream Christians. The mainstream churches, one Charismatic mission leader insisted, "have taken their stand with the upper-caste elite government. . . . They have name and fame and they have the largest property. They have a lot to lose. . . . They don't want to disturb the system. . . . And so they don't even see the Pentecostal as a genuine Christian." Adopting a more sociological perspective, Arun Jones argues much the same. The Syrian Orthodox of Kerala are considered high castes, he writes, and mainstream Protestants are generally part of the Indian middle class. To preserve their status, these groups are careful about who they accept into their folds. But Pentecostals will, according to Jones, "welcome whoever they can get."[17]

The marginalization of Pentecostal Christians by other Indian Christians makes them more vulnerable to attack. Numerous Indian Christians with whom I talked pointed out that most mainstream Christians, particularly mainstream Christian leaders, seemed relatively unconcerned with the riot violence in Kandhamal, which preyed upon lower-caste Christians, and only became exercised about the issue of anti-Christian violence when, a few weeks after the second round of riots had begun in Kandhamal, violent nationalists began attacking upper-caste Christians in Mangalore and elsewhere in Karnataka.

If upper-caste Christians resent the social advance of low-caste Christians, then it should come as no surprise that many upper-caste, wealthy, and powerful Hindus do as well. As I have argued elsewhere,[18] for example, it seems clear that riot violence in both the Dangs, Gujarat, and Kandhamal, Odisha, represented, at least in part, the perturbed response by upper-caste, merchant, and land-owning Hindu communities and the local tribes with whom they allied, to the growing assertion, economic competitiveness, and social advance of lower-caste and tribal Christians.

The same must surely be at least partially true in the case of everyday incidents of anti-Christian violence. Christianity contributes to socially and economically ameliorative processes among lower-caste and tribal converts by speaking of equality and human dignity and provoking

---

[17] Jones, "Faces," 509.
[18] Chad Bauman, "Hindu-Christian Conflict in India: Globalization, Conversion, and the Coterminal Castes and Tribes," *Journal of Asian Studies* 72, no. 3 (2013): 633–53.

demands for the same (if not always living up to the quality of its own rhetoric), and by providing lower-caste and tribal groups with greater access to economic, educational, and vocational development opportunities. These processes often help lower-caste and tribal Christian communities transform themselves from marginalized, exploited victims of the local economy to bona fide competitors, thereby provoking consternation from all other local communities (Christian and non-Christian) who must compete with them.

Social transformations frequently create turmoil and resistance. Pentecostals and Pentecostalized Evangelicals both provoke social transformations and have a large presence in places where such transformations have been particularly noticeable. Moreover, Pentecostals are frequently unashamed to flaunt the signs of their newfound success (in the form of new cell phones, vehicles, sound systems, houses, and churches). It would be somewhat perplexing, therefore, if they did not arouse at least some degree of resentment and jealousy (which is, of course, not the same as saying that a violent backlash to social change is inevitable, in India or elsewhere, or that Pentecostals somehow deserve their special targeting.)

Another factor in the marginalization of Pentecostals is the prominent participation and activity of women in their churches. While Pentecostal women in India may less frequently than elsewhere occupy positions of formal authority, they remain quite visible. In most Pentecostal churches, they comprise a clear majority of congregants (often as much as 70%), and they often participate openly and enthusiastically in worship. There are a number of possible explanations for their greater participation. Women are generally considered more pious and religiously active than men in India (as is true elsewhere, e.g., in the United States), and so in many ways the greater participation of women in Pentecostal worship reflects broader social and religious trends. But women may also be disproportionately drawn to Pentecostalism because at least some Pentecostal communities afford women more opportunities for participation in leadership and/or worship than is available in other religious contexts. Pentecostal healers are also considered particularly skilled at addressing the underlying spiritual and personality sources of family dysfunction, a skill that might have particular appeal to women, who are often disproportionately affected by such dysfunction. In any case, as alluded to earlier, women's participation in the Pentecostal brand of more expressive worship alone is perceived as somewhat scandalous in certain Indian contexts. And the confidence that many female Pentecostal converts gain to relate more freely to others, particularly to other men, is conceived by many traditional Indians as a foreign, western liberty that therefore places them in contravention of certain traditional taboos.

After a Catholic friend of the family told her that her daughter had "joined a cult" and had been surreptitiously attending a Pentecostal church in Chennai, one Hindu mother marched straight to the church in question on a Sunday morning, accosted the pastor outside and, while sweeping dust up off the road at him, bellowed, "You are a drunkard. You are inviting women. You are running a brothel!"[19] In calling the pastor a drunkard, the mother drew upon popular stereotypes of Christians, who, because they lack the teetotalism of upper-caste Hindus, are supposed by others to be more avid boozehounds. But in accusing him of running a brothel, she may in fact have been making certain kinds inferences that made sense, given her social location. Women came to the church in large numbers, they worshipped freely, and they interacted openly with men in the church, all of which might suggest (to more conservative Indian observers) a lack of chastity and propriety.

The Pentecostal woman who speaks in tongues and gives testimonies in church is a threat to more conservative notions of Indian female propriety far more than the average mainstream Protestant, Catholic, or Orthodox Christian woman, who may push the edges of propriety along with other middle-class and urban Indian women, but who does not challenge them in so fundamental a fashion. Like the visibility of lower-caste Christians in Pentecostalism, then, the visibility of women contributes to the marginalization of Pentecostals at the hands of "respectable," higher-class, and higher-caste Christians and non-Christians.

Countercultural Posture

In their analysis of neo-Pentecostals, Paul Parathazham's survey group deployed a working definition that included, as a key feature, "an antagonistic attitude towards the world."[20] At first, and when one expects definitions having to do with the centrality of the Spirit, this seems a rather odd inclusion. But anyone who spends time among Indian Pentecostals comes rather quickly to realize how central, common, and distinctive a feature of their religious life this really is. In fact, Pentecostals globally tend to promote radical "rupture," according to Joel Robbins, with what

---

[19.] The story was told to me by the daughter.
[20.] Parathazham, "Survey," 81.

came before. Their transformations are not gradual affairs, but are, rather, effected by "a series of ruptures with the ways in which they have lived up to the time of their conversion."[21] Robbins's argument is surely intended, in part at least, to interrogate and disrupt the analytical assumptions of those studying global Christianity today, many of whom—including me, in my earlier work—have tended to (over-)emphasize its continuity with pre-Christian religions and cultures (e.g., through processes of inculturation, syncretism, etc.). And certainly the rhetoric of rupture is one of the factors that accounts for the disproportionate targeting of Pentecostals in anti-Christian violence.

While acknowledging the importance of Robbins's intervention, Birgit Meyer has cautioned that we not forget that "rupture necessarily implies some kind of discursive continuity, if only because 'being against' always entails some degree of 'being with.' "[22] The way to reconcile these two positions, it seems to me, is to keep in mind that the "rupture" advocated by Pentecostals works primarily at the rhetorical level, and while the rhetoric of rupture has real and significant effects on the behavior of Pentecostal Christians—in part because it is frequently enacted in ritual[23]—it does not preclude the possibility of syncretisms and assimilations, particularly those that operate at the unconscious level.[24]

Indian Pentecostals, like Pentecostals worldwide, tend to encourage each other to make a radical break with all things non-Christian. This involves notions of personal transformation, of course, particularly for converts. But it also entails communal rupture with "non-Christian" elements of culture, past and present. Birgit Meyer has noted that "Pentecostals tend to mobilize a diabolizing stance toward indigenous gods, which are recast as demons operating under the aegis of Satan."[25] For many Pentecostals the appropriate strategy for dealing with their religious past prior to conversion is not merely to avoid or forget it, but rather to actively combat it. Pentecostalism therefore tends to contour a culture "against culture."[26] In India, this Pentecostal culture against culture is propped up by a dualistic cosmology that simplifies the gradated Hindu realm of the supernatural

---

[21] Robbins, "Anthropology," 159. See also Joel Robbins, "Continuity Thinking and the Problem of Christian Culture," *Current Anthropology* 48 (2007): 5–38.

[22] Birgit Meyer, "Pentecostalism and Globalization," in *Studying Global Pentecostalism: Theories and Methods*, ed. Allan Anderson et al. (Berkeley: University of California Press, 2010), 121.

[23] Robbins, "Anthropology," 161.

[24] See also Ma, "Pentecostal Theology," 70–71.

[25] Meyer, "Pentecostalism," 121.

[26] The phrase is Kirk Dombrowski's, quoted in Robbins, "Anthropology," 159.

into a binary of fully good, and fully evil (but more on that in the next chapter).

A number of Indians I interviewed identified this antagonistic, countercultural stance as the primary reason for the disproportionate targeting of Pentecostals. As one commentator suggested, "They're the ones, Pentecostals . . . who very strictly follow, 'I won't take any *prasadam*,[27] I won't go to the [temple], I won't worship the idols' . . . Which in a way detaches them from [their cultural context]. It is they who have been mostly attacked." Fashion is also an important factor. More so than other Indian Christians, for example, Pentecostals intentionally dress and present themselves in ways that set them apart from other Indians. One young man who arrived at a North Indian Pentecostal seminary, for example, was told that he could not wear the *dhoti* and *kurta* he was accustomed to wearing in his central Indian village, because these were examples of "Hindu" dress. The distinction between "Hindu" and "Christian" dress was further clarified and essentialized at the seminary by the fact that the student was allowed to wear the *dhoti* and *kurta* during "cultural programs" celebrating the ethnic and cultural diversity of India.

Many Indians I interviewed maintained that the intentionally distinctive dress of Pentecostals was one factor in their being disproportionately targeted. Hindus saw members of the mainline denominations as culturally similar, one female North Indian Pentecostal indicated, because they dressed and decorated themselves as most Hindus did. Indian Pentecostals (particularly female Pentecostals), however, were clearly distinguishable because they sometimes dressed fully in white, and in almost all cases refused to wear the dots (*tikkas*) that commonly adorn the foreheads of Hindu women as a mark of piety and, for some, of marriage.[28]

This refusal alone occasionally emerges as a bone of contention in anti-Christian violence. In September 2011, in a village around 100 kilometers northeast of Hyderabad, members of a Pentecostalized independent Christian church were assaulted while conducting a cottage prayer meeting. According to the pastor, the attackers accused him of "making women widows" (because his female converts refused to wear the *tikka*), before driving away with his motorcycle, a precious possession in rural India.

---

[27] *Prasadam* is food offered to the gods, made sacred thereby, and then taken back and enjoyed by Hindu worshippers, who often share it with their friends and neighbors (which is how Pentecostals and other Christians are given an opportunity to take it).

[28] On jewelry as a special obsession of South Indian Pentecostals, see Bergunder, *South Indian*, 181.

(Many Indian Christians expressed frustration at what they experienced as a double-edged sword. Critics of Christianity in India deride the assimilationist and inculturative tendencies of mainstream Christian missionaries and theologians as little more than a ploy to attract non-Christians to the faith by making it seem more like Hinduism and thereby obscuring its "foreign" origins. Yet in the situation just described, Pentecostals, who clearly demarcate their distinctive religious culture in very visible ways, are targeted for censure, and sometimes violence, for being overly denationalized.)

The Pentecostal response to attacks such as these may aggravate the problem. Many religions are marked by tension with what exists or existed alongside or before them. "The existence of cultural tension," according to Robbins, is therefore "not in and of itself what makes Pentecostal culture unique." Rather, what "distinguishes Pentecostal culture from others is that it does little to reduce such tensions but rather encourages and feeds off them."[29] Some might even say that Pentecostalism thrives on cultural tension. Among evangelistic Indian Pentecostals, this cultural peculiarity produces a willingness and a proclivity to provoke, even to provoke violence, for there is no greater—or, for some, prouder—mark of having made a complete break with the dominant culture than to suffer martyrdom. More than one Indian mission leader told me that any Christian evangelist worth his or her salt should be "getting some slaps." Only the martyr represents, in effect, a full and complete rupture.

While many Pentecostals maintain that the purpose of their countercultural stance is to allow fidelity to true "Christian" culture, that is, a lifestyle in line with biblical prescriptions and similar to that of the early church, outsiders often perceive this "Christian" culture to be rather suspiciously western (and especially American) in orientation. The signs of at least superficial westernization are everywhere in Indian Pentecostal churches. Males and females frequently dress in jeans, and even, though less regularly, t-shirts. Most of the worship songs are written using common western rather than Indian scales and tuning, and the vast majority of them, at least in English-speaking Pentecostal churches, are imported from the West and performed by worship teams[30] using western-style keyboards, guitars, and drums. Although it seems implausible, in one worship

---

[29] Robbins, "Anthropology," 161.
[30] Worship teams are groups of musicians and singers (much like rock bands) who lead congregations in singing and other forms of worship. They are characteristic of the contemporary Pentecostal and Charismatic movements.

team's rendition of "The Old Rugged Cross,"[31] I swear I even detected the southern twang American Christians often adopt when singing it, probably the result—on the part of the Indian Pentecostals—of unconscious imitation rather than conscious affectation. The influences of western musical and worship styles extend even outside the church doors; "Awesome God," seems to be the Indian Pentecostal ringtone of choice.[32]

Western influences are one element of Pentecostalism's appeal to the masses. When I asked a central Indian Pentecostal evangelist why villagers were attracted to his churches, he said it was because of his guitar playing. Similarly, but on a larger scale, one leader of the South Indian Assemblies of God interviewed by Miller and Yamamori explicitly acknowledged that the American origin of his church was attractive to many Indians. Generally, such connections are not seen by Pentecostals as a bad thing, because "they indicate that Pentecostal spirituality is firmly set in western culture and so might serve as a gateway to the scientific-technical age with western culture as its guarantor."[33]

Nevertheless, many critical or otherwise indifferent outsiders find the western style of Pentecostal worship and music jarring, even grating, and an indication that Pentecostals do not respect "Indian" culture. This is true even for non-Pentecostal Christians. One non-Pentecostal mission leader in rural Andhra Pradesh complained, "The sound and the screaming . . . [and] the anti-cultural style" of Pentecostals is "like fuel on fire. . . . They go with tight jeans, tight shorts and tops. But in mainline churches you will not find them. They will come with *salwar kameez*.[34] . . . People get irritated . . . when our culture is diluted [and] defamed."

In fact, as the commentator just quoted implies, the volume and raucousness of Pentecostal worship itself is a substantial and frequent

---

[31.] "The Old Rugged Cross" is an early twentieth-century hymn written by American evangelist George Bennard (1873–1958).

[32.] "Awesome God" is a popular contemporary Christian song written by native Hoosier, Rich Mullins, in the 1980s. The lyrics of the chorus are, "Our God is an awesome God / He reigns from heaven above / With wisdom pow'r and love / Our God is an awesome God." For a critical comment on "Americanization" among Indian Christians as another form of western "cultural imperialism," see Robert Frykenberg, "The Gospel, Globalization, and Hindutva: The Politics of 'Conversion' in India," in *Christianity Reborn: The Global Expansion of Evangelicalism in the Twentieth Century*, ed. Donald M. Lewis (Grand Rapids, MI: William B. Eerdmans Publishing Company, 2004), 129.

[33.] Donald E. Miller and Tetsunao Yamamori, *Global Pentecostalism: The New Face of Christian Social Engagement* (Berkeley: University of California Press, 2007), 129.

[34.] The commentator is clearly referring primarily to women, as this reference to the *salwar kameez,* an increasingly hip but modest women's outfit including loose pants and a long, usually embroidered shirt, indicates.

irritant. Pentecostal worship is loud, often amplified with the aid of massive speakers and powerful sound systems (which many Pentecostal congregations procure long before they build or purchase their own, dedicated-purpose church structure). Such sound systems seem a rather universal element of global Pentecostal worship, an essential element in the production of the Pentecostal experience. As Meyer affirms, in Pentecostal worship:

> Loudness . . . and also pastors' use of microphones in rhythmic sayings induce a certain trancelike atmosphere that conveys a sense of an extraordinary encounter with the divine force that is experienced to be present and that can be reached by opening up and stretching one's arms.[35]

What many non-Pentecostals perceive to be the gaudiness and clamor of Pentecostal worship, therefore, compounds the negative effect of its imported, alien nature on unsympathetic observers.

Making matters worse, of course, is that many new Pentecostal churches (that is, the majority of Pentecostal churches) meet in homes or in residential areas where their amplifiers are separated from the homes of others by only a few meters, a particularly prickly issue in climates where buildings built to maximize the flow of air also maximize the travel of sound. In fact, the emergence and presence of house churches in neighborhoods that do not want them is frequently a central issue in Hindu–Christian conflict, where legal maneuvering, police harassment, and mob violence (or the threat of violence) is used to enforce what in other parts of the world might be regulated by zoning laws. In cacophonous urban India, it is easy to be sympathetic to those who desire to reduce the din in their own residential neighborhoods. On the other hand, Muslim muezzins and Hindu temple bells are quite frequently a feature of those same neighborhoods, suggesting that the complaints are, sometimes at least, less about noise than about Christian noise. Because of the tensions created by unofficial house churches, some local and state governments and law enforcement agencies have encouraged Christians to officially register these house churches as churches, so that they can better protect them. Christians, however, are often suspicious of the law officers' motives, and resist complying with their requests out of fear that registering would facilitate targeting in times of violence.

[35.] Meyer, "Pentecostalism," 124.

Many of the themes of this section are instantiated by the following story, told by a Pentecostal pastor from North India, who had been attacked by violent nationalists in several separate incidents. A church he had established was renting a private hall on Sunday mornings. The hall was in a residential area, next to the home of a retired army Colonel who complained about the noise. The pastor agreed to turn down the volume. Nevertheless, one Sunday, the Colonel sent for the police and asked them to do something about the noise. The police arrived during worship. Youth from the church told the pastor that the police were waiting for him outside. He said to the police, "I am with the Lord; I'll not come out until after the service." The police didn't want to disturb the service, so they told him to come to the station afterwards. He did, and found that there was a report lodged against him there for disturbing the peace. He made excuses, saying that they were only temporarily worshipping in that hall, and that they were looking for a permanent place. He assured them that they would shut the windows, and not use microphones, and reminded them that their worship happened only once a week, and the singing lasted only half an hour. The police let the pastor go, which did nothing to mollify the Colonel, who believed the Pentecostal worship was still too loud, even without amplification. So he told the pastor, "Now you will see what I can do." The next Sunday, the Colonel erected his own, massive sound system. As the Pentecostals began to sing, he started blasting Bollywood film songs in their general direction. But less than a half a minute passed before the electricity in the entire neighborhood went off. The congregation kept singing; the film songs fell silent. The Pentecostals, of course, interpreted it as a miracle.

The forms of westernization so evident in Pentecostal worship could be construed as rather superficial and therefore insignificant, or even as something other than westernization. As one North Indian Vineyard pastor insisted, "Jeans aren't western, they're just what the youth wear!" Nevertheless, the very notion that western styles could be considered universal in this way offends the sensibilities of many Indian traditionalists. What is even more troubling for them, however, is the fact that Pentecostalism also introduces certain elements of what we might call "deep Westernization," or "deep modernization." The putative affinity (á la Weber) of Pentecostalism and capitalism has been much discussed and probably overstated. While Pentecostalism does tend to promote hard work, entrepreneurship, and the accumulation of wealth, it does not as consistently promote austerity and thrift, or censure ostentatious spending. In fact in its "health and wealth" manifestations, it does quite the opposite, sanctifying luxury as a gift from God. For this reason, only half of the "Protestant ethic," as Weber described it, obtains, because in Weber's formulation, the Protestant ethic required both (1) dedication to work and the accumulation of wealth, and (2) proscriptions against spending that wealth ostentatiously. Only if both were present could excess wealth that could be invested—capital—accumulate.[36] On the issue of whether it promotes Western gender norms and arrangements, Pentecostalism's record is also mixed.[37]

But on the issue of individualism, the evidence is somewhat clearer. Pentecostalism demands personal responsibility, independent decisions, and individual reform. Whether because of its Western Protestant influences, or because of its belief in universal access to the charismatic gifts and divine guidance, Pentecostalism promotes individualism wherever it travels.[38]

In fact, the imagery of "travel" is key. As Meyer observes, drawing upon the work of David Martin, "Pentecostalism launches an alternative understanding of the person as a mobile self with a 'portable identity' and concomitant 'portable practice' and 'transportable message,' all being conducive to spatial and social mobility."[39] One must be careful not to exaggerate or over-essentialize the difference, but individualism does, of course, challenge the community-oriented ethos of much of India (especially rural India), where individual identity is more commonly construed as something that emerges from within and as part of networks of family, caste, religion, and region.

The portable and transportable message of Pentecostalism is also a challenge to widespread Indian notions of religion. Indians (especially, again, rural Indians) often conceive of religion as something spatially bounded and focused on gods and goddesses ruling specific geographical spaces. The worship of some deities, for example, extends no further than the village boundary, and certain sects of Hinduism still observe strictures against crossing the *kala pani* (the "black waters," i.e., the ocean). In this sense, then, many Indians tend to think of religion as something stationary, given, and static, rather than—as Pentecostalism (and particularly conversion to Pentecostalism) promotes—mobile, contingent, and changeable. And so, while it must be kept in mind that Pentecostalism is not alone in doing so, the fact that it does tend to promote individualism and "portable

---

36. Cf. ibid., 116–19.
37. Robbins, "Anthropology," 169.
38. Ibid., 168.
39. Meyer, "Pentecostalism," 121. See also David Martin, *Pentecostalism: The World Their Parish* (Oxford: Wiley-Blackwell, 2002), 24.

identities" is certainly an important reason why it is perceived—and more so even than other forms of Christianity—as somehow "anti-cultural."

Conclusion

The most obvious explanation for why Pentecostals and Charismatics should be disproportionately targeted in the violence against Christians is their more aggressive evangelizing. In this chapter, I have tried not only to problematize that assumption (somewhat) but also to suggest that there are a range of other important additional factors, including the greater presence and participation of marginalized peoples among Pentecostals, and their "countercultural posture."

Whether the targeting of Pentecostals is conscious is another matter altogether. To suggest that there are reasons why Pentecostals are disproportionately targeted is not to suggest that the violent nationalists who target them do so with any significant knowledge about how Indian Christians differ from one another. While some do, the disproportionate targeting of Pentecostals appears, generally, to be an unconscious response to certain kinds of provocation that are more likely to come from Pentecostals than from other kinds of Christians.

When I asked a Christian *dalit* rights activist in New Delhi whether the targeting of Pentecostals was conscious or unconscious, he replied, "If a cockroach lands on your shoulder, what will you do?" The implication, of course, was that while those committing anti-Christian violence often (but not always) did so as a response to general or specific provocations—e.g., harshly critical or assertive evangelism, the growth of Christianity, the relative social and economic advance of Christians, the newfound self-assertion of low-caste and tribal converts—they did so primarily instinctually, unconsciously, and without any clear targeting rationale. Pentecostals therefore fall prey to anti-Christian violence more than other Indian Christians because, to a relatively higher degree, they either (1) are involved in, embody, enact, or motivate the provocations, or (2) are more accessible and vulnerable when violence occurs.

While this chapter has highlighted a number of interreligious factors in Hindu–Christian violence, the internal Christian dynamics are also worth noting. There is, in fact, a rather intriguing intra-Christian cycle of blame that manifests itself in the context of controversies about conversion and Hindu–Christian conflict. The mainline churches blame independent Pentecostal and Pentecostalized churches for provoking conflict with Hindus through their assertive programs of evangelism, harsh criticism of

Indian cultures and religions, and "anti-cultural" stance. Their contempt is fueled both by the knowledge that they themselves occasionally have to suffer the consequences of conflict provoked by Pentecostals, and by a fair amount of unacknowledged resentment stemming from the fact that large numbers of their own members have abandoned the mainline denominations in favor of these churches (or visit them on the sly).

Expressing their distaste for Pentecostals, they stereotype and castigate them with language that Hindu nationalist critics of Christianity echo and borrow. Worldwide, argues André Droogers, mainstream Christians, "have been the most important outsider source of essentialist and normative images regarding Pentecostal believers," labeling them "fanatic, schismatic, heretics, and sectarian."[40] To these epithets we can add many more. Mainstream Indian Christians condescendingly accuse Pentecostals of being fundamentalist, hysterical, emotional, ecstatic, ostentatious, uneducated, boorish, cultish, crass, and uncouth. For example, a Catholic nun in the Punjab reproved Pentecostal evangelists in an interview with journalist Shafi Rahman: "These preachers are not trained in theology," she said. "They often play with the sentiments of people and lure them with incentives and create communal tension. We are forced to take the blame for their wayward preaching methods."[41] "[B]oth mainstream churches and Hindutva parties," Rahman accurately reports, "love to hate" these independent pastors.[42]

But so do India's secularist writers and journalists. Suspicious of all religion, but especially the more enchanted and emotional kind, they, like many of their western counterparts, often join in on the flaying of Pentecostals. In fact Rahman traffics in some blatant stereotyping himself. One congregation he describes repeated "puppet like" after its pastor, while outside the church sat a "bragging generator." Moreover, independent churches, he writes, "attract . . . Christians . . . through mass prayers marked by hysterical outbursts of faith."[43] None of these descriptions is particularly inaccurate, of course, but in context it is clear that there is a (negative) judgment implied.

If India's mainstream Christians blame independent Pentecostalized and Pentecostal Christians for anti-Christian violence, the more "respectable"

[40.] André Droogers, "Essentialist and Normative Approaches," in *Studying Global Pentecostalism: Theories and Methods*, ed. Allan Anderson et al. (Berkeley: University of California Press, 2010), 38.

[41.] Shafi Rahman, "Freelancers of God," *India Today International*, May 9, 2011, 38.

[42.] Ibid., 37.

[43.] Ibid., 40.

among these latter groups, those with a more positive view of Indian religions and cultures and a more indirect approach to evangelism, often blame the violence on the more openly, consistently, and aggressively evangelistic, particularly the street preachers and all those who boldly proclaim the gospel outdoors, away from Christian spaces, and to people with whom they are unacquainted.

Finally, then, these more consistently, assertively, openly, and critically evangelistic Christians (among whom most Pentecostals can be counted) blame all other Christians for not doing their job. All Indian Christians essentially agree that a significant factor in anti-Christian violence is the offense cause by Christian evangelizing and the "anti-cultural" ethos of certain kinds of Christians. The difference lies in whether they believe the end justifies the means. For most Pentecostals, life lived according to the Bible and the Holy Spirit requires open evangelization and a countercultural stance. Other Christians, they conclude, have shirked their responsibility to evangelize and have accommodated themselves to a non- (or, perhaps for Pentecostals, anti-) Christian culture in order to protect and increase their material assets and social status.

Indian Pentecostalism therefore offends the sensibilities not only of non-Christians but also of mainstream Indian Christians as well. As a result, the latter find Pentecostals somewhat embarrassing and distance themselves from them in both obvious and subtle ways. This is particularly true in times of violence, when mainstream Christians tend to blame Pentecostal and Pentecostalized Christians for provoking the ire of non-Christians and turn a blind eye to their suffering. The disproportionate targeting of Pentecostals is therefore exacerbated by their marginalization within the broader Indian Christian community, which increases their vulnerability to attack.

Many and varied are the reasons why Pentecostals bear the brunt of anti-Christian violence in contemporary India, and this chapter has outlined those reasons in great detail. But Pentecostals do not in every way embody or enact the negative stereotypes about Indian Christianity developed and perpetuated by its critics. In particular, both the claim that Christianization leads to denationalization and the assumption and complaint that Christians use their allopathic medical facilities to lure non-Christians to their faith are called into question by the centrality, within Pentecostalism, of faith healing. The next chapter therefore both explores this intriguing and increasingly prominent phenomenon, and discusses its relationship to the contemporary public discourse about conversion and Hindu–Christian conflict in contemporary India.

CHAPTER 4 | Force, Fraud, and Inducement?

Recuperative Conversions and the Growth of Indian Christianity

70% of the converts are converted because of physical or spiritual healing. The other 30% also get healed of something.

—PENTECOSTAL PASTOR FROM CHENNAI

THE MAGNITUDE AND MOMENTOUSNESS of the faith healing revolution in Indian Christian missions has been very little noted, both because of its relative novelty and because of the ignorance (or feigned ignorance) about it of many Indian Christian leaders themselves. Two contrasting interviews I conducted near Valathi, in rural Tamil Nadu, could not have been more instructive in this regard. First, I met with the administrator of a Christian mission that had planted churches in a few nearby villages. The reserved, demure administrator, sitting in his well-built office, assured me that the primary reason why people converted to Christianity in the area was because of the fine Christian example set by Christian converts, who upon conversion immediately, it seems, ceased lying, stealing, and using abusive language. An hour later, however, I was sitting on the floor of one of the village churches his mission had planted. In the chaotic interview that ensued, eight feisty old Christian women, some of them converts, pinched my cheeks repeatedly and spoke enthusiastically and often over top of one another of one miraculous healing after another, and of how these healings had led non-Christians to begin affiliating with the Christian church in which we met.

As indicated in chapter 2, the Niyogi Committee largely endorsed the claims of witnesses appearing before it in the 1950s that Christianity was growing in India through subtle, pernicious, and illegitimate forms of "force, fraud, and allurement." The Committee's *Report* played an important role in popularizing this view, and did so in part by way of a thorough, and thoroughly critical analysis of Christian medical missions. These missions, according to the *Report,* inappropriately mixed up western scientific achievement and economic might, on the one hand, with Christianity and the proclamation thereof, on the other.

While there were at the time of the Niyogi Committee's work Christians in India who believed strongly in the power of supernatural healing without biomedical intervention, and others who would have even gone further to suggest that resort to biomedical care itself was a sign of unbelief, such Christians constituted at the time such a small minority of the larger Indian Christian community that they did not make any substantial appearance in the *Report*'s voluminous archive of testimonies and analyses. More recently, however, with the rise of Pentecostal and Pentecostalized Evangelicalism in India, the work of Christian faith healers has become far more prominent. It has also emerged, it is my contention, as the primary reason why non-Christians first affiliate with Christianity in India today. Because of this, faith healings have begun to elicit the attention of Christianity's critics there, and to alter, inform, and influence conversations about conversion and Hindu–Christian conflict.

The rising prominence of faith healing as a provocation toward conversion to Christianity also calls into question certain scholarly assumptions about how and why non-Christian Indians convert to the faith. As I describe below, for example, the adherence to Christianity that results from supernatural healings is in many cases ephemeral, a matter of temporary convenience. Yet such conversions do lead, in other cases, to significant transformation and permanent, formal affiliation with Christianity. These latter cases undermine the force of what is the most common scholarly explanation for why non-Christian Indians convert to Christianity, that is, as a protest, on the part of lower-caste and tribal peoples, against their debased status and marginalization within broader, Hindu-inflected Indian society.[1]

---

[1] For examples of this argument, see J. Boel, *Christian Mission in India: A Sociological Analysis* (Amsterdam: Graduate Press, 1975); J. W. Gladstone, *Protestant Christianity and People's Movements in Kerala* (Trivandrum, Kerala, India: The Seminary Publications, 1984); Dick Kooiman, *Conversion and Social Equality in India* (New Delhi: South Asia Publications, 1989); and Gauri Viswanathan, "Religious Conversion and the Politics of Dissent," in *Conversion to Modernities: The Globalization of Christianity,* ed. Peter van der Veer (New York: Routledge, 1996). See also Chad Bauman, *Christian Identity and Dalit Religion in Hindu India, 1868–1947*

This is not to say, however, that caste plays no role in the realm of supernatural healing. In fact, caste might be a significant factor in determining whether the affiliations with Christianity initiated by miraculous recuperation last or fade away. In at least one church I visited, for example, a Jain family that attended the church's weekly fasting prayer services refused to convert or affiliate with the church more formally because they considered Christianity a lower-caste faith. Nevertheless, it would be difficult to argue persuasively that those who approach Christian healers for help with physical or spiritual ailments have at the forefront of their minds the amelioration of their social and cultural ailments. The increasing prevalence of faith healing in India, then, both alters scholarly and more popular debates about Indians' motivations for conversion to Christianity and undermines the accusation, by Indian Christianity's critics, that it grows primarily through the promise of material or social advance.

Recuperative Conversions and the Growth of Indian Christianity

"Healing, power encounters, [and] casting [out] of evil spirits [are] a major factor in church growth throughout India," General Secretary of EFI Richard Howell asserted in one of my interviews with him. "You cannot do mission today, irrespective of your denomination, if you are not equipped to handle the issues of demonic power." Similarly, a Pentecostal evangelist working in rural Karnataka told me that the primary reason non-Christians were converting to Christianity there was because "They have been healed . . . [The possessed and the sick] will try their own goddess and so many other ways [to find healing]. But finding there is no[t] any possibility of healing, they will come to Jesus Christ, they will come to know the truth. . . . The problem they were facing previously, after coming to Jesus they will not have any problem."

With respect to the historical growth of Christianity in the Dangs, Gujarat, the top administrator of Gospel Christian Workers (GCW)[2]

(Grand Rapids, MI: Eerdmans Publishers, 2008), 94–98. These works are primarily historical, which may explain their lack of attention to healing as a factor in the growth of Christianity. Nevertheless, healing remains a blind spot even for many scholars working on conversion in contemporary India. For a somewhat tendentious argument, which nevertheless artfully attends to both social protest and healing as factors in the growth of Christianity today, see Amalendu Misra, "The Missionary Position: Christianity and Politics of Religious Conversion in India," *Nationalism and Ethnic Politics* 17, no. 4 (2011): 361–81.

[2] "Gospel Christian Workers" is a pseudonym, the same pseudonym chosen by Sushil Aaron, "Emulating Azariah: Evangelicals and Social Change in the Dangs," in *Evangelical Christianity*

asserted, in an interview with me, "When we preached the gospel to tribal peoples [there], there was a tremendous response to the gospel, incredible response to the gospel, and it all happened through power encounters. People were liberated from demon possession, people were miraculously healed, the blind began to see, even the dead came to life. . . . As a result, people responded in large numbers and we had no option but to build churches for them."[3] It bears mentioning here that GCW's evangelists tend to be members of mainstream Protestant denominations not otherwise inclined toward an emphasis on power encounters. And yet the expectations and demands of those with whom they worked forced them to feature such phenomena more prominently in their evangelical work, a major factor in the Pentecostalization of non-Pentecostal Indian Christianity.

In one recent Indian survey, 80% of Pentecostal pastors surveyed identified "power evangelism" in worship services, that is, evangelism focused on healings and encounters with demonic forces, as the primary reason for Christian growth in the areas where they worked.[4] Healings (and rumors of healings) also often contribute positively to the success of individual pastors or congregations.[5] And my own fieldwork confirms the impression that the primary reason non-Christian Indians first begin to affiliate with Christianity today is because they believe they have received physical healing, liberation from evil spirits, or solutions to family problems after the intercession of Christians. (Problems within the family are often attributed by Indians to the work of nefarious spirits, and to find solutions, then, they frequently seek help from spiritual healers.) As the young Pentecostal pastor in Chennai quoted in this chapter's epigraph illogically, yet revealingly and unintentionally humorously put it, "70% of the converts are converted because of physical or spiritual healing. The other 30% also get healed of something."

Not all of those I interviewed agreed with this assessment, and in fact some denied it outright. But those who did deny or disagree with it were generally either adherents of urban, mainstream Christian communities who evinced a striking degree of ignorance about what was going

and Democracy in Asia, ed. David H. Lumsdaine (New York: Oxford University Press, 2009), 104. Both Aaron and I use the pseudonym to avoid making the mission group vulnerable to attack for the mere fact of its evangelistic success in the region.

[3] For scholarly confirmation of the administrator's views, see Aaron, "Emulating," 104.

[4] Jonathan D. James, McDonaldisation, Masala McGospel and Om Economics (Washington, DC: Sage, 2010), 195.

[5] Michael Bergunder, "Miracle Healing and Exorcism in South Indian Pentecostalism," in Global Pentecostal and Charismatic Healing, ed. Candy Gunther Brown (New York: Oxford University Press, 2011), 298.

on beyond the walls of their own churches, or had theological or ideological reasons to suggest otherwise, such as their own ambivalence and embarrassment, particularly, perhaps, in the presence of a western interviewer, about the prevalence of miraculous healing in Indian Christianity today. Those in this latter category frequently distinguished, in one way or another, between "true seekers," whose conversion careers followed a more intellectual path, and those apparently not-quite-so-true seekers who began affiliating with Christianity due to what was sometimes denigrated as an "emotional" response to miraculous encounters. "We don't play on people's emotions," declared one Vineyard pastor in Dehradun who disapproved of ministries emphasizing supernatural healing. Similarly, a mission leader in Hyderabad contended that to "tempt a man" with healing was to "put the cart before the horse."

Yet it is clear from stories like the one with which I started this chapter that what happens on the ground, so to speak, is not always what church and mission leaders, entombed in their climate-controlled offices in larger towns and cities think or wish were happening. Yet the disparity between their views and the views of those living or working on the growing edges of Christianity may also have to do with the fact that what I in this chapter call "recuperative conversions" (that is, "conversions" that take place after and due to physical or spiritual healing) often do not endure. While I am therefore confident that the vast majority of non-Christians who begin affiliating with Christianity in contemporary India do so because of healings of various kinds, it may be the case that those who first begin affiliating for reasons other than healing comprise a disproportionately larger percentage of those who actually remain Christian in a more formal sense.

In the preceding paragraphs I have generally used the term "affiliate" (rather than "convert") to signal a "conversion careers" approach. "Conversion careers," Henri Gooren writes, involve a religious person's passage "within his or her social and cultural context, through levels, types, and phases of . . . participation."[6] Gooren's model—there are others—employs a five-level typology of religious participation involving

---

[6] Henri Gooren, "Conversion Narratives," in *Studying Global Pentecostalism: Theories and Methods*, ed. Allan Anderson et al. (Berkeley: University of California Press, 2010), 94. See also Henri Gooren, "Conversion Careers in Latin America: Entering and Leaving Church among Pentecostals, Catholics, and Mormons," in *Conversion of a Continent: Contemporary Religious Change in Latin America*, ed. Timothy J. Steigenga and Edward L. Cleary (New Brunswick: Rutgers University Press, 2007), 52–71; and Henri Gooren, *Religious Conversion and Disaffiliation: Tracing Patterns of Change in Faith Practices* (New York: Palgrave Macmillan, 2010).

"pre-affiliation," "affiliation" (what most people think of when they hear the word "conversion"), "conversion" (used in a more limited sense of radical change of worldview), "confession" (a level involving active participation and profession), and "disaffiliation."[7]

The great strength of the conversion careers approach is that it acknowledges that "conversion" is a palimpsest, a term that can refer to a broad assortment of social activities involving varying degrees of social or psychological transformation. The conversion careers approach also avoids the quasi-teleological assumption that conversion is a unidirectional and irreversible process, an assumption embedded implicitly in many contemporary theories of conversion (and even in alarmist anti-conversion propaganda).[8] The conversion careers approach is therefore particularly useful in the analysis of recuperative conversions because they sometimes do not progress beyond Gooren's stage of "affiliation" and quite regularly end in "disaffiliation." Yet sometimes recuperative conversions do lead to permanent affiliation or even to radical psycho-social transformations (Gooren's stages of "conversion" and "confession"). Because of this, and because recuperative conversions have become so common, even though they do not always endure, they remain the primary source of Christian growth in India today.

One of the reasons recuperative conversions do not always lead to permanent or transformative affiliation with Christianity is that they emerge from a common Indian socioreligious source over which Christians have no monopoly. Belief in demons and other malignant spiritual forces is widespread in India, and not just in rural areas. Similarly widespread is the etiological conviction that sickness and misfortune are related to the malice, mischief, or displeasure of spiritual beings. In contemporary India, few would deny the viral causes of smallpox or the veracity of meteorological explanations of droughts. But the question, *Why?* (*Why* did I get smallpox? *Why* did my crops fail), is quite frequently answered with reference to spiritual beings.

Divine displeasure is, of course, always one possible explanation, and Indians of all religious affiliation are careful to worship their deities according to sacerdotally prescribed fashion, particularly when dealing with deities known to be quick-tempered, violent, or vengeful, among whom a significant proportion of goddesses (e.g., Kali or the goddess of

[7] Gooren, "Conversion Narratives," 94.
[8] Chad Bauman, "Conversion Careers, Conversions-For, and Conversion in the Study of Religion," *The Religion & Culture Web Forum*, May 2012, http://divinity.uchicago.edu/martycenter/publications/webforum/052012/bauman_response.pdf.

smallpox called Shitala in the North and Mariamman in the South) can be counted, at least if one does not obey and worship them correctly. Yet because the highest gods are perceived by most Indians to be primarily beneficent, explanations for sickness and misfortune involving generalized divine displeasure are relatively less common than those involving the specific activity of misanthropic witches and sorcerers, maleficent demons, mischievous demigods, disturbed spirits, and disgruntled ghosts.[9] In North India, the spiritual agents most frequently blamed for ailment and calamity are *bhuts* (the ghosts, usually, of prematurely deceased or killed men) and *churails* (the ghosts of women who die while pregnant or in childbirth). In South India, these and other vengeful spirits of the unexpectedly, inauspiciously, or unhappily dead are usually referred to as *pey* (*peey*), or *picacu* (*picaacu*). Belief in the activity of spirits such as these remains nearly universal throughout India.[10]

In both North and South India, there are shamanistic figures who trade in elaborate rituals, mantras, and amulets for healing, the maintenance of health, and the avoidance of mishap, a kind of shadow priesthood specializing in evasion rather than adulation. In the North, these figures are called *ojhas, guniyas,* or *baigas*; in the South, *mantiravati,* or sometimes *cami-yati,* are the more common terms. In almost every case, these figures manage and maintain the wellness and good fortune of their paying clients by identifying threatening witches, sorcerers, or spirits, and then neutralizing, manipulating, or removing the source of trouble (through, respectively, counter-magic, propitiation, or exorcism).[11]

Pentecostal Healing

By the late colonial period, most western missionaries in India had, under the influence of rationalist and scientific trends, rejected etiologies

---

[9] Aaron, "Emulating," 105; and Lionel Caplan, *Religion and Power: Essays on the Christian Community in Madras* (Madras: Christian Literature Society, 1989), 56. In this way, the Indian religious situation reverses the pattern among Western Christians, who tend, when involved in etiological speculation, to think first in terms of generalized divine displeasure if they progress beyond purely scientific explanations at all.

[10] Bauman, *Christian Identity*, 137; and Michael Bergunder, *The South Indian Pentecostal Movement in the Twentieth Century* (Grand Rapids, MI: Eerdmans Publishers, 2008), 126, 46–47. On the *pey*, see Caplan, *Religion*, 52–55; and Michael Moffat, *An Untouchable Community in South India: Structure and Consensus* (Princeton: Princeton University Press, 1979), 113.

[11] Bauman, *Christian Identity*, 136–39; and Bergunder, *South Indian*, 149. In the right circumstances, these shamanistic figures will engage in black magic on behalf of their clients, so the line between witch/sorcerer and *baiga/mantiravati* is not always clear. On this, see Bergunder, "Miracle," 289.

of sickness and misfortune involving the activity of witches, sorcerers, and/or spiritual beings other than God. This is true, as well, of many contemporary mainstream Protestant, Catholic, and Orthodox Indian Christians, especially among their upper-class congregants and their clergy (on which, more below). The popular Indian views on evil and suffering described above, however, resonate with many Evangelicals in India, and particularly with Pentecostals.[12]

Among Pentecostals and Pentecostalized Evangelicals, belief in the causative function of personal and specific (as opposed to abstract) spiritual beings in ill health and bad fortune is ubiquitous. Pentecostal demonology allows for this, as does the Bible itself. In Tamil, for example, the terms *picacu* and *pey* are used to translate the Greek terms *daimonion* and *diabolos*. Although some Pentecostals demonize all of Hinduism and consider the Hindu high gods themselves demons, it is more frequently the case that Pentecostals deploy a demonology similar to that of other Indians, wherein the evil spirits they fear are none other than those feared by their non-Christian neighbors. Only those who have sinned or are not in a right relationship with God are vulnerable to spiritual attack, according to Pentecostals, though sickness and misfortune is also sometimes interpreted as divine testing, as in the biblical book of Job. Nevertheless, according to Pentecostal theology, Christians need not fear evil spirits and the havoc they spawn, for they are powerless before Christ, and flee from the mere mention of his name.[13]

In their perambulations, Christian priests and pastors of all stripes are frequently asked by both Christians and non-Christians to pray for the sick or demon possessed. Yet more than other Indian Christians, Pentecostals are enthusiastic combatants in this spiritual warfare. They play a role, therefore, that resembles that of *baigas, mantiravatis*, and the like. They often employ very similar methods, such as identifying maleficent spiritual beings or occult objects and then eliminating them. And those they heal frequently manifest similar signs (e.g., rolling in the floor, convulsing, etc.)

---

[12] Bergunder, *South Indian*, 147. And here it may be useful to remind the reader that I use "Pentecostal" in this book to refer both to self-identified Pentecostals and to Protestant "Charismatics" (e.g., neo-Charismatics) with whom they share many characteristics. I reserve the term "Charismatic" primarily for Catholic Charismatics, that is, for members of the Charismatic Renewal within the Roman Catholic Church.

[13] Bergunder, "Miracle," 287–88; Amos Yong, "The Demonic in Pentecostal/Charismatic Christianity and in the Religious Consciousness of Asia," in *Asian and Pentecostal: The Charismatic Face of Christianity in Asia*, ed. Allan Anderson and Edmond Tang (Costa Mesa, CA: Regnum Books, 2005), 96; Bergunder, *South Indian*, 147–49; and Caplan, *Religion*, 58; and Nathaniel Roberts, "Anti-conversion Law," 14.

as those healed by non-Christian healers. It surely is not at all surprising, then, that Christian prayers like "In the name of Jesus, be healed!" are perceived by many Indians to be little different than the efficacious mantras utilized by non-Christian healers.[14]

In fact, while Indians generally recognize that Christian pastors, on the one hand, and *baigas, mantiravatis,* and so on, on the other, adhere to different religious traditions, many make very little distinction between the work of these various figures, and some perceive no differentiation at all.[15] Indeed, in the religion of healing, there are no meaningful religious distinctions, a fact that undermines the assumption (or affected assertion) of Hindu nationalists who claim that conversions are inherently socially disruptive. They can be, of course, but the shifts in affiliation caused by spiritual healing are quite frequently more subtle and less dramatic than those imagined by critics of "conversion" to Christianity.

In the course of his excellent ethnographic work in a Tamil slum, for example, Nathaniel Roberts discovered that evangelism and interreligious disputations were rarely disruptive at all, in part because in that context, religion was not about marking an identity through adherence to a mutually exclusive religious practice. Rather, religious practice in the slums was ultimately a pragmatic, practical affair. And in this context, "the defining characteristic of gods and the standard by which they are assessed is what they can *do* for those who worship them."[16] What matters most to the suffering, in the end, is what works, and the Indian market of physical and spiritual healing is a bustling, cacophonous, and competitive one with much demand and many suppliers, due to the absence of effective biomedical care in much of India.

"Healing is very important," said Suresh, a Pentecostal church-planter who worked among an ST group in Jharkhand, "because village people are sick many times. . . . And this is God's way to work there. [The ability to heal] is a gift of God. And I use this gift . . . and I heal people by the grace of God also . . . I cast [out] evil spirits, also, which is [a problem that is]

[14.] Arun Jones, "Faces of Pentecostalism in North India Today," *Society* 46, no. 6 (2009): 504–9; Mathew Schmalz, "A Space for Redemption: Catholic Tactics in Hindu North India" (PhD diss., University of Chicago, 1998), 44–48; Bergunder, "Miracle," 292–93; and Bergunder, *South Indian*, 156.

[15.] Muslim *maulvis* also perform similar functions in some Indian contexts.

[16.] Roberts, "Anti-conversion Law," 16, 18. For a similar argument in a different context, see Corinne G. Dempsey, "Lessons in Miracles from Kerala, South India," in *Popular Christianity in India: Riting between the Lines*, ed. Selva J. Raj and Corinne G. Dempsey (Albany: SUNY Press, 2002).

very familiar to village people." In the healing market, Christ does well, and even many non-Christian Indians consider him a specialist of sorts in physical and spiritual healing. Yet he has by no means cornered the market, and this helps explain why recuperative conversions do not always result in permanent alterations of religious affiliation.

Among other issues, because Indian popular religiosity does not distinguish strongly between the various therapeutic religious traditions, acknowledging the power of a Christian healer need not demand a break with one's own non-Christian tradition. A figure like the famous Christian healer Dhinakaran is little different, in the view of many Hindus, than the late but even more famous wonder-working Hindu God-man, Sathya Sai Baba.[17] And as one Pentecostal preacher put it, when given the choice of offending the Christian God of mercy or offending popular Indian deities, some of which have a more developed (or at least more frequently acknowledged) wrathful streak, one will logically choose the former![18]

A second factor is that popular Indian attitudes toward health care are in fact quite experimental, pragmatic, and itinerant, such that it is common for the sick to move from one healer to the next, from one religion to the next, and from one form of medicine (e.g., allopathic, ayurvedic, shamanistic) to the next in search of cures for what ails them. Even Christians, and even Pentecostals are known to do this. Finding a cure in Christianity one day, therefore, need not preclude the possibility of finding one in the presence of a *baiga* or *mantiravati* the next.[19]

For these reasons, even in the case of healings that do result in recuperative conversions to Christianity, the initial enthusiasm that accompanies the original healing often wanes if and when the healings cease. For many in India, in religion as in the marketplace, relationships are based on pressing but ephemeral needs that lead to temporary arrangements more

---

[17.] Bergunder, "Miracle," 295.

[18.] The putatively more wrathful nature of many Indian deities, vis-à-vis the Christian God, may be more perception, or propaganda, than reality. Certainly the Christian God, as attested in the Old Testament, can be quite jealous, wrathful, and even violent. But only the disobedient, the unrighteous, and non-believers experience this side of God in negative ways. And that, in the end, is not so different from how many Hindus understand the "wrathfulness" of their own Gods and Goddesses. Although I had intuited this at some inarticulate level, it was an informal personal conversation with the anthropologist Gillian Goslinga that helped me recognize that the two ways of thinking about the divine were not as distinct as Christian missionaries and scholars have often, historically, suggested that they were.

[19.] Chad Bauman, "Miraculous Health and Medical Itineration among Satnamis and Christians in Late Colonial Chhattisgarh," in *Miracle as Modern Conundrum in South Asian Religious Traditions*, ed. Selva Raj and Corinne Dempsey (Albany: SUNY Press, 2008); and Bergunder, *South Indian*, 162.

frequently than binding and eternal contracts. And this provides a constant source of irritation for the kind of Christian evangelist who proclaims a religion that requires exclusive and faithful allegiance in the presence of people who are hesitant to relinquish their attachment to healers and Gods the evangelist considers false, demonic, or at the very least ineffective.

Although Indian Pentecostals would deny charges of syncretism, it remains clear, therefore, that there is much they have in common with ordinary Indian non-Christians.[20] Moreover, because Pentecostals are well-positioned to address and take advantage of it, the widespread demand for spiritual healing is one factor in the Pentecostalization of all Indian Christianity. Evangelists and missionaries working in new fields find themselves constantly confronted with requests for healing, and in this way, Christian workers that might not otherwise consider themselves Pentecostal, as well as workers sponsored by non-Pentecostal mission societies in India, the United States and elsewhere, find themselves working in the mode of Pentecostal thaumaturges.[21]

Despite their similarities, it is important to highlight some of the ways in which Pentecostal and other Christian healers differ from their popular Indian religious competitors. It is in the context of healing and exorcism, Michael Bergunder argues with reference to South India that "one can most convincingly show that the . . . pentecostal movement is a quite contextualized version of Indian Christianity. Multicontextuality must also be kept in mind, however, since in most cases, parallels to popular Hinduism are not one-to-one, but are simultaneously found in Indian Christian popular religiosity and elsewhere in the global Pentecostal movement."[22]

One difference between Christian and non-Christian healers that Christians regularly adduce is that non-Christian healers charge for their services whereas Christians do not.[23] In my view, however, this distinction is overblown. Among other issues, the practice of expressing gratitude for healing through gifts of money, produce, or livestock is so widespread— neglecting to do so risks angering the very deity who has just healed you, and providing the gift is considered an important and even catalytic element of the therapeutic transaction—that gifts are even, on occasion, offered to

---

[20.] Yong, "Demonic," 102.

[21.] For one example involving GCW, see Aaron, "Emulating," 104.

[22.] Bergunder, "Miracle," 287. Emphasis added.

[23.] Even scholars often make much of this difference. See, for example, Bergunder, "Miracle," 294. The fact that Bergunder makes the distinction, though, is curious, since he also acknowledges that those healed frequently press a few rupees into the hand of Pentecostal healers. See Bergunder, *South Indian*, 217. The distinction between Christian and non-Christian healers in this regard is therefore one of degree, not in any significant way of kind.

allopathic doctors at biomedical clinics and hospitals.[24] Moreover, those healed by the prayer of a Christian, particularly by the prayers of a priest, evangelist, or pastor, often immediately or later tender an offering of some kind to the healer or the healer's church. While Christian healers do not require or explicitly expect payment, therefore, they quite frequently receive something very much like it.

There are theological differences, however, that do seem to me rather more significant. I have already alluded to the first, which is that while sickness and misfortune are, for many non-Christian Indians, a result of the malfeasance of sorcerers, witches, or evil spirits, they are often interpreted, by Pentecostals, to also be the result of sin and a sign of divine displeasure.[25] A second theological difference concerns conceptions of the divine and its relationship to evil spirits. Many Hindus, as Caplan has lucidly demonstrated with reference to South India, perceive there to be multiple levels of spiritual beings arranged in a hierarchy and increasing in both power and the consistency of their benevolence moving up from the lower to the higher levels.[26] This divine gradation has two important consequences.

The first is that in popular Hindu understandings, as in more recent Hindu mythology, many spiritual beings, with the exception of the highest, represent a mixture of benevolence and maleficence, depending on the situation. Moreover, many "evil" beings (e.g., Ravana in *The Ramayana*) are evil only temporarily, as it were, and only because of disputes with, or the neglect and mistakes made by the putatively more benevolent, "higher" gods. In addition, even at the lowest levels, some spiritual beings are perceived to be more mischievous than malevolent. The second important consequence is that among popular non-Christian Indian healers it is quite common to call upon the mid-level Indian gods and goddesses for help in neutralizing or expelling troublesome lower-level (or just less powerful) spirits.[27]

There is therefore an ambiguity in popular Indian notions of divinity, an uncertainty about where to assign evil, that does not obtain, at least officially, for Pentecostals, whose hierarchy has only two tiers, purely good and purely evil (middling Hindu gods like Murugun and Ganesh often being assigned to the latter category, along with any "high" Hindu gods

---

[24.] On this practice in colonial-era missionary hospitals, see Bauman, *Christian Identity*, 156.

[25.] Bergunder, "Miracle," 289, 91.

[26.] Caplan, *Religion*, 56.

[27.] W. D. O'Flaherty, *The Origins of Evil in Hindu Mythology* (Berkeley: University of California Press, 1980), 57; and Caplan, *Religion*, 58.

and goddesses Pentecostals consider anything more than pure illusion), and who call upon the one and only God, as they understand it, or the God-made-man Jesus, to eradicate evil. This lack of ambiguity, incidentally, seems to give Pentecostals a level of fortitude and courage in their dealings with evil spirits that some of their non-Christian neighbors lack, a courage that might, in addition to other factors, help account for the growing popularity of Pentecostalism.[28] But again, it must be stressed that this difference is one asserted primarily in official, theological, and formal ways, and may not actually be as prominent a feature of Indian Pentecostal life at the more popular level.

While Christian healers do sometimes borrow the methods of non-Christian healers in India, as noted above, there are elements of Christian spiritual warfare that are unique to Christian healing, as is evident in the general description of Pentecostal exorcisms provided by Caplan. "Pentecostal exorcism calls on the power of the Holy Spirit to confront and defeat the evil spirits," he writes. Once identified, the spirit is "roundly abused" and driven out using the name of Jesus. Sacred oil (blessed in the name of Jesus) is often used by the exorcist and/or given to the possessed. Sometimes the exorcist places a Bible on the head of the possessed person. Sometimes the exorcist speaks in tongues.[29] The Holy Spirit, the Bible, the name of Jesus, sacred oil, glossolalia—these and other ritual objects and elements distinguish Christian healers from their non-Christian competitors.[30]

Healings are, as I have argued above, a significant factor in the growth of Indian Christianity today. But the enthusiasm that Pentecostals have for spiritual combat also helps explain why it is that Pentecostalism and Pentecostalized Evangelicalism are growing more quickly than other forms of Christianity. Speaking historically, Vinson Synan writes,

---

[28] Bergunder, "Miracle," 294; Roberts, "Anti-conversion Law," 14; and Caplan, *Religion*, 65–66; and Bergunder, *South Indian*, 158.

[29] Caplan, *Religion*, 67.

[30] Healing within Catholic Charismatic contexts in India resembles that among Pentecostals, though with certain Catholic particularities. And, of course, Catholics who seek guidance in the case of deliverance ministries (e.g., exorcisms) have recourse to the official rite of exorcism. For intriguing work on the globalization of Charismatic healing, which, when paired with the element of syncretism found in Indian and other forms of Catholic healing, is "symptomatic of the simultaneous pull toward universal culture and postmodern cultural fragmentation that characterizes the global condition of religion," see Thomas J. Csordas, "Catholic Charismatic Healing in Global Perspective: The Cases of India, Brazil, and Nigeria," in *Global Pentecostal and Charismatic Healing*, ed. Candy Gunther Brown (New York: Oxford University Press, 2011), 335; See also Thomas J. Csordas, *The Sacred Self: A Cultural Phenomenology of Charismatic Healing* (Berkeley: University of California Press, 1994).

"In emphasizing and experiencing the charismata or gifts of the Spirit, Pentecostal/Charismatics have tended to single out two gifts above all others, glossolalia (speaking in tongues as evidence for receiving the baptism in the Holy Spirit) and divine healing as a 'signs and wonders' gift useful for edification and evangelization."[31] In fact, Synan argues, belief in miraculous healing in Pentecostal history actually predates the emergence of tongues as a central, distinguishing Pentecostal phenomenon (though this, of course, brings us back to some of the issues involved in identifying the origins and "central, distinguishing Pentecostal phenomena," discussed earlier).[32]

Mainstream Protestant missionaries in the colonial era were largely unwilling to engage in spiritual warfare, and many performed the prayers for supernatural healing that Indians expected of them only awkwardly and ambivalently, particularly since one significant aspect of the civilizing mission in which missionaries participated was convincing the natives to give up their idolatrous "superstitions" and put their *faith*—the double entendre is appropriate here—in biomedicine rather than in supernatural healings of any sort.[33] Similarly, Mosse describes how the Catholic Church progressively condemned elements of Indian popular religiosity deemed "diableries" to its disavowed margins as it imposed more forceful, central control over Indian Catholics and Indian Catholic saints' shrines beginning in the late nineteenth century.[34] And even though popular expressions of both Protestantism and Catholicism in India today acknowledge the possibility of miraculous healing, members of the clergy associated with churches planted by Protestant and Catholic missionaries often—though not always—conceive of it as something that happens primarily in pill bottles, doctor's offices, and hospitals.

One likely factor in the phenomenal growth of Pentecostalism in recent decades, therefore, is that Pentecostals acknowledge the activity of evil spirits (an activity that is simply taken for granted at the level of popular Indian religiosity) and provide an officially endorsed method for

---

[31.] Vinson Synan, "A Healer in the House? A Historical Perspective on Healing in the Pentecostal/Charismatic Tradition," *Asian Journal of Pentecostal Studies* 3, no. 2 (2000): 189.

[32.] Ibid., 190.

[33.] On the paradoxical position of Christian missionaries vis-à-vis the etiology of disease and the causes of its cure, see Bauman, "Miraculous Health." See also Bergunder, *South Indian*, 126; and Caplan, *Religion*, 60.

[34.] David Mosse, "Possession and Confession: Affliction and Sacred Power in Colonial and Contemporary Catholic South India," in *Anthropology of Christianity,* ed. Fenella Cannell (Durham, NC: Duke University Press, 2006), 110.

managing and circumscribing it more than most of their Christian religious competitors. Lay members of mainline Indian Protestant denominations also generally accept the active presence of the supernatural, but because their clergy do not, they are, as Jones puts it, "left to fend for themselves theologically and ideologically," which leads them, in some instances, to Pentecostalism. While the desire for supernatural healing within the Roman Catholic Church has often led Indian Catholics to the shrines of Catholic saints, sporadic official suppression and routinization of activities at these shrines may have rendered at least some of them somewhat less attractive to those seeking liberation and safety from the work of evil spirits. Mosse, for example, poignantly describes the blossoming of Pentecostal healing ministries in close proximity to the popular Catholic shrine of St. John de Britto, with which the Pentecostal healing ministries now compete. Nevertheless, official suppression of such practices is not everywhere the rule, and many Catholic shrines still buzz with the activity of popular religious healers visited by both Christians and non-Christians (though their activity might in some cases take place somewhat more on the periphery than it once did). But in such Catholic shrines, the focus appears, in general, to be on the healing and boon-granting power of saints, rather than on countering the negative effects of evil spirits. Even when they have official sanction, therefore, they are often unable to address popular religious demands for exorcism and protection from the evil spirits as directly as their Pentecostal counterparts, and this may be one of the reasons why efforts appear to be underway, within the Catholic Church, to more fully revive and support long-established Catholic rituals or exorcism.[35]

It is, moreover, a widely acknowledged fact that many who retain their membership in mainstream Protestant, Catholic, and Orthodox denominational churches supplement worship in them with visits to Pentecostal healers, prayer cells, services, or television channels. To the extent that Protestant, Catholic, and Orthodox Indian Christian communities deny the effectiveness and repress manifestations of miraculous healing and liberation from spirit possession, then, Pentecostal spaces become more and more popular venues for what Foucault termed the "insurrection of

---

[35] E-mail correspondence with Corinne Dempsey, January 20, 2014. On the revival of exorcism within the Roman Catholic Church, see Thomas J. Csordas, "Hammering the Devil with Prayer: The Contemporary Resurgence of Exorcism in the Catholic Church " (paper presented at the Department of Religious Studies, University of California, Santa Barbara, May 1, 2013). A video of the lecture is available at http://www.youtube.com/watch?v=YObVse3KM6c.

subjugated knowledges."[36] But it is important to acknowledge that even in Protestant, Catholic, and Orthodox Christian spaces such denials and repressions are never perfectly consistent or absolute, as the prominence of spiritual healing within the Catholic Charismatic renewal demonstrates. Yet even here, the ambivalence of many clergy within the Catholic Church regarding the Charismatic movement betrays a larger institutional ambiguity about how to properly regulate (and circumscribe?) the supernatural and Christian dealings with it.

It is worth pausing to note here the ways in which Pentecostal approaches to evil, sickness, and misfortune undermine many commonly held, scholarly assumptions about the impact of Christianity's rise in places like India. Webb Keane has pointed out that missionary Protestantism often preached the "moral narrative of modernity," which promoted as a goal the emancipation of individuals from tradition and other social entanglements in order to create freely acting "agents."[37] Theologically speaking, such agents could be (and were, of course) held responsible for their own actions. Yet the promotion of this moral narrative often failed, at least in part, because it encountered (and still encounters) popular traditions like those in India that locate the source of evil, sickness, and misfortune in supernatural entities other than (if not always wholly outside) the individual human. "Thus," writes Caplan, "a popular tradition that externalized evil and sought thaumaturgical solutions was met by a western Protestant tradition that urged instead individual responsibility and the notion of personal guilt—what Hill calls the 'internalization of the struggle against the forces of evil'."[38]

Pentecostalism complicates this historical narrative by occupying a mediating ground between missionary Protestantism and popular Indian religiosity. With missionary Protestantism, Pentecostalism does accept the notion of individual moral responsibility and the theological concept of sin. Yet what sin does, in Pentecostal thought, is make one more vulnerable to the mischief or ill will of personalized supernatural entities, the

---

[36] Bergunder, *South Indian*, 126; Jones, "Faces," 509; Mosse, "Possession," 99, 126; and Caplan, *Religion*, 82, 89–90. Foucault's discussion of subjugated knowledges appears in Michel Foucault, *Power/Knowledge: Selected Interviews and Other Writings, 1972–77* (New York: Pantheon, 1980), 81. It is also discussed in Caplan, *Religion*, 92.

[37] Webb Keane, *Christian Moderns: Freedom and Fetish in the Mission Encounter* (Berkeley: University of California Press, 2007), 6, 201.

[38] Caplan, *Religion*, 61. The quotation is from Christopher Hill, "Science and Magic in Seventeenth Century England," in *Culture, Ideology, and Politics: Essays for Eric Hobsbawm*, ed. Raphael Samuel and Gareth Stedman Jones (Boston: Routledge & Kegan Paul, 1983), 183. See also, Keane, *Christian*, 183.

reality and activity of which is asserted by both Pentecostals and in the context of popular Indian religiosity.

Further complicating the usual narratives is the fact that Pentecostalism and its demonology emerged and were articulated most forcefully (if not exclusively) in the West. For a variety of reasons, then, the interaction of Christian and popular religious traditions in India, as Mosse maintains, "should not be read as the story of a tension between Western (Christian) and Eastern modes of personhood. Rather, it draws attention to different therapeutic movements present in many societies, which are to degrees either centripetal (confessional), focusing on the individual moral agent, or centrifugal (possession-oriented), expanding and dispersing agency."[39]

The Varieties of Christian Healing

Christian "healings" can be of various sorts. Thus far in the chapter I have used the term to cover the entire range of ailments for which Indians commonly seek treatment—physical, reproductive, spiritual, familial, relational, and so on. In this section I devote a few paragraphs to each of them, drawing primarily from the testimony of Indian Christians themselves. Most of the Christians quoted below are Pentecostal for reasons that earlier sections of this chapter make clear. However, as we shall see, Pentecostals are not the only Indian Christians to claim miraculous healing in the name of Jesus. It is also important to keep in mind that while many associate miraculous healings with the large-scale "crusades" of figures like Benny Hinn[40] and D. G. S. Dhinakaran, the vast majority of Christian healings in India take place far more inconspicuously, during the daily peregrinations of Christian pastors, or in the context of regular Christian worship.

Although Christian pastors receive a steady stream of requests for prayer from uninvited guests who appear at their doors, many Christian congregations that believe in the possibility of miraculous healing also sponsor regular sessions of fasting prayer. The fasting with which those who attend prepare for the service is believed to increase the potential for divine healing.[41] Because the sessions focus on healing, many non-Christians

---

[39.] Mosse, "Possession," 127.

[40.] For an excellent description of a Benny Hinn healing crusade in India, see Pradip Ninan Thomas, *Strong Religion, Zealous Media: Christian Fundamentalism and Communication in India* (Los Angeles: Sage, 2008), chapter 8.

[41.] Spiritual austerities are commonly believed, by Indians of all kinds, to increase the power of holy men and women. Fasting is one common austerity, but so too is celibacy. While the former is

who would not otherwise attend a Christian worship service will come for fasting prayer in search of healing. If they receive it, they are likely to consider affiliating with the congregation or pastor that sponsored the service more formally, but many continue to attend only the healing services.[42]

When westerners hear the term "healing," they tend to think first of the physical, and in India, too, physical sickness, pain, and discomfort often lead the ailing to religious healers. Henry, an Assemblies of God pastor in Bangalore, said that non-Christians were attracted to his church primarily through physical healings: "The number one thing that drew them was when my wife went over to their slums and heard their problems. . . . She just empathized with them. And she said, 'Can I pray for you?' The Spirit of God came down upon them. . . . We have seen God heal them left, right, and center. We have seen tumors . . . disappear, cancers disappear, people with heart problems healed."

The trope of the sympathetic pastor's wife is a common one, and interestingly male Christian healers frequently speak of visits from their wives preceding their own prayers for the sick. In fact, in the story just recounted it is difficult to tell who (the pastor or his wife) was actually doing the healing. It is not at all uncommon for lay Christian women to be considered healers.

Prem, an evangelist associated with Henry's church who worked in village areas outside of Mysore, told me of an older woman who was until her son also became Christian the solitary convert in a village that does not allow any outsiders to evangelize in its environs. People come to her for healing. She takes a tumbler of water and prays over it, saying, "Make this water the blood of Jesus." Then she gives it to the ailing and they are healed. "With faith she does this thing," Prem averred, with obvious admiration.

Given the lack of access to sophisticated and affordable healthcare in much of India, it is perhaps not surprising that illnesses requiring complicated medical intervention are high on the list of maladies for which Indians seek miraculous healing. And no condition seemed more prevalent in the stories people told about healing than cancer. At another Assemblies of God church, this time in Chennai, I heard of a Hindu who had stomach cancer. An evangelist approached him and he began coming to church. He converted, and then so did his wife, who was a devotee of the

---

extremely common among Indian Christians, particularly those of the Pentecostal variety, celibacy is less so, except in the Catholic Church, the Ceylon Pentecostal Mission, and in a few other small churches which require their priests and pastors to be celibate. Bergunder, *South Indian*, 159, 63.
[42] Bergunder, "Miracle," 297.

famous Venkateshwara, in nearby Tirupati. Some time later the man visited his oncologist, who declared him fully cured. Similarly, a Hindu woman who also had stomach cancer visited the same church for prayer after she had been given only seven days to live. Members of the church prayed for her, and she was, they say, fully healed.

Another malady for which Indians frequently seek divine intervention is infertility. In a rural CSI church in Karnataka, a young farmer told me a story the likes of which I heard frequently, and all over India. Before he was born, he said, his mother was barren. She began attending church in hopes of finding a cure. Immediately, and miraculously, as he told it, she got pregnant and had a baby girl, then a second girl, and then him. At the same church, a woman named Shashi testified to having becoming a Christian because, having struggled with infertility for six years, she became pregnant with a male child after merely seeing an image of Christ through the windows of a nearby church. At a Pentecostal church in Chennai I heard of another Hindu couple who had been trying to have children for four or five years, but without success. The couple began attending church and came to believe that God would "bless them." Soon afterwards, the woman gave birth to a male child. Several hours by car from Chennai, in rural Tamil Nadu, I heard of a man who visited a mission church for fasting prayer, during which he manifested and was delivered from possession. After he recovered from the episode, he related to others present that he and his wife had been trying to have children for six years. Church members prayed for him, putting their hands on his wife's womb. The pastor prophesied that she would become pregnant. Today they have a baby boy. (Not surprisingly, given the enduring preference for male children in much of India, most of the testimonials given about "successful" Christian interventions in cases of infertility ended, eventually, in the birth of a boy.)

Christians also sometimes interpret infertility as a punishment for lukewarm faith, and several times I heard of Christian couples becoming pregnant after having renewed their faith in God. Additionally, miraculous healings are often sought and provided by Christian healers for barren livestock or farmer's fields. Fecundity, in general, then, is something that many Indians consider a spiritual concern, and the ability of Christian healers to find solutions for sterilities of all kinds has both spiritual and material dimensions.[43]

The pursuit of miraculous cures for infertility is not merely a rural or lower-class affair in India. After the ritual dedication of a Christian baby boy in an upper-class, urban Pentecostal congregation in Bangalore, for

---

[43] Cf. Aaron, "Emulating," 107.

example, the dedicated baby's mother testified: "Several months after getting married, we came to know that my mother and father-in-law were expecting a child." This caused her and her husband some concern, since they were having difficulty getting pregnant. But, she said, they "took comfort in the words of Genesis 21:1," in which the barren wife of Abraham, Sarah, is given the child she had been promised by God. And now, "by God's grace," she said, we have gotten "pregnant and can dedicate our son to the church."

From this woman's testimony, it is clear that infertility is not viewed merely as a physical problem for many in India but also as a familial and social issue. In fact, many Indians make little distinction between physical and social ailments, both of which are considered spiritual problems. As with poor physical health, then, many Indians consider poor familial relations a problem requiring consultation with those known to be able to manage and manipulate the evil spirits. In one sophisticated survey of converts to Pentecostalism, more than half admitted having faced problems within their families before becoming Pentecostal, and 77% reported experiencing greater familial love and harmony afterwards.[44]

Many Christians and converts to Christianity I interviewed reported receiving what they considered miraculous healing for family squabbles and conflicts, stubborn or irresponsible children, and/or the alcoholism of irresolute husbands. The last of these is of particular concern for many Indian women, and especially those in tribal communities where teetotalism is not idealized as it is in some Hindu contexts, and the reportedly generally positive effect of Pentecostal conversion may be part of its allure for women. In the Dangs, for example, according to Aaron, "Deliverance from alcohol addiction ranks next to healing as a cause for allegiance to Christianity, particularly among women, who readily accept Christ after their husbands give up drinking."[45]

Here again, note the positive material consequences of spiritual healing; when a husband breaks his addiction to alcohol it not only decreases the dysfunctionality of relationships but also usually helps the family achieve higher levels of financial prosperity. In fact, many Pentecostals consider it perfectly appropriate to approach supernatural healers for matters of material interest, such as when they find themselves in legal or financial stress. For example, Rajesh, an independent Pentecostal pastor near Hyderabad,

---

[44] Paul Parathazham, "Neo-Pentecostalism in India: Preliminary Report of a National Survey," *Word and Worship* 29 (1996): 85, 96.
[45] Aaron, "Emulating," 109.

told me of a Hindu family that sought his help with a legal case. "They were paying *lakhs* and *lakhs* of rupees to judges and lawyers," he said, "but were not coming out of it. They fasted and prayed. After 7 days, the case was completely over and done. Now they come to church."

In all of the ailments discussed so far (i.e., physical, reproductive, familial, financial, legal), the machinations of witches, sorcerers, and evil spirits are generally suspected. Appropriately, then, Christian healers almost always employ strategies designed to mitigate the effects of the spiritual malfeasance involved. Sometimes this is done without exorcism, for example, through a simple prayer to God, who is believed implicitly to be able to overcome the work of any other spiritual agent. In other cases, however, those with the gift of discernment deem demonic possession to be the primary issue, and not just the source of secondary problems. In these cases, those involved in "deliverance ministries" prescribe and perform exorcisms. While all supernatural healings therefore demand attention to the spiritual world, exorcism constitutes a subcategory of healing, for it is not always required. Nevertheless, as with miraculous recoveries from sickness, infertility, alcoholism, or financial and legal misfortune, the spiritual healings that result from exorcisms often prompt those healed to consider affiliating in some way with Christianity.

Explaining why his village church outside of Dehradun was growing, Satish, an independent Pentecostal pastor said, "People are so much disturbed, and they have a lot of problems. In our church, some people were demon-possessed, and they used to worship the spirits, and they were tormented by the spirits. They were violent, anti-social. They went to witch doctors, [and] got no help. But they came to church and they got deliverance in Jesus' name. So then they realized there is truth and power in Christ, and they gave their lives [to him]."

The ineffectiveness of *baigas, mantiravatis*, or other shamanistic healers is a common trope of Christian testimonies involving exorcisms (and healings in general). At a mission church in rural Tamil Nadu, Christians told me about a *mantiravati*'s daughter who had come to one of the church's fasting prayer services to seek healing for chronic joint pain. The family had previously paid a sizeable sum of money to a local non-Christian healer to provide some relief for the girl, but to no avail. During the prayer service, the girl fell down, began writhing on the floor, and then fainted. The congregation kept praying, and when the girl woke up, she felt better, and started coming back regularly for more prayer. At this point, her father, the *mantiravati*, began to oppose her association with the church. Yet her mother argued with him, saying "Even your power didn't work."

Christian, another evangelist in Dehradun who claims to specialize in deliverance ministries, was approached by a young couple. According to Christian, they said, "Please save us and we will convert. In three days' time, an evil spirit [had] killed their one son. And they were afraid because another daughter was possessed, and the evil spirit was upon her and she was suffering many times in a day." Christian went to their home and began to preach and pray. Gradually the family came to embrace Christianity. The spirit left the daughter, and now, some years later, as any feel-good Indian Christian story should end, the daughter is married to a Christian boy, pregnant, and attending church.

In another case, the parents of a boy who could not sleep for three days called for Christian, who reported being able to "feel the heaviness of the boy's evil spirits" even as he stepped on the verandah of their home. The evangelist entered and began praying. Before he could say more than a few words, the boy fell fast asleep.

During interviews I conducted at a CSI church in rural Karnataka, I met a humble, unassuming young man named Prakash, who had become a village evangelist after himself experiencing a series of miracles. Prakash had gained a reputation for healing, and during his evangelistic visits he was often approached for prayer. Although he admitted to struggling with a lack of confidence in his dealings with the demonic, he drew courage from an incident in which he had delivered a young boy from demon possession. I recount the incident as Prakash conveyed it to me through a translator.

The possessed boy's Hindu family had tried a variety of other non-Christian methods, but unsuccessfully. Friends told the Hindu family to believe in Jesus and call Prakash, who came with his evangelistic associates to pray for the boy. But the demon was not immediately expelled. In fact, things got worse, and afterwards the demon spoke to the boy's parents through the possessed boy, telling them, "This boy will be alive for only seven days, and those who came earlier to pray will not be able to do anything now." The family relayed the message to Prakash, who gathered his friends and went to pray again for the boy, returning over and over again during a six-month period. Whenever they walked to the boy's village, strange things would happen, like trees making unusual noises. But they kept going, and finally, one day after they sprinkled consecrated water and oil on the house and the boy, he was healed of his possession.

Belief in the workings of evil spirits, and action to combat their influence, extends far beyond Christians who specialize in such work. For example, Prakash's mother, Jyothi, who was present for the interview just described, said that during the six months when her son and his friends were visiting the boy, she was praying for them at her home, asking God to bind the evil spirits that possessed the boy. Just before the boy was delivered, she had received a vision. In the vision, she saw a white-washed wall behind which there were many evil spirits. She interpreted the vision as a communication from God assuring her that the spirits had already been bound, and instructing her that rather than praying for them to be bound, she should instead be thanking God for having already done so.

As these stories suggest, children are considered particularly vulnerable to spirit possession. One of the reasons is that, according to popular Indian religious belief, fear and a lack of psychological fortitude provide openings for evil spirits. For this same reason, women, who are stereotyped as weak-willed, fearful, and more neurotic and emotional than men, are also considered more vulnerable to demonic attack and possession. Christians also sometimes presume women to be more "sinful" than men, a reference to their ostensibly greater sexual desire. For this reason, female beautification and adornment are believed to increase vulnerability to attack, and this may help explain why some Indian Christian, and particularly Pentecostal communities prohibit women to wear jewelry, makeup, or colorful dresses.[46] In every place where I conducted fieldwork, I heard stories of women and children being cured of demon possession far more regularly than I heard of men suffering from the same condition.

For example, one Hindu grandmother in rural Tamil Nadu was delivered by her grandson's Pentecostal pastors of what they identified as a demon that had possessed her within the confines of the temple her family maintained (to the chagrin of the priest there, who believed her to be possessed by the temple's tutelary goddess—an auspicious kind of possession, according to popular Hindu belief). Another young woman in the same region was exorcised of the spirit of a psychotic man who used to live and wander around naked before eventually hanging himself in the house where her family now resided. Yet no story was as disturbing to me as that of a young businesswoman in Dehradun, who, after visiting a series of religious healers to find relief from a demon that she could actually see, and that, she reported, raped her violently and repeatedly, finally found deliverance through the work of a Christian exorcist.[47]

[46.] Mosse, "Possession," 117.

[47.] This story drew forth my skepticism and raised in my mind some concern about what was actually going on. But it would have been impertinent for me to voice these concerns, particularly since I heard the story from the exorcist, not the young woman.

Along with deliverance from spirit possession and healings from all manner of ailments and injuries (e.g., ulcers, poison snake bites, paralysis, diabetes, comas, even death), protection from harm, injury, and misfortune is viewed, by Indian Christians, as an integral aspect of divine healing, as another story provided by Prakash and his mother Jyothi suggests. Several years ago, the family was sleeping in the village home they rented. Prakash, who was lying on the floor, awoke in the middle of the night, sensing that something was crawling on him. Rodent visitations in village India being relatively common, Prakash—and here I am horrified by his nonchalance—was not terribly concerned, because he assumed what was on him was a rat that he could just swat away. Yet when he tried to move his arm toward the rat, he discovered that he was paralyzed, feeling like his hands and legs had been bound. His mind was by this time alert, though, and in the dim light of the television, which had been left on, he watched what he finally discerned to be a very large, poisonous snake slither a meandering path from his bed to that of his sister, who was also sleeping on the floor nearby. Coming fully to his senses, he started shouting, "Snake! Snake!" Jyothi and her husband came running and discovered the snake lying just beside the body of their still sleeping daughter. They burst into spontaneous prayer, saying the name of Jesus over and over while slowly dragging their daughter, who was still somehow sound asleep, out of the room. When they came back in, the snake was on her bedding. They quickly but carefully trapped it in her blanket, took the blanket outside onto the street, and beat it until they had killed the snake inside.

By this time, the neighbors, all of whom were Hindu, had been awakened and had come out of their homes to see what had transpired. When they found out, they were distressed, since in popular Hindu belief snakes are sometimes worshipped as manifestations of the snake-god Nagaraja ("The king of snakes," or the "snake-king"), and to kill one, even one that has bitten you, is to invite the wrath of this potentially dangerous deity.[48] "Nagaraja," they said, fussing over the corpse of the snake, "if you had come into our house we would have treated you better!" Then, turning to the Christian family, they said "Since you've killed a god, there's going to be vengeance. People in your house will die of blood." Yet the Christians believed they had been kept safe by God himself and interpreted Prakash's perceived paralysis to have been particularly miraculous, since it prevented

---

[48] Early Christian missionaries often took Indian Christians' reticence to kill snakes as a sign that they had not been fully converted. For an example, see Bauman, *Christian Identity*, 158.

him from provoking the poisonous snake. Afterwards, the family remained in that house for three more years without incident, and their very survival instigated some of their Hindu neighbors to seek their prayers, which they happily offered, effecting, they report, several healings.

The Function of Miraculous Healings

For those Indian Christians who believe in them, healings and other miraculous events perform several important functions. Below, I focus on three: (1) confirming faith, (2) provoking conversions, and (3) activating ministry. In the story just told, for example, Prakash's family interpreted protection from the serpent, and the fact that no harm befell them after they killed it, as confirmation of their Christian faith and the power of Jesus Christ. In fact, before they told me this story, as I was getting to know them, Jyothi began to give an unprompted testimony of faith that focused on a series of miraculous recoveries within her family. According to her testimony, her children had been miraculously healed of chronic and potentially debilitating conjunctivitis, about which doctors could do nothing, after she offered the children, in prayer, to God. Her husband, a day laborer, had recovered from an acute, untreated appendicitis that doctors thought would leave him permanently disabled. And she herself was cured from asthma after receiving a vision in which she saw herself as a young girl, crying and being picked up and placed on a high pedestal by God.

The sharing of such testimonies is ritualized in churches where faith healings occur. In these churches, worship services almost always include expressions of gratitude for experiences of miraculous recovery. No problem is too big (e.g., cancer, cholera, typhoid, heart disease) or small (e.g., difficulty studying for exams or toothaches) to expect or report supernatural intervention.

If experiences of supernatural healing and other miraculous events confirm faith, the inverse is also true. Many Christians I interviewed interpreted the misfortune that befell non-Christians who harassed or opposed them as proof of Jesus' power and a confirmation of the validity of their Christian faith and ministry. For example, when the ringleader of a mob that repeatedly disrupted his VBS and had threatened to break his arms and legs got in a fight and had both of his own legs broken, Satish, the North Indian evangelist mentioned in the Introduction, interpreted it as a sign of God's judgment upon the thug.

Similarly, when Rajesh, the Pentecostal pastor from Hyderabad, purchased land and began constructing his church, a group of local rowdies kidnapped him, and then held and beat him for an entire night. According to Rajesh, during the beatings, the ringleader said, "You should not be a pastor; we will give you money to do a big job." Rejecting their offer, Rajesh reportedly responded, "Anna [uncle], if you built a temple we wouldn't stop it." Unconvinced, the ringleader said, "We will give you one month to stop or we will break your legs and hands and kill you." Several months later, however, the ringleader himself became paralyzed in his hands and legs. The doctor gave him one week to live. Rajesh and other members of his congregation visited the man, prayed for him, and invited him to become a Christian. But he did not, and Rajesh interprets the man's subsequent death as the natural result of his obstinacy.

Belief in the supernatural powers of the spiritually disciplined and particularly pious is common in India, so common, in fact, that the interpretations given to events like these by Christians are quite frequently shared by their non-Christian neighbors. After the death of his primary opponent, for example, Rajesh came to be respected among non-Christians in the area as a man of supernatural power. And since it is well-known that one should not provoke or meddle with men (and women) of power, opposition to his ministries quickly dissipated.

Miraculous events, as we have seen above, can also instigate conversions to Christianity. The miracles can even be quite small, as in the case of Vivek, a recent Assemblies of God convert in South India. Vivek's sister had converted to Christianity and was encouraging him to do the same. He told her, "That's what you believe, but I don't want to do anything about it." She persisted, telling him to ask Jesus to help him understand. Impetuously, according to Vivek, he decided to test Jesus, saying, " 'Jesus, I have this pen that doesn't write. If you are God and you are one, I want you to make this pen write.' You won't believe it," he said, "but miraculously the pen started writing!" (Having deemed this particular miracle "quite small," I must nevertheless admit to considering India a graveyard for pens. It may therefore require substantially more supernatural power to revive a heat-smitten ballpoint than I have implied.)

Instances of miraculous cures and protection from harm also function to activate an interest in ministry, and this is particularly (but not exclusively) true for Pentecostals.[49] In many Pentecostal testimonies, Bergunder writes, "pastors and evangelists report that their devotion to full-time ministry resulted through an illness and miraculous recovery,"[50] and these reports

---

[49] Cf. Bergunder, *South Indian*, 151.
[50] Bergunder, "Miracle," 291.

generally follow one of two models. In the first, the future minister is sick and promises to enter the ministry in exchange for a cure. In the second, the future minister becomes sick after refusing a call to ministry. My own fieldwork bears this out, though it also suggests several other common models (e.g., that of miraculous and inexplicable protection from harm, or of supernatural visions) and reminds us that such testimonies are not unique to Pentecostals.

After he and Jyothi had recounted the saga of their brush with the snake, for example, Prakash—who was, remember, a member of a rural CSI church and not a Pentecostal—told me that the experience had propelled him from his previously nominal faith into active Christian evangelism. Similarly, Suresh, a young Pentecostal evangelist and Bible college graduate from North India, testified that God had miraculously saved him from death on multiple occasions. "I died three times," he said. The first was when he contracted cholera as an infant. The medicine was not working and the doctor declared him a lost cause. His mother took him from their home and put him on the verandah of the church, where the family prayed for him throughout the night. At 4:00 in the morning, he awoke from his stupor and began singing a familiar Hindi tune with the words, *jab se pyara yesu aya, mera jiwan badal gaya* ("My life has been transformed since [my] dear Jesus came"). The second time, Suresh was on a bus that crashed into live electric wires carrying a massive amount of current. His brother and cousin died in the accident, and others were permanently injured or disabled. But he emerged unscathed. The third time, he was speeding on his motorbike, and arrived at a bridge just as a lorry, rounding a blind corner, suddenly appeared at its opposite end. He doesn't know how he escaped being hit by the truck, and the next thing he remembers is lying on the ground below the bridge. "I got a vision from there," Suresh said, "I felt that someone was picking me up . . . as I was falling. I was going 70 [km/h] and dropped 15 feet. I should have been injured, but I had only scratches." Not surprisingly, he came away convicted that God wanted him to enter the ministry.

Sometimes, the miraculous protection of loved ones can also instigate a person to explore Christian ministry. Satish, mentioned above, said that he had rejected a call to ministry for some time. But then his mother fell ill and needed surgery. Everyone, including her doctors, thought she would die. So he prayed to God, saying, "Lord, if you save her, I will know you want me to serve you." His mother recuperated, and he now carries on an active church-planting ministry around Dehradun.

The testimony of Ravi, a 20-something, lower-caste village evangelist who works outside of Hyderabad, demonstrates both the converting and activating functions of miracles in the life of India's Christians and also illuminates quite clearly the risks involved in Christian conversion. Ravi grew up Hindu, but had a Christian friend who witnessed to him. The friend gave him a copy of the New Testament. Ravi threw it on the ground and stepped on it to express his contempt for the message contained therein. But then, desperate after having failed to properly prepare for exams he was taking to become a government accountant, he took his Christian friends' advice to pray at a nearby Mennonite Brethren church. He prayed there daily for eleven days and then took the exam. Certain he had failed, he took another, less prestigious job. But when the marks were returned, he discovered he had passed with what he deemed miraculously high marks. So he converted, but only "internally" since his family would not have approved.

Finally, he decided to get publicly baptized. Following the church's prescription, he fasted for three days before the ceremony. Someone told his father about the impending ceremony, and as it was about to take place, the father arrived on the scene, beat Ravi, abused the officiating pastor for trying to convert his son to the "SC faith," and dragged Ravi away, beating him the whole way home. When they arrived back at their house, the father stripped off the son's clothes, tied up his hands and feet, and left him on the roof of the house from 11:00 a.m. to 6:30 p.m., in the heat and glare of the midday sun. At 1:00 p.m., the father appeared and put chilies and salt in Ravi's eyes. At 2:00 p.m. he came and did it again, and this time also beat Ravi with a belt. It went on like this until 6:30, when Ravi received a vision of a person with shiny clothing, whose face he could not see. The person untied him, attended to his wounds, and released him. Then the person offered him a prince's outfit. Ravi put it on, and the person lifted him up and put him on a golden throne, gave him a diamond crown, and said, "I have chosen you; this is your crown. Make certain no one takes it from you."

Just after the vision began, his sister-in-law, a nurse, had come to check on him. She found him unconscious and could not find his pulse. He laid there from 6:30 p.m. to 7:30 p.m., and he believes, in retrospect, that his spirit had left his body. At 7:30 p.m., he awoke and found that he actually had been untied. He turned to his mother, who was sitting nearby, and told her that God had given him a crown. She gave him a slap in return, but that was the last of the beatings. Within days he had left his home and become an evangelist.

For Christian ministers like Ravi, visions and other miraculous events not only activate ministry, they also direct it. Some years after his conversion, Ravi received a vision of people crying for no reason. He asked them why they were crying, but they wouldn't answer him. He asked Jesus, who was there, why they were crying. Jesus said, "They have money and food, but not eternity." He said to Jesus, "Where are they?" and Jesus gestured toward a house in the village that he recognized. After the vision, he went to the house and found a woman who had just poured five liters of kerosene over her body and was on the verge of lighting herself on fire to commit suicide.[51] He shared the gospel with her, he said, and she converted. Now several members of her family have as well.

Visions, as these stories indicate, are considered by many Indian Christians instances of miraculous divine intervention, and appear regularly in Christian testimonies. They prompt conversions, confirm faith, and activate/direct Christian ministry, particularly among Pentecostals and the Pentecostalized.[52] But, in this sense, Indian Christians are little different than Christians in other parts of the world, and visions, of course, have been an important element of Christian faith from the very beginning.

It is clear, then, that healings and other miraculous events are a significant factor in Christian, and particularly Pentecostal growth in India. They also, however, play a role in the maintenance and preservation of Christian communities by confirming Christian faith, activating otherwise apathetic believers, and propelling them into lives of committed ministry. Healings, by any definition of the term, then, clearly constitute an "allurement" to Christian faith, and in the conclusion we turn to questions of how this reality informs and/or complicates conversations about conversion and Hindu–Christian conflict.

Conclusion: Does the "Divine Physician" Have an Unfair Advantage?

The Niyogi Committee concluded that missionary medical facilities constituted an illegitimate allurement to the Christian faith, particularly when those who ran them consciously or unconsciously conflated the efficacy of allopathic medicine with the power of Jesus Christ, the Divine Physician, or when—more problematically—they offered Christians (and only Christians) priority or discounts in their allocation of medical care.[53] The

---

[51.] Dousing oneself with and then igniting cooking fuel is a common method of suicide in India, particularly for women.

[52.] Bergunder, *South Indian*, 139; and Caplan, *Religion*, 105–6.

[53.] Sections of this conclusion appeared first in Chad Bauman, "Does the Divine Physician Have an Unfair Advantage? The Politics of Conversion in Twentieth-Century India," in *Asia in the Making of Christianity: Agency, Conversion, and Indigeneity*, ed. Jonathan Seitz and Richard Fox Young (Leiden: Brill, 2013). Reprinted with Permission. Copyright Brill, 2013.

complaints of those who appeared before the Niyogi Committee, however, emerged from the intuition or conviction that the provision of missionary medicine represented primarily a scientific and financial achievement that missionaries nevertheless illegitimately tried to claim and utilize as a religious one. Missionaries, as the argument went, were therefore guilty of increasing the attractiveness of their faith by associating it with demonstrations of material and scientific power.

Many contemporary observers would perhaps acknowledge that the influence of Christianity in Europe and North America helped produce a sociocultural environment conducive to the development, in the last century or two, at least, of biomedical science. Yet few today, even among Christians, would accept the widely embraced colonial-era missionary view that biomedicine was Christian science.[54] For these reasons, I imagine that most readers would agree with the Niyogi Committee's criticism of Christians who tried to claim biomedical science as Christian science, thereby borrowing its allure in an effort to attract converts.

The mere ability of Christians to heal in missionary hospitals, to make whole what was broken, to provide succor for suffering, was appealing to non-Christians. It was a demonstration of potency, of ability, and power. And Hindus perceived in this aphrodisiacal power to heal a kind of allurement to the Christian faith, a perception not at all unjustified in the context of postcolonial imbalances of wealth and power, and in the context of an ongoing lack of access, for many Indians, to secular biomedical care. Missionary medicine, therefore, did surely provide Christians with a competitive advantage.

In this chapter, however, we meet with a more complicated kind of healing: supernatural healing. Good health is the default and expected state for many of India's Christians, particularly those of Pentecostal persuasion. Among such Christians, illness, addiction, misfortune, and family dysfunction are considered signs of sin and/or spirit affliction to be overcome through the operations of Christ the Divine Physician and his human assistants. The promise of good health and good fortune is in and of itself attractive and alluring, particularly in places where satisfactory and advanced biomedical care is inaccessible and/or unaffordable (that is, in most of India).

In addition, there are also, as I acknowledge above, material benefits that result from good health, cordial family relationships, and the breaking of

---

54. On which, see Bauman, "Miraculous Health."

addictions like alcoholism. Because of this, without a doubt the Christian claim to ensure good health, through divine intervention (and the widespread belief that this claim is in fact true), draws people toward the faith.[55]

The fact that many begin affiliating with Christianity after receiving healing or help with addiction draws the ire of Hindu nationalists, who raise against faith healings the accusation of allurement. In fact, Hardiman interprets the anti-Christian riots in the Dangs, Gujarat, at least in part as a response to a surge in recuperative conversions.[56] And here again, the common portrayal of Christianity as a purveyor of modernization in the context of more traditional religions gets turned on its head, for very often Hindu critics of Christians have accused them of being "guilty of [superstition], by duping credulous "tribals" into conversion through what they depicted as trickery . . . [Christian missionary] activities were contrasted to the Hindu religious workers who were seen to provide . . . "legitimate" health care.[57] There is, of course, a certain irony in the claims of Hindu nationalists that Christians are not adequately modernized, since in many other situations Indian Christians are accused, by dint of their presumed connections to western Christianity, of being peddlers of a "foreign" (and threatening) modernity.[58]

Nevertheless, many urban, well-educated and upper-class Hindus today consider Christian faith healings little more than quackery intended to dupe the simple-minded and desperate, and a form of allurement that would never work within their own communities. "The whole thing is a fraud, and we have established it," Mr. Venkatanarayan, advisor to the Hindu Dharma Acharya Sabha, told me, adding sarcastically and with an ornery grin, "If Jesus Christ can rectify my knees without surgery, either directly or through the medium of Mr. Baptist Missionary, I am willing to become a Christian!"

Similarly, in the last few years, a number of articles have appeared in the RSS's official organ, the *Organiser*, which deem Christian healing a fake and claim that it is being held out as an illegitimate inducement to the faith. In these articles, the grand healing crusades of televangelists like Benny Hinn bring forth the most consistent contempt. But the articles also demonstrate an informed if partisan awareness of the kinds of

---

[55] Aaron, "Emulating," 108–9.
[56] David Hardiman, "Christianity and the Adivasis of Gujarat," in *Development and Deprivation in Gujarat: In Honour of Jan Breman*, ed. Ghanshyam Shah, Mario Rutten, and Hein Streefkerk (London: Sage Publications, 2002), 190.
[57] Ibid., 190–91.
[58] Ibid., 191.

smaller-scale healing activities that take place at the local level. Christian "agents," one article claims, "play a major role during ill-health of Hindus and offer a free prayer meeting to get rid of diseases only to get them converted to Christianity with a bogus healing power of Jesus."[59] Another tells the story of two brothers who were "allured to convert by fake healers . . . along with all members of the family" because they were assured "that their younger sister Indu, who was suffering from an ulcer in her stomach, [would] be cured by prayers. Now nineteen long years have passed, the patient is still suffering."[60]

Sangh organizations, these articles demonstrate, have at least on occasion responded to Christian healing ministries with violence, such as that perpetrated against one Father Anthony, and reported approvingly by the *Organiser*, in 2006. According to the story, Father Anthony and his followers were "thrashed by some Bajrang Dal activists when the former was organising a healing prayer meeting at his residence in Kathua," a thrashing which occurred after the Bajrang Dal had "repeatedly warned him to stop his anti-Hindu activities."[61]

While from a skeptical perspective, one might label Christian supernatural healing a kind of "superstition," as do these RSS authors and the critics of Christianity Hardiman paraphrases, it would be impossible to deny that Hindu and other popular Indian healers engage in quite similar activities. To be consistent, then, Indian critics of Christian faith healers would need to be equally disparaging of all forms of "bogus healing."

It may be useful, at this juncture, for me to acknowledge my own prejudices in this regard. Whereas, it had been for many decades the tendency of scholars of religion to declare beyond their investigative abilities and purview the question of whether the supernatural was really there, and really active in the possessions, exorcisms, and healings claimed by religious people, there is a growing trend, particularly among anthropologists dealing with such phenomena, to grant to the supernatural some form or degree of objectivity, or at least to find some way of speaking about it that

[59] R. Guru Prasad, "Cash Prize for Hindus to Throw Photos of Hindu Gods: Extra Money for Wearing Cross Lockets," *The Organiser (Online)*, 3 April 2011, http://organiser.org/archives/historic/dynamic/modules4a3b.html?name=Content&pa=showpage&pid=391&page=7. The grammatical errors appear in the original.

[60] Ajai Srivastava, "The Pastor Reveals the Truth: Reconversion to Hinduism," *The Organiser (Online)*, 11 March 2007, http://organiser.org/archives/historic/dynamic/modulesb72e.html?name=Content&pa=showpage&pid=174&page=30.

[61] Khajuria S. Kant, "Bajrang Dal Saves 42 Families," *The Organiser (Online)*, 5 November 2006, http://organiser.org/archives/historic/dynamic/modules6ef4.html?name=Content&pa=showpage&pid=155&page=11.

avoids the extremes of skeptical denial, on the one hand, and attributing to supernatural entities full agency and individuality, on the other. The works of Susan Harding, Thomas Csordas, and Matthew Engelke have been instructive in this regard, though tentative, each in their own way.[62]

The challenge is to acknowledge the power that supernatural entities (real or imagined) have in and over the lives of those who believe in them without simply dismissing belief in the supernatural as superstitious bunk, or theoretically reducing it to uninformed misattribution/misrecognition of agency and causality. Very often the latter has been done with the best of intentions (that is, to avoid the former), and by the best known names in the field. For example, attempting to avoid dismissing the religious claims of the Australian aborigines he studied, Émile Durkheim suggested they were correct to recognize that some objective reality had power over their lives. Their error was not in this recognition, but rather in misidentifying this objective reality as the supernatural, when in fact the powerful objective reality was society itself.[63] Similarly, the careful wordplay that concludes William James's *Varieties of Religious Experience* is intended (but does not successfully manage) to explain religious belief without dismissing or reducing it to the "medical materialism" he so forcefully (in the opening pages of *Varieties*) deplores. "God is real since he produces real effects" (517) writes James, but only five pages after proposing:

> that whatever it may be on its *farther* side, the "more" with which in religious experience we feel ourselves connected is on its *hither* side the subconscious continuation of our conscious life. Starting thus with a recognized psychological fact as our basis, we seem to preserve a contact with 'science' which the ordinary theologian lacks. At the same time the theologian's contention that the religious man is moved by an external power is vindicated, for it is one of the peculiarities of invasions from the subconscious region to take on objective appearances, and to suggest to the Subject an external control.[64]

---

[62] See, for example, Susan Friend Harding, *The Book of Jerry Falwell* (Princeton: Princeton University Press, 2001); Csordas, *Sacred Self*; and Thomas J. Csordas, *Language, Charisma, and Creativity: The Ritual Life of a Religious Movement* (Berkeley: University of California Press, 1997); and Matthew Engelke, *A Problem of Presence: Beyond Scripture in an African Church* (Berkeley: University of California Press, 2007). Thanks to Gillian Goslinga for helping me sort through some of the issues in this and the succeeding paragraphs in personal e-mail communication (March 10, 2014).

[63] Émile Durkheim, *The Elementary Forms of Religious Life*, trans. Karen E. Fields (New York: Free Press, 1995), 226–27.

[64] William James, *The Varieties of Religious Experience* (New York: Mentor Books, 1958), 512–13.

Both Durkheim's and James's formulations strike me as genial but in the end somewhat glib attempts to obscure what is really being suggested, which is that religious people misidentify the agent of the effects they experience in life as the supernatural, when in fact the real agent is (for Durkheim) the social or (for James) the psychological/unconscious. The supernatural is therefore not really "real" at all, for Durkheim or James. It is just a misattribution. Moreover, in both cases, the "informant's" appraisal of reality is rejected in favor of the scholar's, effectively and inevitably placing the scholar's rationality, epistemology, and ontology hierarchically above that of the informant.

In a theoretically rich article, Gillian Goslinga has suggested that "the stakes of what gets to count as 'real' in anthropology have had and continue to have profound consequences for how we imagine sociality as well as practice encounter across ontological difference."[65] For reasons articulated above, then, Goslinga might criticize Durkheim and James as she does a variety of other well-known contemporary anthropologists, whose "most sensitive and ethnographically rich readings of the uncanny transpose as their *first* and *last* analytical move the ontology of their subjects onto their theoretical constructs as if these theoretical constructs have the *same* ontological make up as spirits, or the same origins and histories."[66]

I must admit that at a personal level, and very much despite myself, I remain a skeptic and find claims of possession, exorcism, and supernatural healing to be difficult to believe. It is for this reason that I am left unmoved by the work of anthropologists (like Edith Turner, Paul Stoller, Frederique Apffel-Marglin, and Kalpana Ram)[67] who ascribe to the supernatural any kind of objective reality. Moreover, I instinctually interpret religious individuals' professed experiences of the supernatural as manifestations of their largely unconscious but socialized tendencies to attribute what may just be mundane affairs—psychological disorders, spontaneous remissions or regressions, unexpected illnesses, interpersonal conflict, the effects of stress—to supernatural etiologies when natural ones might be

---

[65.] Gillian Goslinga, "Spirited Encounters: Notes on the Politics and Poetics of Representing the Uncanny in Anthropology," *Anthropological Theory* 12, no. 4 (2012): 386.

[66.] Ibid., 404.

[67.] See, for example, Kalpana Ram, *Fertile Disorder: Spirit Possession and its Provocation of the Modern* (Honolulu: University of Hawaii Press, 2013); Paul Stoller, *In Sorcery's Shadow: A Memoir of Apprenticeship among the Songhay of Niger* (Chicago: University of Chicago Press, 1989); and Frederique Apffel-Marglin, *Subversive Spiritualities: How Rituals Enact the World* (New York: Oxford University Press, 2012); and Edith Turner, "A Visible Spirit Form in Zambia," in *Being Changed by Cross-Cultural Encounters: The Anthropology of Extraordinary Experience*, ed. David E. Young and Jean-Guy Goulet (Toronto: Broadview Press, 1994).

perfectly adequate. But as a scholarly theory this simply will not do, for all of the reasons just articulated, and therefore it strikes me as important to remain open to the possibility of supernatural agency and objectivity in my scholarly research, even if my personal instincts might encourage a different course.

Moreover, when interacting as a scholar with Pentecostals or others who believe in the possibility of supernatural healing (among whom are many of my Hindu interviewees as well), I do not generally publicize my skeptical views. My hesitation derives not from any desire to dupe my interlocutors into thinking I embrace their worldview, but rather from two altogether different sources. The first is that in the end, it could very well be *I* who is engaged in misattribution (i.e., of what is in reality super-natural agency to natural causation). The second reason is my firm belief that those who expect supernatural healing do often experience it (whatever the nature or source of that healing), and perhaps significantly more than random chance might suggest they should. I have no doubt, then, that Pentecostal faith may play a role even in the most fantastical forms of healing (e.g., from cancer). Whether the agency involved in that healing is supernatural or "merely" psycho-somatic, I see no reason to set about intentionally to undermine it.

In the end, for the purposes both of our discussion here, and the public debate in India, what matters is not so much whether the claims that Pentecostals make about supernatural healing are true, but rather whether they represent something we might call "force, fraud, or inducement," and since supernatural healings in India are not unique to Pentecostals, or even to Christians more generally, the question of their authenticity and source seems (to me, at least) ancillary to the matter at hand, except in the limited, hypothetical ways indicated below.

The Niyogi Committee's criticism of missionary medicine rested on what it perceived to be the illegitimate conflation of scientific/material power with Christianity, but in the context of supernatural healing, this conflation does not appear to exist. Is there any way, then, that one could claim that the miraculous interventions Christians expect and experience gives them what could be considered an unfair advantage? Surely the ability to offer access to efficacious biomedical therapies in contexts where they are otherwise unavailable constitutes a greater (and therefore a more unfair) advantage than the assertion that illnesses can be cured through prayer and faith in Christ. Whereas, the former requires access to wealth, technology, and scientific power, the latter does not; local non-Christian healers can presumably compete with Christian faith healers on a relatively level playing field. Of course, this presumption requires that one share with the *Organiser* authors quoted above their skeptical materialism and treat all claims to spiritual healing as equally spurious.

But what if it could be shown scientifically that Christian faith healers were more effective than their non-Christian counterparts (or vice versa), even if only marginally so? That would certainly constitute an advantage, but would it be an unfair one? Could one be faulted for engaging in superior faith healing practices if the superiority of those practices did not in any way depend on having greater access to material wealth or medical equipment? Or is the ability of Christians to heal, and the perception that they can, somehow, quite indirectly, related to the great mass of foreign funding that supports those who engage in it?

Questions such as these lay bare the thorniness of this issue. For even if it could be proven, for example, that Christian faith healers were more effective than their non-Christian counterparts, how could one know whether their greater effectiveness was rooted in the superior power of their particular faith or in the superior power of their rhetoric to convince people that they can be cured through prayer? And if it were established that the salient factor was the power of the rhetoric, could it be conclusively determined whether this was purely the result of their persuasive techniques or, instead, related somehow to their putative association with the great might of Western nations? And then, if their greater effectiveness were determined to reside not in their God but in their more effective psycho-social manipulations, would this constitute an illegitimate allurement to the faith?

Do the partisans of the Divine Physician, then, have an unfair advantage? Clearly they have an advantage of some kind. That is to say, Christians have an advantage, in terms of attracting people to their faith, when superior biomedicine is offered by them in contexts where it is otherwise unavailable, or when people are convinced that Christians possess the power, through prayer, to heal (and heal better than others). But whether that advantage is deemed an unfair one will, of course, depend on many factors, most important among them how one decides which kinds of advantage—spiritual, material, rhetorical, psychological, scientific—are fair and which are not. And these questions are rooted in larger ones about the nature of religion and conversion itself, questions to which I return in the Conclusion.

As is clear from the foregoing discussion, then, the conversation about "allurement" in the context of healing is undergoing a slow transformation, spurred on by the increasing prominence and importance of faith healing in Indian Pentecostalism, and indeed, in all of Indian Christianity. No longer is the focus of the critique of missionary medicine focused solely on the work done in biomedical facilities. In fact, that debate seems to be slipping somewhat into a state of irrelevance, partly due to the pluralization of options within the Indian healthcare system. There are now more private and public players in the Indian healthcare market, and though it remains largely ineffective throughout much of India, missionary hospitals no longer maintain the monopoly on rural medicine they once enjoyed. But just as important as this factor in the transformation of the debate about medicine and allurement to the Christian faith is the rise of faith healing, which undercuts many of the assumptions on which it had for many years rested. Nevertheless, the fact that Christians are decreasingly accused of using their biomedical facilities to induce conversion does not portend a decrease in violence. As the *Organiser* articles suggest, in the right context, even faith healing is deemed, by the RSS at least, sufficient cause for a violent response. Although the rise of faith healing alters the debate about conversion and Christian evangelism in India, then, it may not have too significant an effect on the frequency of anti-Christian violence.

For a variety of reasons outlined so far in this book, the presence and practices of Pentecostalism in India indeed seem to correlate with increased risk of anti-Christian violence. And we might reasonably expect, then, that the growth of Pentecostalism would lead to greater violence. As indicated earlier, Pentecostalism in India has enjoyed a healthy growth rate for some time, partly at the expense of other forms of Christianity, and partly due to the conversion of non-Christians to Pentecostal life and faith. But it is somewhat more difficult to predict the future of Pentecostalism in India. Will it grow or decline in the immediate future? In the next chapter, I consider the state, extent, and foreign support of Christian missions in India, and suggest that several trends in the Christian missionary movement favor the growth of Pentecostal and Pentecostalized Christianity in India.

CHAPTER 5 | Missions and the Pentecostalization
of Indian Christianity

IN THE RHETORIC OF Indian critics of Christianity, "missionaries" often symbolically stand in for Christianity more generally. The work of missionaries, it is implied by these critics, reveals the true, and truly sinister, nature of Christianity as an expansionist and anti-national religion. Such critics frequently argue that the work of missionaries "provokes" violence against Christians, or at the very least proves that Christians disrespect India's religious traditions, and are, for this reason, not sufficiently "Indian." "We demand immediate ban to aggressive and violent Christian missionary activities in Orissa and India which threatens religious harmony and is a threat to national security," reads an online petition that appeared after the killing of Swami Lakshmanananda Saraswati in the context of Hindu–Christian violence in Kandhamal. "The aggressive proselytization activities which teach hatred, coerce newly converted to go against customs of the land by forcing them to slaughter cows and to eat beef, cut down sacred trees, denigrate Hindu gods, is against the pluralistic and tolerant nature of India."[1]

Such assertions, and the rejection of them, depend upon conflicting perceptions of the nature and legitimacy of contemporary Christian mission work in India. While it is no doubt the case that some portrayals of that work (on both sides of the debate) are pure propaganda, disagreements about the nature, value, and appropriateness of Christian missions emerge at least in part from a dearth of reliable information about the actual state of Indian

_____

[1] http://www.ipetitions.com/petition/missionaryaggression/. The grammatical errors appear in the original.

missionary affairs. This chapter addresses that dearth, and by doing so, hopefully, provides a perspective from which the accuracy and legitimacy of these claims and counterclaims can be more intelligently considered.

The term "missionary," when deployed by Indian critics, is intended (often with great effect) to evoke an image of the colonial-era, white, foreign missionary. In the popular imagination (if not always in actual fact), colonial missionaries are believed to have supported, enjoyed the protection of, and contributed to the perpetuation of colonial rule in India. They were therefore, in this view, intrusive meddlers with foreign loyalties who used their colonial advantage to impose a "foreign" faith on hapless natives while captiously criticizing Indian religions.

By continuing to speak of "missionaries," and especially "foreign missionaries," opponents of Indian Christianity therefore aim to suggest that the era of colonial Christian missions still persists. The suggestion serves their purposes well, but the portrait of a "typical" Indian missionary as a white-skinned European or American is no longer accurate. Today, the "typical" Indian missionary, at least in terms of numbers, is in fact an Indian. In this chapter, I therefore resist the rhetorical misrepresentation of missions in India as an entirely foreign affair by paying considerable attention to the work of Indian missionaries themselves, and I do so, *inter alia*, by referring to Indians doing mission work in India as "missionaries," and not making the common distinction between foreign "missionaries" and native "evangelists."[2]

If the misrepresentations promoted by the critics of Indian Christianity must be resisted, however, so too must those of others. Among those studying worldwide Christianity in the wake of postcolonial theory, it has become *de rigueur* to emphasize (or "recover") "native agency" in the telling of Christian history. This trend, which typifies the "global Christianity" school today, is admirable for remembering that the story of the expansion of Christianity around the world in the last few centuries is not merely the story of white European and American missionaries doing things (as it was almost universally told until the 1970s). I myself was trained in this school—Andrew Walls, now considered one of its "fathers," was one

---

[2] As elsewhere in the book, and though it would be relevant, I decline to provide much specific information about the largest American and Indian mission agencies at work in India in order to diminish the likelihood that they might be targeted in anti-Christian violence. The one exception to this rule is Gospel for Asia (GFA), which is already fully on the radar screen of anti-missionary forces because of the large amounts of funds it sends (from the United States) and receives (in India). GFA is also quite open, on its website and through the publications of its president, Dr. K. P. Yohannan, about its evangelistic focus and methods.

of my dissertation advisors—and my own work, particularly my earlier work, bears the mark of the school's influence in its preferential focus on Indian Christians over the missionaries with whom they interacted.

One must be careful, however, that when one engages in corrective retellings of history, or what Bergunder calls "emancipatory historiography,"[3] one does not overcorrect or overstate the case. One of the important early observations of those in the "global Christianity" school (which now includes better known and more popular, widely read authors like Philip Jenkins and Lamin Sanneh), was that Christianity's center of gravity was shifting southward (that is, away from Europe and North America). And it has, significantly, in demographic terms. Yet focusing on this fact can obscure another, which is the enduring theological and missiological dominance of western, particularly American Christians in the worldwide Christian community.

In fact, as pointed out by Robert Wuthnow, one of the reasons the focus on "native agency" is so appealing to contemporary scholars is that it downplays the continued power and influence of westerners within the worldwide Christian community, a power and influence that we (i.e., western scholars studying nonwestern Christianity) have come, after postcolonial theory, to find embarrassing.[4] The image of Christianity is therefore somewhat rehabilitated by the global Christianity approach, which makes Christianity a more appealing object of study for scholars, particularly Christian scholars, who are sensitive to such issues. (Almost all of those who now advance the global Christianity paradigm work at Christian schools or seminaries, and Philip Jenkins, who had earlier been a notable exception, recently moved from Penn State to the Evangelical stronghold of Baylor.)

It is important to note, however, that in the case of Christian missions in India, the work of "native Christians" who have, of late, become the focus of research, is only half the story. Foreign Christians and foreign missionaries continue to be influential in India, even if their boots, to use a military metaphor the appropriateness of which will become apparent later, are decreasingly "on the ground." Among these foreign missionaries, none are more powerful than the Americans. And so we cannot explore the nature and future of Pentecostalism in India, and in the context of anti-Christian

---

[3.]Michael Bergunder, "The Cultural Turn," in *Studying Global Pentecostalism: Theories and Methods*, ed. Allan Anderson et al. (Berkeley: University of California Press, 2010), 58.
[4.]Robert Wuthnow, *Boundless Faith: The Global Outreach of American Churches* (Berkeley: University of California Press, 2009), 51–54.

violence, without reference to global missions, and in particular to the state of American missionary involvement in India.

The central aim of this chapter is to show how a variety of trends within worldwide Christianity, and particularly within the American missionary establishment, favor the growing Pentecostalization of all Indian Christianity. In the context of this book, which explores the disproportionate targeting of Pentecostals and Pentecostalized Evangelicals in the violence against India's Christians, one important question, of course, is whether the violence is likely to increase or decrease. Making predictions is notoriously risky, and there are simply too many factors at play to do so with any degree of confidence. However, because the presence and activity of Pentecostals often provokes violence against Christians (which, it bears mentioning, is quite different from asserting that it is responsible for it), the future of Pentecostalism in India, that is, whether it will grow or decline, is among the most important of these factors. And that, thankfully, is something about which we can make at least some relatively informed predictions.

That said, the future growth or decline of Pentecostal Christianity in India will not be determined merely by internal Indian factors. Rather, transnational flows of Christian wealth and theology, and changing western missionary strategies, have and will continue to have a tangible impact on Indian Christian demographics. In this chapter, then, I focus in particular on the American missionary establishment, and its influence over its Indian counterpart. Not only do recent changes in the extent and style of American missions (and western missions more generally) favor the continued Pentecostalization of Indian Christianity. So, too, do realities on the ground (e.g., the growing demand for supernatural spiritual and physical healing).

Among the most salient of these changes are two. First, the declining mainstream Protestant and Catholic investment in direct evangelism (as opposed to social service and relief work) leaves the field of evangelization, and its potential "harvest" (on which, see below) open almost exclusively to Pentecostals and Evangelicals. Second, the dramatic shift in foreign support from foreign to native missionary workers favors Pentecostalization because of the fact that native Indian workers are frequently far more Pentecostalized, and less constrained by denominational barriers, than those that support them financially. In what follows, I consider these two factors, and several others, in the context of a broader discussion of the nature of missionary work in India, and the impact that global (and particularly American) mission trends has on it.

American Christian Involvement in Foreign Missions

Those critical of missionary work in India understandably perceive it to be a neocolonial enterprise, a cultural invasion engineered, directed, staffed, and funded by the West, or, more specifically, by the United States. Indeed, the extent of American Christian involvement in missions is staggering. According to *Operation World* ("The Definitive Prayer Guide to Every Nation"), America's 93,500 missionaries (foreign and domestic) rank second only to China's 100,000 (again, foreign and domestic, but in China's case, mostly the latter). The roundness of the Chinese figure should give us pause and remind us that any estimate having to do with religion in China is a very rough estimate, indeed. Moreover, China's estimated 100,000 missionaries are mostly deployed in China, leaving America the largest producer of foreign missionaries by a substantial margin.[5] India is third on the list for total domestic and foreign missionaries, with 82,950, the majority of whom are deployed in India. South Korea is fourth, with 19,950, a large number of whom work abroad, including, in substantial numbers, in India. In terms of the number of missionaries sent abroad, then, South Korea is second only to the United States.

The most recent edition of the *Mission Handbook* provides information on 800 Protestant American mission agencies at work overseas. In 2008, these agencies spent $5.7 billion dollars annually (more than the Gross Domestic Product of several small countries). Although this amount represents a slight decrease since 2005, due presumably to the worldwide financial crisis, it represents an increase of over 80% since 1996. With these funds American mission agencies supported 263,583 missionaries in 217 countries. Of these, 139,269 were full-time missionaries, and 47,261 were US citizens.[6]

---

[5] Although clearly an Evangelical document, the massive *Operation World* is based on generally reliable statistics. Jason Mandryk, *Operation World: The Definitive Prayer Guide to Every Nation* (Colorado Springs: Biblica Publishing, 2010), 951; and Todd Johnson and Kenneth Ross, *Atlas of Global Christianity 1910–2010* (Edinburgh: Edinburgh University Press, 2009), 294.

[6] Linda J. Weber, *Mission Handbook: U.S. and Canadian Protestant Ministries Overseas,* 21st ed. (Wheaton, IL: Evangelism and Missions Information Service, 2010), 36. These statistics include support for all missionaries doing all forms of workw (both evangelism and service, for example), but neither the support which comes from large churches which sponsor their own independent missions nor that represented by individuals or groups that eschew the "missionary" label and association with mission agencies for theological reasons, or to gain access to areas where missionaries are forbidden. They also do not include statistics for Christian agencies like World Vision that are involved in relief and development but do not consider themselves "missionary."

American Catholics were also active in giving for worldwide missions, though at a considerably lower rate. In 2008, American Catholics gave 57 million dollars to the Pontifical Mission Societies in the United States (i.e., The Society for the Propagation of the Faith, the Holy Childhood Association, the Society of St. Peter the Apostle, and the Missionary Union of Priests and Religious).[7] While American Catholics account for roughly a quarter of worldwide Catholic donations for mission, their contributions to the Pontifical Mission Societies represent only 1% of the total Protestant figure. That said, contributions funneled through the Pontifical Mission Societies probably constitute a minority, maybe even less than a third of total American Catholic contributions for missions. Individual missionaries, orders, and dioceses receive contributions of considerable size directly from American Catholic individuals, churches, and dioceses. These are not, unfortunately, so far as I know, publicly tracked at the denominational level. The facts that Catholic giving is harder to track, and that Pentecostalism influences and is influenced more significantly and obviously by Protestant mission work, account for the overwhelming focus on Protestant missions in the pages that follow.

This massive American investment in foreign missions is facilitated not primarily by the budgetary prioritization of foreign missions (which continue to make up a rather small portion of Christian giving) but rather by the size of American incomes, the strength of the American dollar abroad, and the breadth of Christian support for the enterprise. (Nearly three-quarters of all American churchgoers say their church supports an overseas mission or missionary.[8]) The magnitude and might of the American foreign missionary movement therefore tells a story about relatively small amounts of money becoming large in the aggregate, and even larger, in terms of their impact, when spent abroad where their impact is compounded by favorable exchange rates. As these statistics indicate, then, while some have identified the first few decades of the twentieth century as the heyday of American missions,[9] the extent, wealth, and influence of the American missionary movement continue to grow in the twenty-first.

Moreover, the varied processes of globalization enable and accelerate the growth of American missionary influence on the world stage. While

[7] Based on figures provided by the Pontifical Mission Societies at http://www.onefamilyinmission.org/images/stories/pdf/pms/Great_Works.pdf.

[8] Wuthnow, *Boundless*, 4, 24–25, 148.

[9] See, for example, William R. Hutchison, *Errand to the World: American Protestant Thought and Foreign Missions* (Chicago: University of Chicago Press, 1987), 1–5.

globalization has many, sometimes contradictory effects, Wuthnow maintains that communication within the global Christian community is easier when more people speak the same language, meet together in person, consume the same music, attend the same conferences, and so on. Moreover, "the fact that English has become at least a second language in many parts of the world is particularly important for understanding the international activities of U.S. churches."[10]

Global diversity is not just a fact, but represents a choice, Wuthnow continues. And what choices people make among the various sociocultural alternatives available to them is affected by global dynamics of wealth and power. Moreover, in a globalizing world, the choices people make are increasingly influenced by their relationships with people elsewhere, relationships in which the more powerful parties often end up the more influential. "If a well-heeled congregation in Illinois sends visitors to Central America to locate pastors who merit its assistance because they have a sufficiently entrepreneurial vision of the kind valued in Illinois, that is an example of such influence," Wuthnow contends.[11]

The reach, wealth, and involvement of American missions then, as one aspect of American cultural influence abroad, creates a situation in which American theological, liturgical, and missiological predilections gain global clout and appeal disproportionate to that justified by the mere number of American Christians. What happens inside the offices of American mission agencies therefore matters, and matters significantly, in places like India, which is why we must devote a substantial portion of this chapter on missions in India to American missions, and their effects abroad.

Several trends in US support for foreign missions are worth noting because of their impact in India. First, among American Protestant mission agencies, the share of budgets devoted to evangelism is declining in favor of relief and development work. Of the agencies surveyed by the *Handbook* in both 2001 and 2008, the total budget reported for "Evangelism/Discipleship" dropped 10.6%, while the budget reported for "Relief and Development" increased 8.7%, bringing spending on the two activities relatively close to parity.[12]

However, the decreased share of mission money devoted to evangelism between 2001 and 2008 can probably be attributed in part to a second important trend, that is, that especially during the early part of that same

---

[10.] Wuthnow, *Boundless*, 91.
[11.] This and the previous quotation appear on Wuthnow, *Boundless*, 92.
[12.] Weber, *Handbook*, 51–52.

period, mission agencies involved in evangelism were still radically shifting their support for missionaries away from Americans and toward native workers. So while spending on evangelism may have dropped, the number of missionaries supported has still risen. Although the origins of this shift were surely diffuse, Christian Aid Mission, which in 2008 reported supporting 11,036 indigenous missionaries worldwide, claims to have been the "first missionary agency to support and promote indigenous mission groups" and "the catalyst behind the present reformation in foreign missions methodology."[13]

There are a number of reasons for this shift. The most obvious is efficiency. Native workers are generally considerably cheaper than American workers, and they do not as frequently require the cultural and linguistic training that their American counterparts do. Many of the American mission agencies supporting Indian missionaries in India openly justify their support in these terms. For example, Gospel Revival Ministries, which supports a few dozen Indian missionaries, says that "native [p]astors know the land, languages, and people, and are more readily accepted into their native countries than western missionaries." In addition, "native [p]astor support [requires] a small fraction of the amount of money it takes for a western missionary to prepare, travel, and become established overseas."[14] Similarly, Spiritual Overseers Service International, which trains native missionaries around the world, including in India, does so in part to "insure a superior return for missionary investment."[15]

Another reason is access. In places like India where foreign missionaries are impeded, restricted, or forbidden, native missionaries are an obvious way forward for eager missionary societies. "Accessing hard-to-reach groups and ethnic minorities in restricted-access areas," says WorldServe Ministries, which has a small investment in India, "is done most effectively through indigenous believers."[16]

A third reason may be the fact that American Christians are increasingly sensitive to, and ambivalent about the politics of cross-cultural mission, particularly mission from the rich and powerful developed world to

---

[13] http://www.christianaid.org/AboutUs/Default.aspx. In 2008, Christian Aid Mission was the second largest Protestant American mission agency in terms of support for native missionaries worldwide. Campus Crusade for Christ, Intl., was first, with 11,404. GFA was third, with 9,523, and AMG International was fourth, with 8,293. Note that all of these work (but not exclusively) in India.

[14] http://www.gogoodnews.com/whynativepastors.html.

[15] http://sosinternational.us/.

[16] http://us.worldserve.org/what-we-do/leadership-development.

the less rich and powerful developing world.[17] The spectacular relative wealth of American missionaries, a wealth that is frequently on display even on the mission field, has come to be seen within missionary circles as an embarrassment, and worse yet (for efficiency minded American missionaries), an impediment to the spread of the gospel.

For example, Jonathan Bonk, who is probably the most widely read critic of Western missionary uses of money, writes: "Western missionaries continue to enjoy and employ their relative affluence as a birthright. They are not unaware of the burden of credibility this places upon their personal mission to the world's poor. . . . But alternatives to relative personal affluence are both unattractive and unnecessary, in the thinking of most missionaries . . . "[18] Seeking to address these and other concerns, then, many American mission agencies have transformed themselves from missionary sending agencies, to "partners" with or "enablers" of autochthonous missions and ministries.[19] Nevertheless, from the perspective of many American missionaries, indigenous missionaries, and their critics in places like India, the shift in support from American to native missionaries does not dissolve the political problems described above, but rather simply ships them abroad, as the dual meaning of the term "enable" implies.

The shift in resources from American to native missionaries appears to have reached a plateau. Support for native missionaries from American Protestant mission societies grew faster (at about 12.3% annually) between 1996 and 2005 than it did between 2005 and 2008 (2.3% annually). And the share of all mission workers supported by American mission agencies who were employed in their own countries actually declined from 66.6% in 2005 to 66.1% in 2008. So it is clear that the trend toward native workers slowed, or perhaps even reversed, after 2005. But the longer term trend in favor of native missionaries remains an important one and helps account for the shrinking of evangelism budgets discernible in the period between 2001 and 2008, especially because the trend toward native missionaries appears to have been stronger among agencies devoted primarily to evangelism than among other mission agencies.[20]

Evangelism therefore remains a major focus of American Protestant missions. In 2008, nearly 90% of all their full-time workers (American

[17] Wuthnow, *Boundless*, 243.
[18] Jonathan J. Bonk, *Missions and Money: Affluence as a Missionary Problem Revisited,* revised and expanded ed. (Maryknoll, NY: Orbis, [1991] 2006), 34.
[19] Wuthnow, *Boundless*, 243.
[20] Weber, *Handbook*, 38.

and native) supported by American mission agencies and working abroad were still engaged primarily in evangelism and discipleship ministries, and between 2005 and 2008, the budgets of American Protestant mission agencies involved primarily in evangelism increased more quickly (12.5% vs. 2.3% annually) than those of agencies primarily engaged in other activities. In addition, while the number of agencies reporting evangelism as their primary activity declined from 62.8% in 1998 to 56% in 2008, the number of full-time workers in agencies devoted primarily to evangelism rose by 5% (to 41,293) for US citizens abroad, and by 42.6% (to 81,890) for non-US citizens working in their own countries.[21]

American Missionary Investment in India

Of the 800 American Protestant mission agencies surveyed by the *Mission Handbook* in 2008, 185 reported operating in India. The only country in which more American agencies were at work was Mexico (and that by only a slim margin). The extent of American mission engagement with India is simply astonishing given the distance between the two countries. But India is an important "strategic" focus of global Christian missions, for reasons I explain below, and this helps account for the size of Christian missionary investment in it.

A survey of marketing materials produced by these 185 agencies suggests that the "typical" American Protestant mission society at work in India is interdenominational and Evangelical. The dominance of interdenominational Evangelical mission agencies over denominational boards reflects a century-long trend of growth for the former, though the latter are still often larger and wealthier.[22] Statements of faith are important in the self-conception of these interdenominational mission agencies, and in them, most profess a belief in the literal, inerrant, or infallible truth of the Bible (often, as noted by my perceptive research assistant, Katie [Kilgore] Harber, even before they profess a belief in God), in non-allegorical understandings of heaven and hell, in salvation through Christ alone, and in his "visible," "personal," "bodily," "imminent," and almost always premillennial return at the end of time. The agencies support a wide variety of activities, among which the most popular are maintaining medical and

[21] Ibid., 51–55.
[22] Hutchison, *Errand*, 128, 69; and Andrew F. Walls, "World Christianity, the Missionary Movement and the Ugly American," in *World Order and Religion*, ed. Wade Clark Roof (Albany, NY: State University of New York Press, 1991), 152.

educational institutions; providing for widows, women, and children; engaging in projects of economic development; and distributing or producing (translating, recording, etc.) biblical literature. Many are also, of course, engaged in direct forms of evangelism, particularly through the agency of native missionaries, which more than 60% of the agencies working in India support.[23]

Collectively, Protestant American agencies supported 683 US citizens at work in India. Americans probably comprise the majority of foreign nationals engaged in mission work in India, though it is difficult to know exactly how many expatriates from other countries still work there. *Operation World* estimates the total at fewer than 1,000.[24] The *Atlas of Global Christianity*, however, suggests that India received about 8,000 foreign missionaries in 2010.[25] The discrepancy has to do with the fact that *Operation World* focuses on Protestant and Evangelical mission agencies and does not count Catholic and Orthodox missionaries (who comprise well over half of the total) or attempt to include in its figures the large and growing number of missionaries sent directly by congregations (i.e., not through a mission agency), as the *Atlas* does.[26] The *Atlas*'s figures are therefore likely to be closer to the actual tally of missionaries from all denominations.

Statistics from the *Atlas* indicate that these 8,000 missionaries place India at the top of the list, along with Japan and the Philippines, among Asian nations in terms of the total number of missionaries received. While the foreign missionary presence in India is large, however, it is actually below the Asian average relative to the size of the population. In fact, in greater Asia, and in proportion to the size of their respective populations, only Bangladesh, Tajikistan, Saudi Arabia, Myanmar, China, Iran, and North Korea receive fewer foreign missionaries than India, according to the *Atlas*. India also sends a substantial number of Christian missionaries abroad, putting it, along with only Turkey, in a select group of Asian countries that both send more missionaries and receive fewer missionaries, per million citizens, than the Asian average.[27]

While the direct impact of US citizens at work in India is therefore arguably relatively small, contemporary American Protestant mission agencies

---

[23.] Weber, *Handbook*, 435–39.
[24.] Mandryk, *Operation*, 414.
[25.] Johnson and Ross, *Atlas*, 269–70.
[26.] Personal e-mail conversation with Todd Johnson (*Atlas* co-editor), June 26, 2012.
[27.] Johnson and Ross, *Atlas*, 269–71.

actually wield far more influence through the large number of Indian missionaries to whom they provide at least partial support. According to the *Mission Handbook,* that number, in 2008, was 19,312. But even this number significantly underestimates the extent of American Protestant support for Indian missionaries since, for reasons I cannot discern, the *Handbook* lists GFA under "Asia-General," but not under India, despite the fact that Indians comprise the largest portion of GFA's 9,523 Asian evangelists. Taking this into account, then, it is clear that the number of Indian missionaries working in India with support of American Protestants is well over 20,000. And while there are five or six agencies that account for a large proportion of this support, as I indicated above, more than 60% of American Protestant mission agencies are involved in supporting native Indian missionaries. Only one mission agency reported sending more than 100 Americans to India, but more than 20 provided at least partial support for 100 or more Indians at work in India. [28]

Among the *Mission Handbook*'s 19,312 Indian missionaries working in India with support from American Protestants, there are teachers, doctors, nurses, agricultural scientists, orphanage directors, widows' home workers, and people engaged in a variety of occupations other than evangelism. Yet the Protestant mission agencies that support the largest number of Indian missionaries are nearly universally engaged primarily in evangelism, so it is safe to assume that most of their employees in India are as well.

The 19,312 Indian missionaries recorded as receiving support from American Protestant mission agencies also represent an increase of 68% in the years since the 19th (2004) edition of the *Handbook,* which reported support for only 11,518 Indian missionaries. Mission work in India has therefore followed the global missionary trend toward significantly greater support of native workers, a trend that has and will continue to have profound religious and political implications for the future of Indian Christianity. The trend also, it should be pointed out, is one which favors independent Evangelical and Pentecostal Christianity rather than the established churches, since the pastors who are supported generally fall within the Evangelical-Pentecostal spectrum.

In addition, the shift in funding from evangelism to service is particularly pronounced among mainstream Protestant groups. Proportionately, then, more and more of the dollars being spent on direct evangelism are

---

[28] Weber, *Handbook,* 435–39.

being spent by those who remain clearly committed to evangelism, that is, by Evangelicals and Pentecostals. Similarly, for reasons I articulate below, the native Indian missionaries hired by western mission agencies to evangelize in India more often than their western counterparts become Pentecostalized in their evangelistic practice, whatever (and sometimes despite) the denominational affiliation of those that support them. Realities on the ground, then, and, in particular, the demands of those among whom missionaries work for supernatural healing and ecstatic experience, turn many Evangelicals into Pentecostals or Pentecostalized Evangelicals. The trends outlined here, then, further favor the process of Pentecostalization.

The trend toward support for native workers is also one that we would expect to be more prominent in the conversations about Christian missionary work in India. But as noted in the introduction to this chapter, opponents of Christianity have reason to ignore it, since it undermines the image of Christianity as a "foreign" religion propagated by "foreign" missionaries. Moreover, the number of American citizens at work in India also increased, and increased more (124%) than the number of Indians in recent years. So the shift in balance from American to Indian missionaries, like the balance between American and native missionaries worldwide, appears to have reached a point of relative stability. If the shift in missionary funding from foreign to native workers goes largely unmentioned in contemporary Indian debates about proselytization and conversion, the same cannot be said for the issue of foreign funding, to which we now turn.

Foreign Funding and Indian Pentecostalism

Echoing a common accusation against Christians in India, Ashok Chowgule maintains that "Christian churches in India are coming up in places where there are no Christians. They are set up by obtaining funds from outside the country."[29] No organization or author, unfortunately, has attempted, so far as I know, to compute the total amount of money spent in India, annually, by all mission agencies. So to develop an understanding of the scale of foreign Christian spending in India, we must rely less on texts like the *Mission Handbook* and *Operation World*, and more on statistics gathered by the Indian government itself as part of the Foreign Contribution (Regulation) Act of 1976 (FCRA), which stipulates that

---

[29] Ashok V. Chowgule, *Christianity in India: The Hindutva Perspective* (Mumbai: Hindu Vivek Kendra, 1999), 19.

charitable organizations receiving funds from abroad must declare their receipt to the Home Ministry, which then tracks and annually publishes a report on them.

When I interviewed Christian leaders, they often countered claims of their critics by alleging that there really is not that much foreign funding for Christians, that the money received from abroad by Christians is used in such a way that it did not encourage people to convert for "material" reasons, or that Hindu organizations receive comparable donations from foreign sources and put them to use in less admirable and less socially beneficial projects (e.g., for political purposes, or to distribute *trishuls*,[30] some presumably very small minority of which end up being used in anti-Christian intimidation and violence).

The assertions of a director of a *dalit* Christian advocacy organization based in Delhi are typical:

> In India, through the Foreign Contribution Regulation [Act], [Indians] get . . . maybe 6,500 crores[31] [annually]. This is the authorized money which we get from . . . foreign sources for social activism, advocacy, for religious purposes, also. Of this, 4,000 crore [400 million rupees] is obtained by . . . the VHP, RSS, BJP, [and other] Hindu fundamentalist organizations. . . . They openly use it for their fundamentalism. . . . The remaining 2,500 crore [250 million rupees], the Christians are getting . . . [With this] 2,500 crore which they get from the foreign country, at least they are doing some . . . social activism. . . . You see, [with] the 2,500 crore rupees, they run 45,000 Christian [service] organizations.

Although this commentator vastly overstates the amount of money received by Sangh Parivar organizations from abroad (at least according to FCRA data), his estimate of the proportion of money received, annually, by organizations that identify themselves as Christians is roughly accurate, according to my calculations, at just above one third of the total.

The debate about foreign funding will not be settled with reference to FCRA data alone, since raw contribution amounts tell us little about how the money is actually spent. And this, in the end, is the crux of the matter. Nevertheless, it may be of some use to glean we can from the data.

[30.] *Trishuls* are tridents, associated iconographically with the God Shiva, and also symbolically with more violent and menacing forms of Hindu nationalism. They are frequently on display in riots, or in the context of anti-minority activities and demonstrations.

[31.] A crore equals ten million, so 6,500 crore equals 65 billion.

In 2010–11, the most recent period for which all the data and a full, final report have been released, 38,436 NGOs (secular and religious, of all religious faiths) were registered under FCRA, of which 21,508 organizations received funding from abroad totaling more than 103 billion rupees (approximately $2.3 billion dollars). This represents an increase of around 250% since 1997–98, when the figure was closer to 29 billion rupees ($636 million). The United States was the source of nearly one-third of that funding, providing almost three times more than its next closest rivals, Germany and the United Kingdom.[32] This data is for all NGOs, including but not limited to Christian missionary organizations. To get a more accurate sense of foreign support for missionary organizations, it is necessary to dig a bit more deeply into the data.

The Ministry of Home Affairs does not include information on individual NGO recipients of donations in its full reports, except for NGOs receiving more than 10 million rupees (about $222,000) whose receipts are reported by the Ministry on its website. The most recent figures available are for 2010–11. The contributions received by organizations receiving more than 10 million rupees comprise only about 10% of the total number of organizations receiving funding. But these larger organizations are the recipients of an impressive 70% of the total receipts, which indicates something about the size and wealth of the largest NGOs. Analyzing the data for just these largest NGOs allows us to compute approximate proportional receipts received by organizations associated with the various religious faiths. In 2010–11, the Indian NGOs individually receiving more than 10 million rupees from abroad collectively received 71.5 billion rupees ($1.6 billion). Of this, 25 billion rupees ($555 million, or 35%) was received by organizations that identified themselves as Christian, or by churches, societies, or orders with obviously Christian names.[33] The funding received by explicitly and openly Christian organizations is therefore considerably lower than many anti-Christian critics and propagandists would have their audiences believe.

[32.] Ministry of Home Affairs, Foreigners Division, FCRA Wing, *Receipt and Utilization of Foreign Contribution by Voluntary Associations Annual Report 2009–2010*, available at http://mha.nic. in/fcra.htm. See also Lancy Lobo, *Globalisation, Hindu Nationalism and Christians in India* (New Delhi: Rawat Publications, 2002), 92.

[33.] Here, and in the currency calculations below, I approximate the average value of the rupee in 2010–11 at 45 rupees to the dollar. These and the FCRA contributions discussed below are based on a database I developed in collaboration with a research assistant, Matthew Miller, with data drawn directly from FCRA's tables, which are available from the Ministry of Home Affairs at http://mha.nic.in/fcra.htm.

However, this figure actually significantly underestimates the extent of contributions received by Christian organizations, if "Christian" is conceived more broadly. For example, it excludes the receipts of World Vision, the largest recipient of foreign contributions in India, which neither identifies itself as a Christian organization in its FCRA report (despite referring to itself, in its own marketing, as a "Christian humanitarian organization"[34]) nor has an "obviously Christian" name. Presumably, World Vision's FCRA self-identification as a secular organization derives from the fact that it understands its relief and development work to be nonsectarian. Nevertheless, World Vision employs a large number of Indian Christians—author Pradip Ninan Thomas contends that it "is home to some of the most fundamentalist Christians in India"[35]—and is open (to the extent allowed by law) about the Christian faith being a source of its charitable motivation. Critics frequently complain, therefore, that World Vision's deployment of massive sums of foreign funding amounts to at the very least a subtle form of allurement to the Christian faith. Some go even farther. For example, with characteristic hyperbole, the writers at ChristianAggression.org allege that "many innocent looking child sponsorship programs, such as Christian Children's Fund and World Vision . . . are guilty of forced conversions. . .[I]nstead of nurturing these children as they claim, they use this money to buy children of poor non-Christian families (like slaves!)" and then "brainwash them with Christian fundamentalist ideas."[36]

World Vision alone received 2.3 billion rupees ($51 million) in 2010–11. Similarly, the fourth and eleventh largest recipients of foreign aid (Caruna Bal Vikas and Compassion East India) are both primarily supported by Compassion International, the Christian child sponsorship program. Together, they receive 1.5 billion rupees ($34.8 million). Including just these three organizations under the "Christian" tally, then, would raise the proportion of foreign funding received by "Christian" organizations to 40% of that received by NGOs receiving more than 10 million rupees from abroad.

---

[34] http://www.worldvision.org/content.nsf/about/
who-we-are?open&lpos=top_drp_AboutUs_WhoWeAre.
[35] Pradip Ninan Thomas, *Strong Religion, Zealous Media: Christian Fundamentalism and Communication in India* (Los Angeles: Sage, 2008), 59. It is important to note, however, that Thomas employs a rather idiosyncratic definition of fundamentalism, which would include nearly every Evangelical or Pentecostal Indian.
[36] "Conversion Tactics," http://christianaggression.com/tactics_charity.php. The grammar, punctuation, and capitalization are retained from the original.

Since there are no data publicly available from the FCRA on the receipts of smaller NGOs, the closest we can get to an estimate of the total receipts received by all Christian organizations in India, large and small, is to assume that "Christian" organizations, as I have defined them (in the broader sense), receive the same proportion (40%) of foreign funding when all NGOs (large and small) are included as they did when only the largest were considered. If so, then in 2010–11, all Christian NGOs in India would have received around $900,000,000 (40%) of the $2.3 billion[37] total received from abroad by NGOs working in India. Without a doubt, this is a staggering amount of money and constitutes an impressive share of the foreign funding market. But if these data are to be believed, foreign funding received by missionaries in India does not begin to approach the proportional levels of funding that their critics contend.

The amount of foreign funding used for evangelism as opposed to relief, development, or other purposes would, of course, be smaller, though how much smaller is difficult to discern from the FCRA data. Table 5.1 lists the ten largest recipients of foreign funds in 2010–11. Among these, only the Believers Church India (the denomination established by GFA) is significantly involved in evangelism. World Vision and Caruna Bal Vikas, as discussed above, are more or less Christian organizations not registered as such and engage primarily in relief and development. Action Aid and Missionaries of Charity, Mother's Teresa's well-known organization, are welfare and relief organizations that self-identify as Christian, but that do not engage primarily in direct evangelism. OXFAM India, Bal Raksha Bharat (supported by Save the Children), Population Services International (which works with HIV/AIDS victims), Rural Development Trust (RDT), and Women's Development Trust (a subsidiary of RDT) promote themselves as secular organizations, though RDT was founded by the ex-Jesuit, Vicente Ferrer.

Absent from the top ten is any organization associated with a religion other than Christianity. The first such organization to appear on the list is the International Society for Krishna Consciousness, the 14th largest recipient of foreign funds (nearly $11 million). In fact, among the roughly 300 organizations receiving $1 million or more in 2010–11, only 9 registered as Hindu.[38] Hindu organizations have not always been absent from

---

[37] This 2.3 billion dollars should not be confused with the 2.3 million rupees received by World Vision alone (discussed in previous paragraphs).

[38] The Tibetan Children's Village, received the most foreign donations ($10 million, the 17th largest overall) of any Buddhist organization. The first Muslim organization appears on the list in 29th place and received just over $6 million.

TABLE 5.1 Foreign Funds Received, 2010–11, Ten Largest Recipients

ORGANIZATION	RUPEES RECEIVED	IN DOLLARS[a]
World Vision of India	2,337,393,809	51,942,085
Believers Church India[b]	1,607,167,620	35,714,836
Rural Development Trust[c]	1,353,801,033	30,084,467
Caruna Bal Vikas	964,371,836	21,430,485
Women's Development Trust	727,510,280	16,166,895
OXFAM INDIA[d]	710,028,416	15,778,409
Bal Raksha Bharat	675,698,093	15,015,513
Action Aid	669,630,005	14,880,667
Missionaries of Charity	622,937,903	13,843,065
Population Services International	602,695,354	13,393,230

[a] Using an exchange of 45 rupees to the dollar.
[b] Believers Church India is the denomination supported by GFA, whose receipts of nearly $10 million are listed separately in the FCRA data. If the two figures were combined the total would approach, but not exceed, that received by World Vision.
[c] Rural Development Trust and Women's Development Trust were both founded by Vicente Ferrer and are both supported by the Fundación Vicente Ferrer.
[d] OXFAM's funds are also received by an organization called "OXFAM India Trust," which is listed separately in the FCRA data. Combined, the two received nearly $22 million dollars, which would make OXFAM the fourth largest recipient of foreign funding.

the top of the list. As recently as 2008–9, the Mata Amritanandmayi Math was among the top three largest recipients, as was the Sri Sathya Sai Central Trust in 2004–5. And in the late 1990s, these organizations, and the Maharishi Ved Vidyan Vishwa Vidyapeetham, routinely claimed the top spots.[39]

Considering only the NGOs that receive more than 10 million rupees, and whose details are published by the Home Ministry, there were only two states (Gujarat and Uttar Pradesh) where Hindu organizations received more funds than Christian organizations. In the rest, Christian receipts outpaced that of Hindu organizations, sometimes quite dramatically so. Christian organizations (defined in the narrower sense, as those that register as Christian or have obviously Christian names) accounted for more than 70% of foreign funding in 9 states and union territories,[40] and for more than 50% in 14 (of 35).

[39] Lobo, *Globalisation*, 92.
[40] Andaman & Nicobar Islands (100%), Chandigarh (100%), Assam (93%), Meghalaya (96%), Nagaland (94%), Kerala (83%), Chhattisgarh (88%), Arunachal Pradesh (77%), and Punjab (70%). Most of these states have relatively large Christian populations. Chhattisgarh and Punjab are the curious exceptions.

Obviously, the fact that a large proportion of Hindus live within India accounts, in part, for the relatively modest levels of foreign funding for Hindu organizations. None of the major Sangh organizations (e.g., the VHP, RSS, Bajrang Dal) appear under their best known names on the list of those NGOs receiving more than 10 million rupees in 2010–11, though they have in the past been accused of receiving (and misusing) donations funneled through front organizations.[41] It is well known that such groups do receive support from abroad, particularly from the United States,[42] but the extent of this support is difficult to establish.

What is clear, however, is that the data do not support the assertion of the Christian commentator quoted earlier that Sangh Parivar organizations receive the majority of foreign funds. Surely these organizations receive funds from abroad, but the amount of the donations they receive appear to be dwarfed, in the FCRA data at least (if not in reality) by funds received by Christian and secular (e.g., OXFAM) organizations. Nevertheless, the data do not sustain the assertion of many critics of Indian Christianity, that the vast majority of donations received from abroad are used for evangelism, that is (from the perspective of critics), for the express purpose of undermining India's non-Christian religious traditions. Even journalist Shafi Rahman's assertion that money received from abroad is used "mostly for missionary activities"[43] seems at best an overstatement, unless groups like World Vision are considered "missionary" (as opposed to just "Christian") and unless "mostly" means nothing more than "around half." So far as I can tell, among the twenty largest recipients of foreign funding, only three (GFA/Believers Church India, AMG International, and the Service Association of the Seventh Day Adventists), regularly support religious services or engage in evangelism. The rest are either secular NGOs, or Christian organizations engaged almost exclusively in welfare, relief, and development operations.

The greatest portion of foreign funding received by Christian agencies, then, appears to be going for relief and service. Nevertheless, it is important to recognize, as well, that great sums of foreign money still go primarily towards evangelism and the support of fledgling native congregations. In 2010–11, the Pentecostalized and highly evangelistic mission agency,

---

[41.] See, for example, Sandesh Prabhudesai, "BJP Ready to Probe VHP Funds, Says Minister," *Rediff on the Net*, October 5, 1999, http://www.rediff.com/news/1999/oct/05goa.htm.

[42.] On this, see Prema Kurien, *A Place at the Multicultural Table: The Development of an American Hinduism* (New Brunswick, NJ: Rutgers University Press, 2007), 144.

[43.] Shafi Rahman, "Freelancers of God," *India Today International*, May 9, 2011.

GFA, for example, received (together with the denomination it founded) around $45 million dollars.

Opponents of Christianity in India are frequently quite critical of the amounts of foreign money received by Christian organizations there. As indicated above, while their rhetoric tends at times toward exaggeration and hyperbole, it would be hard to find anyone who was not impressed, either positively or negatively, by the magnitude of the foreign Christian investment in India. Moreover, even those who support foreign missions in India and Indian Christians themselves regularly raise concerns about the effects of foreign funding. Among these latter groups, some fear that the increased levels of support for Indian evangelists creates pressure to produce, that is, to produce converts, a "superior return" on the investment of wealthy foreign donors. "Donors want numbers, pictures," said one Assemblies of God Pentecostal pastor in Chennai, and sometimes (still today) even remunerate evangelists for every convert. This tempts Indian pastors to exaggerate their successes, to baptize "converts" as quickly as possible, even, in some cases, before the baptized understand the import of the ritual.

If you were to add up all of the Hindus Indian evangelists claim to have converted, quipped John Dayal, "then there [would be] no Hindu left in India." Occasionally, native missionaries supported through foreign donations, or desiring more foreign donations, are even tempted, according to Indian Christian observers, to stage or fabricate conversions and persecutions, reports of which often bring a flood of new funding. Foreign funding therefore encourages evangelical entrepreneurship in both its positive and negative connotations. And Christians of all stripes are relatively unanimous in their assertion that Pentecostals are the most entrepreneurial of all Indian missionaries (again, in both the positive and negative sense).

Similarly, a desire to provide foreign donors with a return on their investment leads, as in the capitalist marketplace, to the streamlining of evangelistic methods (i.e., using only those known to rapidly produce converts) and the strategic targeting of "ripe" populations. "Western funders," said one CSI Christian mission leader with long experience as a village evangelist, "want very strategic, organized plans," and regular reports detailing the numbers, names, and locations of converts. "Sometimes these kinds of documents have to be prepared in . . . formats [that are] more appealing to the West," but then they end up being used against Christians by those who oppose them. "It's a big struggle. It's a vicious cycle," he said. In this way, then, the American gospel of efficiency through statistics, maps, and strategies, as described below, becomes manifest in ways most Hindus—and not just nationalists—consider uncouth or even offensive.

Seeking an efficient return on their investment, foreign donors who support native missionaries also generally desire to support as many missionaries as their funds will allow. This creates a downward pressure on evangelists' salaries. And here, Christians perceive themselves to be in somewhat of a double bind. As the Assemblies of God pastor quoted just above put it, if the evangelists are paid too little, for the sake of efficiency they "become beggars," forced to live among the poor in low-caste neighborhoods where they work. When they do, "immediately the upper castes won't touch [them]." Such evangelists make only 2,000 rupees (about $50) a month around Chennai, and the only people who will work for so little are untrained and uneducated, and therefore more likely to cause offense: "You throw peanuts," he said, with little regard for political correctness, "and you get monkeys!" The solution he recommended was to make a monthly salary of around 10,000 rupees (about $200) the minimum.

But then the antipodal problem arises, which is that evangelists' salaries alone become a kind of allurement to the Christian faith, or at least to a more assertively evangelistic kind of Christian faith than those taking the salary might be otherwise inclined. "There is truth in the foreign money claim," said one Pentecostal Indian missionary:

> The problem is, the native missionary, he was [wearing his native clothes, but when he becomes a Christian missionary], within two years he will become a suit wearer . . . and then you will give the [motor]bike, and his economical growth will be . . . quicker than [that of] other people. Normally the neighbors will get jealous of that. They are thinking that the shortcut to become a rich man is to embrace Christianity. This is the cultural ignorance, or innocence [might he have meant "naiveté"?] of the mission.

The vast economic inequities between India and places like Europe and America play a role here, because when foreign donors see the Indian evangelists they support, they often perceive them to be destitute. Yet when these evangelists are provided with what western agencies consider "minimum" support, the resulting economic disparity distances the evangelists from those they seek to serve and/or convert. The funding agencies "are thinking that this missionary is suffering a lot," the evangelist quoted above continued, "but this fellow is not at all showing love to his neighbors."

The concern about allurement is not, of course, limited to Indian missionaries on the foreign funding dole. Many Indian critics of Christian missionaries complain that the massive amount of foreign funding used to support Indian Christianity generally, and Indian Christian institutions in particular, itself constitutes an allurement to the Christian faith. The relative wealth of Christian institutions and Christian workers serves as a demonstration of financial power, critics argue, and it is attractive.

This complication has been recognized for some time even within western missionary circles. Jonathan Bonk, for example, writes that the effects of western missionary wealth are compounded by the fact that many western missionaries have believed it to be a sign of divine approbation. For them, "the overwhelming racial, material, and political ascendancy of the 'Christian' nations was not simply a fact, but—in missionary thinking— a *providential* fact."[44] Missionaries have also generally recognized that their wealth contributed to the missionary mystique and could buy access, admiration, and attention: "Missionaries then, as now, recognized that . . . astonishment [at missionary wealth] could be parlayed into Christian conversion. With their pale skin and their extraordinary material culture, missionaries constituted a kind of Great Exhibition, attracting Africans [and, we might add, Asians, etc.] from great distances."[45]

As I have already indicated, the relative number of western missionaries at work in places like India is declining as the number of native missionaries rises. Yet rather than avoid the complications of foreign funding, this trend merely relegates it to another location. Today, it is just as often the native missionary, relatively wealthier than his (and sometimes, rarely, her) neighbors, and brimming with the borrowed impudence of his foreign benefactors, who is tempted to use his substantial resources to draw people to the faith.

Indian Christian concerns about the effects of foreign funding arise not only out of disinterested reflection and critique but also from interdenominational and inter-caste tensions within the Christian community. The most obvious individual (as opposed to institutional) Christian beneficiaries of foreign funding are the native missionaries supported from abroad. Because of the Evangelical bent of the foreign agencies that support native Indian missionaries, most of the missionaries supported in India are Evangelical or Pentecostal. A significant portion, probably even a majority

---

[44] Bonk, *Missions*, 25, see also, 3. In the context of America, of course, this thinking is clearly related to the notion of Manifest Destiny.
[45] Bonk, *Missions*, 22.

of Evangelical and Pentecostal congregations and evangelists in India are at least partially or indirectly funded from abroad. This support, and the growth (of various kinds) it enables, creates jealousy among mainstream Christian communities, with whom the Evangelicals and Pentecostals are already embroiled in what I earlier called a "cycle of blame" fueled by inter-caste, inter-class, and interdenominational rivalries.

According to many Indian Christians, however, the actual presence of foreign missionaries in India is far worse than the presence of their funds. "I for one am clear," declared a Mar Thomite missionary working in rural Karnataka, "that it is not the time for westerners to do evangelism in India." According to them, the presence of Americans, particularly those associated with funding agencies, exacerbates all of the complications associated with foreign funding, and tempts Indians to perform for their pleasure and approval by staging conversions or attacks on Christians.

Yet worse, according to almost all Indian Christians I consulted, are the foreign televangelists and revival-meeting thaumaturges, like (respectively) Joyce Meyer and Benny Hinn, who buzz through India using their massive financial and institutional might to create evangelistic spectacles, and then leave almost as soon as they come. Western evangelistic networks like Pat Robertson's Christian Broadcasting Network, and even Christian programming produced in India (usually on American models), is funded almost entirely from abroad. This programming has gained massive exposure in terms of availability on satellite stations (if not in actual viewership). According to James, for example, on at least one recent early morning in Bangalore, Joyce Meyer appeared on three stations at once.[46] Such programs proportionally skew Pentecostal, and so they represent yet another source of Pentecostalization.

Not only does the presence of foreign missionaries make Indian Christians more vulnerable to claims that Christianity is a "foreign" faith entirely dependent on western Christianity, but, Indian Christians complain, they are also terribly ineffective as missionaries. Foreign missionaries rarely live for very long in India any more. So they don't know how to communicate with Indians. And even when they do appear to provoke conversions, the conversions are generally short-lived. One commentator for this reason compared foreign-sponsored healing and revival meetings in India to speeding trucks (an image more poignant, no doubt, for those

---

[46] Jonathan D. James, *McDonaldisation, Masala McGospel and Om Economics* (Washington, DC: Sage, 2010), 150; and Thomas, *Strong*, 112, 24.

who have traveled on Indian roads). As they drive by, in a hurry, leaves (i.e., converts) get caught up in the gusty draft they create, but then rather quickly fall away.

Moreover, many Indian Christians are as sensitive to and concerned as their critics about the ways in which foreign funding encourages Indian Christians to adopt both the theological and cultural trappings of western Christianity. Such issues are not unique to India, of course. As Wuthnow puts it, "the missionaries bring American radios and Bibles, the television stations broadcast American films [and, we should add, American revivalists], and the visiting evangelist from the United States helps raise money to build the new church. It becomes hard to disentangle the Christian message from images of US wealth and power."[47]

For all of the good it does, then, for all of the hospitals, schools, and orphanages it has constructed and maintained, foreign funding also creates complication and generates critique, particularly among opponents of Christianity in India, many of whom need no more evidence of the continuing dependency on foreign funds (and therefore of the continuing "foreignness") of Indian Christianity than the annual FCRA reports. Foreign funding for Christian individuals and organizations clearly contributes to Hindu–Christian tensions. Proving, through state-by-state statistical analyses, whether it correlates with anti-Christian violence, as is the occasional claim of Hindu nationalists, would be considerably more difficult, particularly since foreign funds received are recorded under FCRA regulations in the states where the recipient's organizational headquarters are located, even if the funds are spent elsewhere.

Indian Missions and Pentecostal Christianity

It is difficult to estimate the number of Indians at work as missionaries in India. There is nothing produced in India like the *Mission Handbook*, for either Protestant or Catholic missions, though there had been before the mobilization of anti-Christian forces in recent years. Mission organizations that collect and maintain statistics on Indian missions have become, because of anti-Christian violence, hesitant to publicize what they know. I spent several hours at the headquarters of India's largest mission association, which keeps detailed statistics on the presence of Christians and missionaries in India. In a three-hour interview, the Director there declaimed

---

[47] Wuthnow, *Boundless*, 94.

for long periods on a variety of topics unrelated to my research, intentionally, it seemed, trying to keep me from asking the probing questions about numbers he knew I had come there primarily to ask. When I finally did ask questions about numbers directly, the stonewalling continued, and it seemed to me that the Director even took some pleasure in his ability to parry my repeated inquiries. At one point he openly congratulated himself on his ability to say nothing on the topic, even though I had already pledged to use the statistics responsibly, and only in consultation with him. Mission groups in India will not give out statistics any more, he finally said, even to foreign scholars, "because everybody is scared," and "most of the information that groups like the BJP collect is from the U.S."

That, surely, is true, due to publications like the *Mission Handbook, Operation World*, and the *World Christian Encyclopedia*. It is, moreover, one of the reasons why I have withheld identifying information wherever possible, including when describing the "mission association" in the previous paragraph. Although the association's Director was unwilling to provide any state-by-state data on Indian missionaries, which is what I really wanted, he did offer estimates of the total number of Indian missionaries at work in India. And since such estimates are available to the public elsewhere (online, in various publications, etc.), it seems appropriate to include them here.

The Director's mission association comprised around 1,200 Indian mission agencies sponsoring about 55,000 full-time, professional Indian missionaries, and he estimated that these missions and missionaries represented 75–80% of the total. Altogether, then, the total number of native Indian missionaries is therefore likely to be around 70,000. It should be noted, however, that this figure does not include Indian Catholic missions (e.g., Catholic Relief Services), for which no reliable statistics appear to be available, nor does the figure include Indian Catholic or Orthodox clergy (e.g., monks, nuns, and priests) working on the frontiers of Christian boundaries, and carrying out a more or less missionary role.[48] If such workers were included, then the RSS's claim that 100,000 Indian Christian missionaries are active in India, which once seemed rather dubious and far-fetched to me, would probably not be very far from the truth.[49]

---

[48] Part of the difficulty in counting Catholic missionaries is that the Catholic model is diocesan. Diocesan funds support priests, nuns, and others who sometimes work in non-Christian or barely Christian contexts, where the line between a priest or nun, on the one hand, and a missionary, on the other, is difficult to discern.

[49] On the RSS claim, see Sushil Aaron, *Christianity and Political Conflict in India: The Case of Gujarat* (Colombo: Regional Centre for Strategic Studies, 2002), 26.

These figures represent an increase of around 20 times since 1973, when there were probably around 500 total Indian missionaries. By 1994, the total number was around 12,000, and by 2009, that figure had likely risen to over 50,000.[50]

While the phenomenal growth in the number of Indian missionaries reflects, to some extent, the growth of indigenous Indian mission agencies, it also, and probably more substantially, is a reflection of the growth in foreign support of native Indian missionaries, as described above. Although there are a handful of Indian mission organizations that self-consciously refuse foreign funding, foreign Christian organizations still represent an important source of funding for Indian mission agencies. "Most of the missions are running with foreign funds," said one Indian, well-positioned mission observer (a Christian), "That is the reality here."

While most of the largest foreign funding agencies would self-identify as Evangelical, the funds they contribute frequently support Indian missionaries that westerners, at least, would perceive to be Pentecostal or Pentecostalized. There are two reasons for this. First, Indian Evangelicalism is largely a Pentecostalized Evangelicalism, and this is particularly true among independent and evangelistic Evangelicals. Many self-identifying Evangelicals in India therefore speak in tongues and conceive of the Holy Spirit's work along Pentecostal lines. Second, belief in the existence of spirits and demons is widespread in India and cuts across all religious divisions. Those with whom missionaries in India work, therefore, expect them to be able to provide physical and spiritual healing in the name of their God, and their perceived ability to do so is probably the most important contemporary factor in Christian growth, particularly in rural India. Although Evangelicals also frequently engage in spiritual warfare, it is the Pentecostals, in India, who are best known for integrating it into the lives of their congregations.

While the typical foreign funding agency is Evangelical, therefore, the typical Indian missionary is of the independent, Pentecostal, or Pentecostalized Evangelical variety. Some of them are involved in social service, of course, but the vast majority of them are engaged primarily in evangelistic activities, and those that are, work primarily among

---

[50] Robert Frykenberg, "The Gospel, Globalization, and Hindutva: The Politics of 'Conversion' in India," in *Christianity Reborn: The Global Expansion of Evangelicalism in the Twentieth Century*, ed. Donald M. Lewis (Grand Rapids, MI: William B. Eerdmans Publishing Company, 2004), 118 n. The figures derive from interviews, and from Johnson and Ross, *Atlas*, 269; Mandryk, *Operation*, 413; and K. Rajendran, *Which Way Forward Indian Missions?* (Bangalore: SAIACS Press, 1998), 48.

lower-caste and tribal peoples. As the number of Indian missionaries grows, then, so too does the tension between these Pentecostals and Pentecostalized Evangelical missionaries, on the one hand, and, on the other, members of the older, mainstream Indian Christian denominations, who watch in condescending dismay as the "new breed" of independent missionaries receives more and more foreign funding, and achieves more and more spectacular rates of growth, often at the expense of membership in the mainstream denominations, and often through methods that mainstream Christians believe provoke and irritate, or even cause a violent backlash from non-Christians that affects all Christian communities negatively.

While the vast majority of Indian Protestant[51] missionaries are engaged in evangelism of some kind, the nature of their evangelistic activities is radically different than it was ten to fifteen years ago, before the mobilization of anti-missionary resistance. Up until about 1998 (i.e., coinciding with anti-Christian riots in the Dangs, Gujarat), open-air preaching—what we might call mission by megaphone—and evangelism aimed at complete strangers in un-Christian areas was not at all uncommon.[52] After that point, however, and due to the growing Hindu resistance to Christian evangelism (the effect, both Christians and non-Christians agree, of Sangh mobilization), Christians were forced to alter their evangelistic approach. While the timetable varies by state—earlier in Gujarat, for example, and later in Karnataka and Chhattisgarh—Christians of all denominations (including Catholic Christians) agreed that sociopolitical realities had caused a significant shift in missionary methods in the last ten to fifteen years.

Nobody does "public street preaching . . . now," said Richard Howell with only minor exaggeration, and echoing views I heard expressed all over India. While ten years ago Indian Christians could stand on a corner and start preaching or singing, "Those days," he said, "I think are over, because of the threat of persecution. You'll be beaten up." Similarly, one Indian missionary in Chhattisgarh said that in an earlier era, non-Christians were often eager to talk to Christians, and interested in taking their pamphlets and discussing religion with them. Today, however, he said, one cannot distribute pamphlets without getting into intemperate arguments and risking assault. Open-air preaching has been largely replaced by a variety of

---

[51.] The same is probably not true for Catholic missionaries, the majority of which are at work in social institutions of various kinds. Nevertheless, John Dayal suggests that there has been an increase in evangelistic activities among Indian Catholics since *Ecclesia in Asia.*
[52.] Aaron, *Christianity,* 79.

techniques (e.g., "Web Evangelism," "Friendship Evangelism," "Care Cell Evangelism") that follow lines of friendship and family relationships, and that put an emphasis on evangelizing only where one is invited.

Another sign of the changing times is the greater care with which some denominations now accept new converts. In Karnataka, for example, the CSI has begun requiring converts to sign an affidavit to preemptively frustrate critics' claims of force, fraud, and inducement. In the affidavit, converts declare:

> I have chosen to become a Christian of my own free will and volition without any coercion, force, inducement of food, clothing, money, or other material benefits. I have hereby of my own free will and volition decided to get baptized by water immersion. I state that no one has forced me to attend any Christian programs. I state that no one forced me to pay any money to the church. I state that it is my choice whether I remain a Christian or reconvert to my parent faith or any other religion. I hereby declare that the details furnished above are true and correct to the best of my knowledge and information.

The affidavit includes the convert's name, signature (or thumbprint), and picture, names of the convert's family members, and a stamp and a notary's signature that officially register the document with the government.

While the Christians with whom I conversed unanimously agreed that the growing opposition of anti-missionary groups was responsible for these evangelistic changes, they differed considerably in their appraisal of the new reality. Some struck a wistful tone. For many, particularly older Indian Christian missionaries, the era of street preaching represented the "good old days." During a worship service in Bangalore, for example, a Pentecostal pastor told his congregation that the church was failing in its witness. "You know, we used to hand out tracks and pamphlets, and preach outside," he said, "That's how my wife and I got our start. . . . We didn't have to poach believers from other churches. . . . But now we can't do that, and so we are beginning some witness through the Internet." Those who found the new situation regrettable were also more likely to attribute it to demonic forces. Evangelists could not go out in public spaces like they used to, said one leader of a large Indian missionary organization, because of the anti-Christian "hate campaign, which is the work of the Devil."

Others attributed the anti-missionary backlash to the sometimes overly aggressive and insensitive evangelizing of the earlier era. As one famous Indian Evangelical leader put it, "I think we have learned our lesson." Still others remained combative, and refused to change their missionary methods in the face of intimidation, harassment, and violence. And this response, I found, was particularly prominent among the Pentecostals. "Even with all of the persecution, people are not afraid," said one Assemblies of God missionary. "[Missionaries] get all kinds of beatings, but they stay there only. [They are not] afraid of this BJP and RSS and all." Many missionaries and mission organizations in fact still ply the old trade, continuing on in the same way because of their confidence in the effectiveness and biblical rectitude of the old methods. And this is true not only of smaller mission organizations, as I suggest below, but even of the best funded of all of them, GFA.

The Consequences of Pentecostalization

So far in this chapter, we have examined a variety of current trends that favor the Pentecostalization of Indian missions and of Indian Christianity more generally. Of these, two are the most important: First, the shifting of funds from evangelization to relief and social services particularly evident among mainstream Protestant mission agencies leaves the funding of direct evangelism and efforts to grow the church primarily to Evangelicals and Pentecostals. Second, because Indian Evangelicals are already Pentecostalized to a significant degree, less concerned (than their western counterparts) about the theological differences between Evangelicals and Pentecostals, and more attuned, both personally and strategically, to Indian popular religious demands for ecstatic experience and supernatural physical and spiritual healing, the global shift in missionary funding from western-born to native missionaries favors ever greater Pentecostalization. What effect this will have on Hindu–Christian tensions and conflict remains to be seen. But for several reasons we may hypothesize that the effect will be primarily negative.

First, as I have already suggested, in India, Pentecostals are perceived by non-Christians and by Christians of all stripes—including Pentecostals— to be the most aggressive and confrontational in their evangelistic style and methods. The disproportionate targeting of Pentecostals in violence against Christians is surely at least partially related to this fact. Second, because of their focus on winning souls for Christ, and because of the urgency they feel in carrying out that task, today's Indian Pentecostals are far more likely than other groups—even other Evangelical groups, it seems—to openly engage in the kinds of strategizing and the targeting of marginalized peoples that critics of Indian Christianity find so objectionable.

But here again, transnational flows of missionary method and theology impinge upon Indian realities. For if Protestant American ways of thinking and doing mission prevail throughout much of the Christian world, their dominance is particularly pronounced in Evangelical and Pentecostal circles. And if aggressively evangelistic Evangelical and Pentecostal Christians in India provoke a hostile backlash from some non-Christian Indians, it is not because they have happened upon their own unprecedented and uniquely offensive missionary style. They do not represent a "new breed" in this sense. Rather, they might more usefully be seen as the natural inheritors and primary torchbearers of certain peculiarly American ways of being missionary that have a very long history, and that remain very much alive in shrinking but still quite influential circles.

Because of their numbers and the extent of their involvement, American missionaries have put their stamp on the global evangelistic project. While European, Australian, and (increasingly) South Korean missionaries and mission agencies are also relatively active in India, it is the American missionary who is generally perceived, by Indians, to be the typical (and model) foreign missionary. Moreover, among Protestant missionaries worldwide, even among South Korean missionaries, the American missionary style predominates.

The peculiar style of the American missionary movement is related to the fact that it was born in the nineteenth century, in the era of westward expansion and the industrial revolution. Others have traced this history and its influence more thoroughly than is possible in these pages.[53] But as a result of its unique historical trajectory, American Christianity was expansionist from the very beginning, and its missionaries particularly inclined to employ rational means (e.g., money, planning, and strategy) toward the speedy and efficient accomplishment of the evangelistic task. In addition, during this same era, American Christians had begun to think of America as a special nation, the new Israel, chosen by God (the term "Manifest Destiny" was coined in the 1840s), lending to the American missionary movement a tincture of triumphalism that was not in other Christian contexts so fully manifest. Not surprisingly, the American missionary

---

[53.] See, for example, Walls, "World"; Hutchison, *Errand*; Andrew Preston, *Sword of the Spirit, Shield of Faith: Religion in American War and Diplomacy* (New York: Alfred A. Knopf, 2012); and Frederick Jackson Turner, *The Frontier in American History* (New York: H. Holt and Co., 1920).

movement therefore grew quickly, efficiently, and confidently, becoming the largest in the world by 1910.[54]

Such thinking is, of course, not exclusively or even originally American. William Carey's 1792 *An Enquiry into the Obligations of Christians to Use Means for the Conversion of the Heathens* is often credited with launching the modern missionary movement, or the "William Carey Era" in world missions.[55] Less known (but unsurprising, given his influence) is the fact that Carey devoted more than a quarter of the text to statistics and information on populations, politics, and the state of religion around the world. In Carey's view, then, one was not only obligated to use means, but to use them effectively.

Carey's example found its natural audience in America. One can trace a fairly straight line of inspiration from Carey's *Enquiry,* through the statistical work of American missions theorist James S. Dennis in the 1880s and 1890s, to statistical texts like the *World Christian Encyclopedia, Mission Handbook*, and *Operation World*, and ecumenical mission strategies like the Joshua Project and AD2000 today.[56] The latter's goal of "A Church for Every People and the Gospel for Every Person by AD2000" was nothing if not a restatement of the watchword for Christians—"The evangelization of the world in this generation!"—at the end of the twentieth century.[57]

American mission agencies—and, significantly, many of the missionaries they support in places like India—frequently employ a distinctive vocabulary derived from such studies and projects. The "10/40 Window" is that part of the world between 10 and 40 degrees north of the equator, where most non-Christians live. The "4/14 Window" refers to the period between ages 4 and 14 when people (children, really) are believed by missionaries to be most receptive to gospel messages and most likely to make a "decision for Christ." "Children are one of the most responsive groups to the Gospel message," wrote Dave Stravers, President of Michigan-based Mission India, "And what better place to 'think smaller' than India—home to over 358 million kids under age 15!"[58]

American mission theorists have also contributed distinctive mission strategies, none now more influential than that of Donald McGavran's

---

[54] Hutchison, *Errand*, 93.

[55] Bonk, *Missions*, 15.

[56] Walls, "World," 165; Wuthnow, *Boundless*, 39; and Bonk, *Missions*, 19.

[57] Although the headquarters of AD2000 closed in 2001, their website is maintained as an historical archive at its original address: http://www.ad2000.org/. North India was a strategic focus of AD2000.

[58] Mission India e-mail to supporters, with the subject line, "Think Smaller!" February 21, 2012.

"Church Growth Movement," which inspires missionaries to enumerate the world's many "homogeneous units" (now better known as "people groups"), and to identify and concentrate evangelistic effort on provoking group movements of conversion among the "unreached peoples." Originally promoted by institutions McGavran helped establish (e.g., Fuller Theological Seminary), Church Growth ideas now pervade the Evangelical Christian landscape, and not just in America.[59] All over India, and including in Pentecostal circles, Christians I interviewed demonstrated an easy fluency with prevailing American mission theories and strategies. According to its current director, for example, GCW, one of the largest indigenous Indian missionary agencies, developed its initial mission strategy along Church Growth Movement lines with help from recent Indian graduates of Fuller Theological Seminary.

All of this lingo, of course, reflects the evangelistic and especially American desire to hasten conversions through the strategic targeting both of those who have not yet heard the message (e.g., the "unreached peoples" in the 10/40 window) and those who are presumed to be most receptive to it (e.g., children within the 4/14 window, or, in India, the lower castes and tribes). This kind of strategic targeting helps explain why India is awash in missionaries and missionary funds. On their sophisticated website, for example, the Joshua Project maintains that India is home to 2,605 people groups, 2,280 (or 87.5%) of which are "unreached."[60] And *Operation World* reports that "the world's least-evangelized peoples are concentrated in India. Of 159 people groups of over 1 million people, 133 are unreached. . . . There are 485 people groups with populations of over 10,000 that are unreached and unengaged, almost three quarters of the world's 639 people groups that come under this category."[61]

Information from *Operation World* and the Joshua Project is widely used and cited by American Protestant mission agencies at work in India. "India Gospel Outreach," writes the California-based agency on its website, "is dedicated to planting a dynamic church in each of India's 3,000 ethnic groups and 28,000+ zip codes."[62] Moreover, with a proportionally large youth population and many socially marginalized groups (i.e., groups presumed to be more receptive and likely to convert), India appears

---

[59.] Walls, "World," 165.
[60.] http://www.joshuaproject.net/.
[61.] Mandryk, *Operation*, 414–15.
[62.] http://www.indiago.org/About-IGO.html.

now, as it has appeared to missionaries for centuries, as a mission field on the verge of a major breakthrough.

While most missionaries would defend the methods outlined above as a responsible and efficient use of resources, their blatant strategizing and boastful vaticination strike many non-Christian Indian observers as crass, cynical, calculating, and generally unseemly, particularly when it openly encourages the targeting of marginalized, less educated, or vulnerable peoples (e.g., minors, women, and the lower castes and tribes, all of whom, with the possible exception of minors, are disproportionately represented in Indian Pentecostalism, and in Indian Christianity more generally). Critics of missionaries in India also object when the urgency and persistence—critics might say obsessiveness—of missionaries, particularly American Evangelical missionaries, drives them to obfuscate their intentions, or to disobey or circumvent local law.

The pervasive or "routinized"[63] triumphalism of foreign and native Indian missionaries and mission agencies continues to nettle many non-Christians in India. Today's triumphalism is generally more subdued than in earlier times, and harvest language is the most regular idiom in which it is expressed. "Now is a time of harvest in India," exclaims a devotional produced by Mission India.[64] Similarly, Roger Houtsma's World Outreach Ministries proclaims, "India is experiencing the greatest harvest in its history. Now is the time that we must reap."[65]

Harvest language is biblical, of course: "When [Jesus] saw the crowds, he had compassion on them, because they were harassed and helpless, like sheep without a shepherd. Then he said to his disciples, 'The harvest is plentiful but the workers are few'" (Matthew 9:37). To most Christians around the world, even to liberal, non-evangelistic Christians, metaphorical harvest language is so common that it seems benign and unremarkable. Assuming conditions have been favorable, after all, harvests are times of feasting, happiness, rejoicing, and plenty. At least if you're the *harvester.*

From the perspective of the *harvested,* however, the harvest has different connotations. Harvest, from this perspective, is a time of slashing, cutting, and destruction. It represents final death, and results in barren, fallow landscapes. It is not without reason that Death is anthropomorphized, in the western imagination, as the Grim Reaper. Critics of Christian missions in India have deftly turned this common evangelistic metaphor against

---

[63.] Thomas, *Strong*, 66.
[64.] http://mypassporttoindia.org/print/110/.
[65.] http://www.wo.org/meetings_vyara.php. The quotation is discussed in Thomas, *Strong*, 144.

those who use it so regularly, as in the title of Arun Shourie's polemically anti-missionary book, *Harvesting Our Souls.*[66]

Christian triumphalism also frequently entails an unshakeable confidence in the rectitude of the Christian evangelical project, as well as in the exclusive ability of faith in Christ to save human souls. This confidence encourages and even—in the view of some—requires audacious behavior. As with the harvest, however, the valence of "audacious" varies depending on one's perspective. To those who approve, it suggests bold and intrepid behavior. But many Indians perceive Christian missionaries, both foreign and native, to be "audacious" along the lines of Merriam-Webster's second definition of the term, that is, "contemptuous of law, religion, or decorum."

Mildly condescending and judgmental attitudes toward non-Christians pervade the American Christian landscape. Non-Christians are commonly referred to as spiritually "ignorant," "the blind," or "the lost," even in relatively non-evangelistic Christian venues. For example, a moderate Methodist church near my home in Indiana recently included a song in its VBS program during which young children sang of inviting "the lost" to God's saving grace while pledging that they would "Spread the truth of God's Word" and not "stop 'til all have heard."[67] Mild, benign, and unremarkable in the view of most Christians, even such language as this vexes many Hindus who encounter it.

Nevertheless, it is certainly true that the radically martial, condescending, and critical language discussed earlier is in decline in the mainstream Protestant and Catholic denominations. American mission agencies decreasingly use such extreme language in public. As part of our research for this project, for example, a research assistant and I perused the websites of all 185 of the Protestant mission agencies listed by *Mission Handbook* as currently working in India. We found very few examples of aggressively critical language of non-Christian peoples, and I have quoted almost every example below. While it remains characteristically pious and conservative, therefore, the language employed in public by the vast majority of American mission agencies, even the Evangelical and Pentecostal ones, is far more conciliatory and irenic.

Similarly, mainstream (e.g., non-Pentecostal) Protestant and Catholic Christians in India have themselves become concerned about the effect

---

[66] Arun Shourie, *Harvesting Our Souls: Missionaries, Their Design, Their Claims* (Delhi: Rupa & Co., 2001).

[67] The song appears as part of the "Operation Overboard" curriculum, which is marketed and sold to VBS organizers around the country by Cokesbury/Abingdon Press. See http://overboard. cokesburyvbs.com/overview/.

that critical evangelistic language has on Hindu–Christian relations. It is important to emphasize that many, many, missionaries in India quietly and respectfully go about their business, avoiding criticizing the faith of non-Christians, and avoiding, as much as possible, offending their sensibilities. General Secretary of EFI (which is broadly Evangelical, and even includes many Pentecostal groups), Richard Howell, told me that EFI discourages the use of "triumphalist language that is likely to be misunderstood." And, Joseph D'Souza, International President of the Dalit Freedom Network and President of the more ecumenical and Catholic organization, the All India Christian Council, at one time appealed to then American President George W. Bush for help in toning down the "bombastic slogans, militant language, and a general demeaning of Indian culture" which he considered particularly characteristic of American missionaries.[68] Likewise, in 2002 the mainstream Christian Indian Theological Association issued a statement suggesting that "the Church should . . . make all efforts to remove every trace of triumphalism, exclusivism and any attitude of superiority in its teachings, structures, evangelizing activities and the styles of the functioning of its institutions."[69]

But many more evangelistic Pentecostals interpret this mainstream Christian hand-wringing as another sign that they (i.e., non-Pentecostal Christians) have become too assimilated, too unwilling to suffer persecution for openly stating spiritual truth and confronting the powers of darkness. Moreover, language harshly critical of Hinduism is frequently employed by well-known evangelists like Pat Robertson, who now appear regularly on Indian television stations, much to the consternation of many mainstream Indian Christians.[70] Because of this, though the number of American missionaries who utilize critical and triumphalist language is relatively small and shrinking, their influence among Indian Christians through radio, television, and the funding of native missionaries and theological/missiological educational institutions, remains quite strong, stronger, perhaps, than that of those who do not.[71] And, of course, as I mentioned earlier, many of the missionaries employed or funded by mainstream American mission agencies do not share their benefactors' misgivings

---

[68.] Aaron, *Christianity*, 33.
[69.] Quoted in Xavier Gravend-Tirole, "From Christian Ashrams to Dalit Theology—or Beyond: An Examination of the Indigenisation/Inculturation Trend within the Indian Catholic Church," in *Constructing Indian Christianities: Caste, Culture, and Conversion*, ed. Chad Bauman and Richard Fox Young (Delhi: Routledge, 2014).
[70.] James, *McDonaldisation*, 148.
[71.] On the way that these factors amplify the voice of American missionaries more generally, see Walls, "World," 152.

about aggressive tactics or harsh and confrontational evangelistic language. Given this, it is not surprising that such language remains common in some Indian Christian missionary circles, and there remain both foreign and Indian Christian missionaries whose audacity is expressed in a more antagonistic idiom. This is particularly true of India's Pentecostals, whose rhetoric of rupture and, in some cases, overt courting of persecution and martyrdom encourages intrusive, confrontational, and antagonistic approaches to evangelism.

Still today, Pentecostal and other Evangelical missionaries occasionally preach the gospel and/or hand out tracts at popular Hindu pilgrimage sites, where they know they are likely to provoke a negative reaction. For example, GFA's website boasts about a group of women who distributed 50,000 gospel tracts in Haridwar in 2007, "despite opposition and threats of beating."[72] Similarly, a Pentecostal pastor in rural Andhra Pradesh (mentioned in the Introduction) told me that in his youth he and his father regularly preached (and regularly got beaten up) during festival times at the popular nearby Yadagirigutta Temple. Evangelistic activities around the famous pilgrimage site of Tirumala (or Tirupati), also in Andhra Pradesh, have recently provoked moves to have them banned in the site's immediate environs, and temple officials now require visitors to sign a declaration of faith in the temple's principal deity, Venkateshwara, before entering (which leads to controversy every time non-Hindu politicians make a VIP visit).[73]

The antagonistic idiom of many Evangelical and Pentecostal missions and missionaries is evident as well in their occasionally harsh and open criticism of Hinduism. Southern Baptists created controversy in 1999 when they published a prayer guide for India that spoke of "900 million people lost in the hopeless darkness of Hinduism . . . slaves bound by fear and tradition to false gods."[74] So did the late Ralph Winter, one-time director of the U.S. Center for World Mission, which "helps to improve strategic decision-making and practice on the frontiers of mission,"[75] when he called the Hindu world "the most perverted, most monstrous, most implacable, demonic-invaded part of this planet. . . . The greatest, biggest, blackest, most hopeless mass of confusion, perversion, deception

---

[72] http://www.gfa.org/news/articles/women-reach-out-with-50000-tracts/.

[73] See, for example, Times News Network, "Jaganmohan Reddy's Tirumala Visit Kicks up a Row," *Times of India Online (Hyderabad)*, 3 May 2012, http://articles.timesofindia.indiatimes.com/2012-05-03/hyderabad/31555281_1_jai-jagan-ttd-executive-officer-temple-rules.

[74] Aaron, *Christianity*, 32.

[75] http://www.uscwm.org/index.php/about/.

and oppression is this massive Hindu bloc. . . . The perversion of Satan in this part of the world is just absolutely legendary."[76]

While these particular statements made headlines, in part because of their colorful language, the sentiments and judgments they express are quite common among the most aggressively evangelistic of American (or Indian) Protestants. "The spiritual darkness in India is evident by the millions of people who worship animals there," declares *Multiply,* a periodical produced by Evangelism Explosion International, a Florida-based mission agency that trains native missionaries in India and elsewhere.[77] And the AD2000 website said of Varanasi, holiest of North Indian cities: "Many consider this city the very seat of Satan."[78] The language of spiritual warfare remains popular among missionaries in India, of course, and provides the primary impetus both for the kinds of criticism of Hinduism I have described above and for missionaries' use of triumphalist and martial language.

Belief in demons and the Christian duty to combat them is common among Evangelicals in general, but especially Pentecostals and Charismatics, whose conceptions of spiritual warfare tend to be considerably more literal and dramatic. And the idea of spiritual warfare has become ever more common in contemporary Asia. Roger Hedlund explains, due largely to the influence of Fuller School of World Missions, and in particular of "Third Wavers" like Peter Wagner and Charles Kraft, in Asian theological circles. Increasingly in Asia, Hedlund writes, "Mission is understood as power encounters. . . . The language of [spiritual] warfare narrowly restricted to the demonic realm has become the dominant mode of expression in mission thinking and practice among many modern Pentecostals and Charismatics."[79] The growing presence and influence of Pentecostal and Pentecostalized Christianity in India suggests, then, that this kind of language is unlikely to go away any time soon, and may in fact increase in the future.

[76.] Quoted in Frykenberg, "Gospel," 108.

[77.] Tom Mangham, "Encompassing the Globe: Reports from our Vice Presidents: Asia," *Multiply,* Summer 2008.

[78.] http://www.ad2000.org/uters4.htm.

[79.] Roger Hedlund, "Indigenous Pentecostalism in India," in *Asian and Pentecostal: The Charismatic Face of Christianity in Asia,* ed. Allan Anderson and Edmond Tang (Costa Mesa, CA: Regnum, 2005), 583–84. The "Third Wave" was a movement of people who came to believe that the "signs and wonders" referred to in the Book of Acts continue to be present and available today, and who tended to be particularly interested in demonology, "power encounters," exorcism, etc.

Conclusion

We have dealt, in this chapter, with broad strokes and general trends and statistics. It may be useful, then, by way of conclusion, to think about the various trends and processes we have considered (and their potential ramifications) by looking closely at a specific group or denomination in which they are particularly evident. No group more clearly embodies the trends and issues discussed in this chapter than GFA. And no single group has been more regularly targeted in the everyday acts of violence against India's Christians.

Gospel for Asia was founded in 1978, in Carrollton, Texas, by K. P. Yohannan, an Indian expatriate born in Kerala who had come to the United States for theological training.[80] While its marketing in the United States positions GFA on the charismatic side of Evangelicalism, in India the organization is identified more clearly with Pentecostalism, and its workers tend to carry out their ministry in that vein. In this sense, GFA provides evidence for the assertion I have made at various points in this chapter and elsewhere, that is, that funds received by Evangelical but not explicitly Pentecostal mission groups in the United States tend to end up supporting far more openly and obviously Pentecostal missionaries in India, and thereby furthering the Pentecostalization of Indian Christianity.

GFA also exemplifies the global shift in missionary support for native-born missionaries. GFA has worked from the very beginning through native pastors. Yohannan has been a sharp critic of non-Indians doing direct missionary work in India, seeing in that work the potential for "religious neo-colonialism."[81] The organization started small, with Yohannan and his wife personally supporting a few Indian missionaries. Today, however, and as indicated above, GFA supports over 9,500 missionaries in Asia, most of them in India. Among American mission organizations, only Campus Crusade for Christ and Christian Aid Mission employ more non-Americans abroad.

In 1993, GFA established a denomination, Believers Church, which claims more than 1.5 million members in India. The size of Believers Church now approaches that even of the CSI, which is the second largest denomination (after Catholicism) in India, and which boasts around

---

[80] Indian expats living in the United States are more and more frequently founding their own missions to India. In this sense as well, then, GFA follows another contemporary trend.

[81] Michael Bergunder, *The South Indian Pentecostal Movement in the Twentieth Century* (Grand Rapids, MI: Eerdmans Publishers, 2008), 53.

2 million members. This made it particularly curious, and controversial, when in 2003 a CSI bishop threw traditional CSI procedures and polity to the wind and consecrated Yohannan archbishop of the Believers Church, a move which many of Yohannan's critics and competitors interpreted, in interviews, as a sign of his, and his church's, growing megalomania.[82] Yet the work of GFA continues apace. Its dozens of missionary training centers are busy equipping around 7,000 workers at any one time. These workers distribute 50 million pieces of evangelistic literature a year, and GFA radio stations broadcast in 92 Indian languages.[83]

The impact and influence of GFA's work, and the missionary model it represents, cannot be overstated. And this is perhaps no surprise, given the fact that it is undergirded by a simply staggering amount of foreign funding. As indicated above, together, according to the 2010–11 FCRA data, GFA and the Believers Church received more than $45 million from abroad in one twelve-month span alone. Despite Yohannan's stated concerns about the influence of western Christians in India, GFA has defended its reliance upon foreign funds. "It is not outside money that weakens a growing church," the GFA website asserts, "but outside control. Funds from the West actually liberate the evangelists and frees [sic] them to follow the call of God."[84] As indicated above, only World Vision received more foreign funding than the combined receipts of GFA and the Believers Church in 2010–11. And whereas the funds received by World Vision go primarily to relief and service, those received by GFA go almost exclusively to missionary and pastoral work.

Yohannan himself speaks regularly against missionary investment in social service. And GFA's website states:

> Reaching the most unreached . . . is the single purpose God gave to Gospel for Asia from its very inception. . . . One lie the devil uses to hinder Gospel work and send people to hell is, How can we preach the Gospel to a man with an empty stomach? Because of this lie, for a hundred years much missions-designated funding has been invested in social work rather than in spreading the Word.[85]

[82.] See, for example, UCANews, "Protestant Bishop Criticized for Ordaining Pentecostal 'Archbishop'," *UCANews.com*, February 18, 2003, http://www.ucanews.com/story-archive/?post_name=/2003/02/18/protestant-bishop-criticized-for-ordaining-pentecostal-archbishop&post_id=22052.

[83.] Mandryk, *Operation*, 407–13; and Thomas, *Strong*, 106.

[84.] http://www.gfa.org/about/faqs/.

[85.] http://www.gfa.org/about/faqs/.

Similarly, Yohannan has criticized the social gospel orientations and what he calls "White think,"[86] that is, the (white) colonial missionary's tendency to be led by sympathy to do works of social service while neglecting the souls of those with whom they worked. Railing against the social gospel for fighting "a spiritual battle with weapons of flesh," Yohannan argues, "When we have plans to fight the biggest problem of the human being, the separation from the eternal God, through supplies of food, then we throw to a drowning person a life-belt, however, we do not take him out of the water."[87]

Naturally, then, GFA's evangelistic methods are more direct, more willingly intrusive, and more confrontational than those of many others. "The most effective evangelism happens face-to-face in the streets," GFA's website proclaims, "Street preaching and open-air evangelism, often using megaphones, is the most common way to proclaim the Gospel. Sometimes evangelists arrange witnessing parades and/or tent campaigns and distribute simple Gospel tracts during the week-long village crusades."[88]

Gospel for Asia missionaries and church leaders are also attentive to the demands of those with whom they work for supernatural healing and assistance in dealing with the nefarious work of spirits and demons. Yohannan's writings are themselves replete with stories of witches, demons, and miraculous healings—even of people raised from the dead by the prayers of Christian missionaries.[89] Implicitly confirming the point I have made several times in this chapter, that is, that native Indian missionaries are generally more willing to engage in these "power encounters" than their western counterparts, Yohannan writes, "Could it be that most Western missionaries, educated into unbelief and powerlessness, are afraid to acknowledge miracles because it reveals their own spiritual weakness? Is the sin of spiritual pride keeping some of God's choice servants defeated and impoverished in their spiritual warfare?"[90] And again, "Missions is not applied anthropology, comparative religion or sociology. It is storming the gates of hell. It is a power confrontation—hand-to-hand combat with Satan and his demons."[91]

---

[86] K. P. Yohannan, *Come, Let's Reach the World: Partnership in Church Planting among the Most Unreached* (Carrollton, TX: GFA Books, 2004), 55.

[87] Quoted in Bergunder, *South Indian*, 54.

[88] http://www.gfa.org/about/faqs/.

[89] For example, see Yohannan, *Come*, 181–82.

[90] Ibid., 184.

[91] Ibid., 185.

In their nondenominational but vaguely Pentecostal orientation, in their confrontational forms of evangelism, in their use of native missionaries and foreign funding, and in their attentiveness to the supernatural and to power encounters, then, GFA missionaries embody many of the trends we have considered in this chapter. Their growth, their size, and the massive amounts of funds they receive from America and elsewhere abroad also confirm that they are no dying breed, no flash in the pan. They are, in many ways, the future of Indian evangelism, at least in the near term.

The fact that they are also, according to my data, the most frequently targeted organization in anti-Christian attacks should therefore give us pause. During 2007, for example, in 23, or 16%, of the 147 incidents of violence in 2007 in which media reports indicated the denominational affiliation, GFA workers or Believers Church members were among the victims, despite constituting fewer than 5% of the Indian Christian population.[92] Without a doubt, the prominence of Christians affiliated with GFA and the Believers Church among the victims of violence reported in the media is due in part to GFA's impressive communications infrastructure, which ensures that attacks against GFA and Believers Church Christians gain more publicity than is possible in the case of smaller organizations or independent Christian pastors and congregations. In fact, the confluence of GFA's antagonistic evangelistic methods, the tremendous sums of foreign funds that support the organization, the disproportionate targeting of GFA workers in incidents of violence, and the publicity that GFA manages to draw to these incidents raises a number of intriguing questions about cause and effect in the violence against India's Christians.

Which is (or are) the driving factors in this confluence? Are the incidents of violence, for example, widely publicized and constantly rehearsed in GFA marketing materials, the cause or the effect of the organization's clearly demonstrated fundraising ability?[93] To put it another way, are GFA workers targeted because the organization's impressive wealth is well-known among opponents of Christianity in India (as it is), or is that very wealth instead the *result* of western Christian donors responding sympathetically to what they might perceive as the targeted "persecution" of GFA and Believers Church Christians? Similarly, is the apparent disproportionate targeting of GFA workers a result of their provocative

---

[92] Mandryk, *Operation*, 147.
[93] On the "endless circulation" of stories of "persecution" in Yohannan's radio broadcasts, see Thomas, *Strong*, 122.

evangelistic methods, or an illusion produced by the fact that the organization is more media savvy, and better able, relative to other Christian groups that suffer violence, to get attacks against their workers noted in Christian and non-Christian media outlets? These questions are difficult to answer, and suggest, at the very least, that any useful analysis of violence against India's Christians must go beyond simple assertions of unidirectional cause and effect. What we can say with some certainty is that if GFA typifies the future and the growing edge of Indian Christianity, as I have suggested it does, then we should expect that the frequency of incidents of violence against Christians will at least hold steady in the near term.

Predictions are, of course, risky, and we can know nothing about the future of Indian Christianity with absolute certainty. But Indian and transnational trends in Christian evangelism do appear to favor the continued Pentecostalization of Indian Christianity. As mainstream Protestant and Catholic groups invest their resources in providing relief and social services and become less concerned about gaining converts, the direct evangelistic vacuum will be filled more and more by Pentecostals and (often quite Pentecostalized) Evangelicals, whose churches are likely, as a result, to see relatively more impressive growth. At the same time, the shift in foreign funding from foreign- to native-born missionaries favors these same groups, and even more so Pentecostal expressions of faith, because of the continuing or perhaps even increasing demands of the evangelized for ecstatic worship experiences and supernatural healing. The Pentecostalization of Indian Christianity is likely, in the short term, to negatively affect relations between Hindus and Christians, in part because Indian Pentecostals are perceived by others to be more antagonistic in their evangelical endeavors, as described above, and in part because of their social location, their expressiveness, their rhetoric of "rupture," and their tendency to seek martyrdom, in ways minor and major, as a badge of honor.

It is important at this juncture to reiterate that suggesting Pentecostal beliefs, practices, and ways of being in the world are "antagonistic" or "provocative," and that at least some of the violence they experience in contemporary India may be a response to their provocations, is not the same as suggesting Pentecostals are somehow responsible for the violence they and other Christians experience. While many mainstream Indian Christians make that claim, they do so largely because of their own theological and cultural reasons that need not guide our judgment here. But in the next, concluding chapter, we do take up the particularly thorny question of culpability.

Conclusion

Conversion Activities, Metaphorical
Cockroaches, and the Question of Culpability

WE BEGIN THIS CONCLUSION with a review of sorts, not only of the
book's primary assertions but also of the "logic" of Pentecostal targeting
in everyday acts of violence. After this review, then, we move on to an
exploration of the presumed "naturalness" of anti-Christian violence, as
well as to the complicated question of culpability, and the larger question
of whether, in secular democracies, aggressive evangelization represents a
form of intolerance that cannot be tolerated.

Many explanations for anti-Christian violence in India focus primarily
on the perpetrators, who are—usually—members of various Sangh Parivar
organizations, others inspired by the Sangh's anti-minority rhetoric, and
still others who exploit the cover of that rhetoric to justify and create support for violence guided by other motives (revenge, pleasure, intimidation,
economic interest, the maintenance of traditional hierarchies, etc.). Such
a focus is important, and no account of anti-minority violence should lose
sight of the fact that it is, in India as elsewhere, tragic and criminal. Full
stop. Let nothing in this book be taken as an exoneration of those who
commit violent crime.

Yet the focus of this book has been on the victims of anti-Christian
violence, and on those it disproportionately affects. One of the disadvan-
tages of focusing too much on those who perpetrate the violence, and on
their agency, is that doing so tends to blind us to the way their violent
actions are embedded within and influenced by a broader historical and
political context, a context that is itself influenced by the agency of many
other actors, from around the world, including even the agency of victims. The disproportionate targeting of Pentecostals and Pentecostalized

Evangelicals in the violence against Christians is not just a matter of contemporary dynamics internal to India, then, but rather takes place at the end of a specific historical trajectory influenced by transnational flows of people, power, and ideas.

Among the most important of these "transnational flows," of course, is colonialism. Anti-Christian violence is related in important ways to the perception that Indian Christianity is a foreign, denationalized, and denationalizing religion. But this is a claim that would have made no sense prior to da Gama's arrival in India in 1498. Afterwards, the Indian Christian affiliation of India's colonial rulers blemished its reputation. And the fact that these colonial rulers frequently allied with, or appeared to ally with India's own Christian communities made the latter vulnerable to accusations of divided loyalties. In addition, the arrival of western Christian missionaries, enabled and at times encouraged by colonial officials, contributed to the Europeanization of Indian Christianity. As a result of these various processes, India's ancient Indian Christian community slowly became disentangled from the popular Indian religious and cultural milieu into which it had been formerly relatively well-integrated, appearing more and more alien, and being ever more regularly suspected of alien allegiances. And while the Syrian Christians have been able to reverse these trends and reestablish their high status and ritual entanglement with high-caste Hinduism, insulating themselves from the negative effects of these processes, the same cannot be said for low-caste Indian Christians, who continue to suffer, to borrow Pandey's phrase, under the sign of the question mark.[1] And this is particularly true of low-caste Christian communities associated with Protestant and Pentecostal movements that do not desire, and often officially prohibit, ritual entanglement with their Hindu neighbors.

The fact that these suspicions survived into the postcolonial era is not proof that they were unrelated to colonialism. Rather, it suggests that certain of the particularly pernicious political, economic, and cultural aspects of colonialism continued more or less unabated after it ended, through the processes of globalization and westernization, and through various forms of political and economic neocolonialism. In the eyes of many Indians, then, the West never ceased, even in the postcolonial period, to represent a threat to the religious traditions, cultural genius, and political sovereignty

---

[1] Gyanendra Pandey, *Routine Violence: Nations, Fragments, Histories* (Delhi: Permanent Black, 2006), 129.

of India.[2] India's Christians, suspected since at least the nineteenth century of divided loyalties, are now often treated as the proxies for (and patsies of) western political power and influence. One explanation for why Pentecostals and Pentecostalized Indian Christians are disproportionately targeted in the violence, then, is that they are perceived to be the most aggressive peddlers of this influence, under the guise of religion. They are also, because of the "rhetoric of rupture," the most forceful in their condemnation of what many Hindu nationalists would consider "traditional Indian culture." And this, of course, makes them more vulnerable than others to accusations of being denationalized, and furthering the process of denationalization among Christian converts.

The global missionary movement represents another important transnational factor in the production of anti-Christian violence. I have already alluded, of course, to the impact of colonial-era, western missionizing on Hindu–Christian relations. And for a variety of demographic reasons, India quickly became, and remains, a special focus of the western missionary movement. Evangelism strikes many Hindu observers as a debasement of religion itself. And the systematic nature of contemporary Christian evangelistic efforts, like the Joshua Project, and AD 2000, only exacerbates the impression, among many Hindus, that Christianity illicitly mixes religion with a cynical political agenda. As with its association with colonialism, then, the Christian association with evangelism brings public opprobrium to all Indian Christians, and not just those who embrace or support evangelistic endeavors; often the anti-missionary critique fails to make a distinction between Christians that do and Christians that do not.

That said, the patterns of anti-Christian violence do suggest some targeting. But the generally unconscious nature of this targeting should be stressed. Few of those who commit acts of anti-Christian violence could provide a detailed disquisition on Christian denominational differences. And yet the attacks disproportionately target certain denominations, and particularly those groups most involved in open, assertive evangelism. In this regard, it is useful to keep in mind the previously mentioned earthy metaphor offered by the Christian *dalit* rights activist in New Delhi: "If a cockroach lands on your shoulder, what will you do?"

The metaphor is a simple one, but conveys a number of important truths. The first, of course, has to do with the disgust that many, particularly

---

[2] On which, see Chad Bauman, "Postcolonial Anxiety and Anti-Conversion Sentiment in the *Report of the Christian Missionary Activities Enquiry Committee*," *International Journal of Hindu Studies* 12, no. 2 (2008): 194–96.

higher-caste (Hindu and Christian) Indians continue to feel for their low-caste compatriots. It is important, therefore, that what metaphorically lands on the metaphorical shoulder is not a speck of dust, or even something annoying, like a mosquito, but rather a positively repulsive insect. There is no doubt that the rise of anti-Christian violence in India is related at least in part to the rise of low-caste Christian communities to places of relatively higher social status and economic position, that is, to extend the metaphor, to their movement from their "proper" place, under foot, to a more equal, competitive, and threatening space on the shoulder. And as I have suggested, to the extent that low-caste, tribal, and other marginalized Indians are more active in Pentecostalism, and particularly in Pentecostal leadership, the targeting of Pentecostals for acts of violence makes some sense.

But the second truth conveyed by the metaphor is the fact that anti-Christian violence is in many cases a response to specific provocation, or to the repeated provocations of a specific person or group. In that sense, then, the metaphor appropriately suggests a kind of unconscious, knee-jerk reaction. Pentecostals are rivaled in their passion for proselytization only, perhaps, by other Evangelicals. And their mode of evangelism tends to be relatively more assertive, aggressive, or even antagonistic. Mainstream Indian Christian communities, on the other hand, have largely withdrawn from projects of proselytization, and do their evangelism (if they do any at all), indirectly, privately, and primarily through social service. They do not, therefore, make themselves visible, like the metaphorical cockroach on the shoulder. Or, to return to John Dayal's metaphor, also quoted earlier, since mainstream churches are not on the frontlines of evangelism, and not working in the countryside, "They're not there to be victimized . . . You can't drown on a mountaintop."

In many ways, then, Pentecostals embody the concerns that Hindu nationalists, and even many more irenic Indians, have about Christianity. They are perceived to be more clearly denationalized than other Christians, and this is related to the rhetoric of rupture, and to the Pentecostals' frequently harsh critique of what many Indians would consider "traditional" Indian/Hindu beliefs and customs. India's Pentecostals and Pentecostalized Evangelicals are, in addition, often quite westernized and/or handsomely supported with funds from western missionary agencies, funds that, it can be legitimately asserted, often serve as a kind of indirect allurement to the faith (and in other, rarer cases, may even be used as a direct kind of inducement). Pentecostals are also, finally, ambitiously, enterprisingly evangelistic. Evangelism alone, in the abstract, strikes many Hindu observers as a sign of an unsophisticated faith. But when it is carried out in intrusive, adversarial, or antipathetic manner, as it often is among Pentecostals and Pentecostalized Evangelicals, then the cockroach, so to speak, makes its presence fully known. And such provocations are likely to increase, because of the fact that current western and internal Indian missionary trends favor the continued Pentecostalization of evangelism, and even of the Indian Church itself.

And yet, there are at least a few ways in which Pentecostalism does not fit the negative stereotype of Christians nurtured by Hindu nationalists and other critics of Indian Christianity. The most important of these has to do with the increasing prominence of faith healing within the Indian Christian Church, a trend that Pentecostals and Pentecostalized Evangelicals clearly lead and perpetuate. There is no doubt that a substantial percentage of those now affiliating for the first time with Christianity in India do so as the result of what I have called "recuperative conversions." And even though such "conversions" do not always endure, they account for a significant proportion, probably even the majority of church growth in India today.

Yet faith healing does not conform to the critical portrait of Christianity cultivated by its foes. Christians have long been accused of using their superior access to western wealth, power, and technology to lure impecunious and powerless Indians to the fold. And this accusation makes a certain kind of sense in the context of missionary educational and medical facilities. But faith healing does not rely upon superior access to western wealth, power, or technology. In fact, in many ways, it rejects their application to matters of health and healing altogether. In addition, the growing prominence of faith healing in Pentecostal and Pentecostalized circles is at least partly due to popular demand for it. Pentecostals are particularly well-placed to respond to this demand because their belief in the involvement of spiritual beings in matters of health, healing, and prosperity aligns, in important ways, with those in the realm of popular Indian religion more generally. At this most fundamental level, then, Pentecostal belief and practice do not further processes of denationalization, but rather, perpetuate popular Indian religious belief and practice in a new spiritual idiom.

While certainly Indian social, cultural, and political realities do matter, it is clear that they cannot fully account for the increasing frequency of anti-Christian violence since the late 1990s. Nor, indeed, can they fully explain the disproportionate targeting of Pentecostals in this violence. Rather, transnational flows of power, technology, and wealth also constitute important factors in these phenomena, as described in the preceding paragraphs. If focusing too much on the perpetrators of anti-Christian violence tends to prevent us from recognizing this, however, it also obscures from view relevant dynamics internal to the victim community.

While I do not wish in any way to exculpate the criminals who carry out attacks on India's Christians, another important factor in the disproportionate targeting of India's Pentecostals in those attacks is the fact of their marginalization by India's mainstream Christians. There are many reasons why mainstream Christians keep their distance from independent Pentecostals and Pentecostalized Evangelicals. One of them, of course, is jealousy, because of the fact that many mainstream Christians are converting to Pentecostalized forms of the faith, or supplementing their mainstream Christian affiliation with open or surreptitious visits to Pentecostal churches, pastors, or faith healers. A second reason is that mainstream Indian Christian communities, which have achieved some modicum of social respectability, do not in some cases wish to associate with the independent and sectarian churches, among whose leadership low-caste and tribal Christians are somewhat more prevalent. And, of course, in addition to this is the fact that Pentecostal and Pentecostalized Christians engage in activity that many mainstream Christians find churlish and classless, and/or lacking theological or biblical approbation. A third important reason why mainstream Christians marginalize India's Pentecostals is because they know that Pentecostal proselytizing activities are sometimes inflammatory, and they wish to avoid suffering the kind of backlash they suspect might follow in the wake of these activities. For a variety of reasons, then, India's Pentecostal communities are marginalized by the larger and more established mainstream Christian communities. This, combined with the fact that many Pentecostal churches do not have a large, networked institutional infrastructure (like the mainstream Christians do), makes them especially vulnerable to attack.

If there is a central argument of this book, then, it is that the disproportionate targeting of Pentecostals and Pentecostalized Evangelicals in India's anti-Christian violence cannot be explained with reference to internal Indian political and interreligious dynamics alone. Rather, a satisfactory explanation must pay attention to the imbrication of these dynamics with historical factors, transnational political and religious currents (e.g., colonization, globalization, and the global missionary movement), and *intra*-Christian tensions, politics, and structures of power.

Attempting to account for anti-Christian violence and why it tends to affect some Christian groups more than others, however, is not the same as justifying the violence. Likewise, demonstrating that the targeting of

Pentecostals and other similar groups "makes sense," in some way, or follows some logic, is not to excuse it, or suggest that it is desirable. Indeed, one of the really disturbing and yet fascinating aspects of the story of anti-Christian violence is how naturalized it has become, and how frequently it is implied, by commentators across the religious and political spectrum, that it is normal, predictable, and even justifiable.

The Sangh view, which is that incidents of anti-minority violence in India are a "natural reaction" to specific provocations, has been well documented. For example, in response to the rape of several nuns in Jhabua, Madhya Pradesh, in 1998, which Sangh forces were initially alleged to have organized—the reality turned out to be somewhat more complicated—the then VHP All-India Secretary, Baikunt Lal Sharma, told an Outlook India reporter, "The attacks on missionaries are due to an awakening among Hindus. The attack is a natural reaction of the local people to the missionary activity."[3] Similarly Swami Dayananda Saraswati's position, quoted earlier, that "religious conversion destroys centuries-old communities and incites communal violence,"[4] expresses the views of many even moderate Hindus about the nature of anti-Christian violence.

But anti-Christian violence appears "natural" even to many Christian commentators as well, especially when it targets groups other than their own. Referring to independent Pentecostal and Pentecostalized Evangelical leaders, for example, one Catholic nun working in the Punjab said, "These preachers are not trained in theology. They often play with the sentiments of people and lure them with incentives and create communal tension. We are forced to take the blame for their wayward preaching methods."[5] Similarly, one of my good friends in India, a wise and thoughtful CNI leader, repeatedly told me that if he should come upon some people assaulting an aggressive Pentecostal evangelist he would tell them to "give him some slaps for me!" There is tacit acknowledgment of the putative "naturalness" and justifiability of violence against such Christians not only among Hindus, then, but also in many Christian quarters.

Even more aggressively evangelistic Pentecostals see violence as a natural response to their work, one predicted by the very Bible on which

---

[3] K. S. Narayanan, " 'The Attack is Only Natural'," *OutlookIndia.Com,* October 12, 1998, http://www.outlookindia.com/article.aspx?206325.
[4] Swami Dayananda Saraswati, "Conversion is an Act of Violence," *Hinduism Today (Web Edition),* November 1999, http://www.hinduismtoday.com/modules/smartsection/item.php?itemid=4308.
[5] Shafi Rahman, "Freelancers of God," *India Today International,* May 9, 2011, 38.

they depend: "If you see in the Bible, it should come—persecution—to Christians," one Jharkhandi Pentecostal preacher told me, "It is one kind of work of God, I think. It is not that I call persecution to come on me. It is because it is written in the Bible that persecution comes." Similarly, by way of explaining the origins of anti-Christian violence, an Assemblies of God missionary working the villages outside of Bangalore (and who claimed himself to have been attacked as a result) referred to John 16:2, in which Jesus predicts a coming period of persecution: "[T]he time is coming when anyone who kills you will think they are offering a service to God."[6] "The day will come, it may happen," the missionary said. "Seriously it may happen. But we are not bothered about that . . . we will do what God has told us to do." As another Indian Christian evangelist who lives near Hyderabad but works in North India put it, when he gets beaten up he responds by praying, "I thank you, Lord, the scriptures have been fulfilled in me." Other Pentecostals and Pentecostalized Evangelicals explained the violent response to their evangelism in practically the same language as Swami Dayananda Saraswati, but, of course, with a different conclusion about whether Christians should continue to engage in it. For example, after comparing the current situation in India to attacks on the Apostle Paul,[7] one Pentecostalized Evangelical mission leader said, "We don't want to disturb the peace as such . . . But when you proclaim the gospel the disturbance in society is natural, it is a natural result, and that itself is evidence that you are preaching the truth . . . Violence is the natural result when you are preaching the truth."

But what is the source of the perceived naturalness of anti-Christian violence? The fact that many consider the antagonistic idiom of Pentecostal preaching offensive is not particularly surprising. And even I am among those who find more assertive forms of Christian evangelization boorish and intrusive. But all manner of annoying, obnoxious, and offensive behavior is tolerated nonviolently in India. Why, then, does it appear so natural to so many observers that those offended religiously should "naturally" respond violently? This, it seems to me, is a question rarely asked and even less frequently addressed.

The presumption that violence is a natural response to being offended religiously rests on a number of widely accepted but largely unexamined assumptions that demand more careful interrogation. The first is that

---

[6.] NIV.
[7.] See 1 Corinthians 15:32, NIV.

religious opinions and sentiments deserve special treatment because they are *sui generis*. Relevant here is Swami Dayananda Saraswati's assertion, quoted earlier, that "the religious person is the deepest, the most basic in any individual. When that person is disturbed, a hurt is sustained which is very deep." Most people would probably agree with this statement. But in my view, it merely begs the question: Why is the "religious" person the "deepest" of any individual? Why not the political person? The ethnic person? Is not insisting upon special treatment for the religious aspect of human personality to make a deeply religious argument, an argument that would only be made by a "deeply" religious person?

As Amartya Sen has argued, though many of the aspects of our identities are given to us, ascribed rather than chosen (e.g., language, ethnicity, nationality), we do have some freedom in choosing which identities to emphasize or highlight. "Given our inescapably plural identities," Sen writes, "we have to decide on the relative importance of our different associations and affiliations in any particular context."[8] And, he continues:

> Central to leading a human life, therefore, are the responsibilities of choice and reasoning. In contrast, violence is promoted by the cultivation of a sense of inevitability about some allegedly unique—often belligerent—identity that we are supposed to have and which apparently makes extensive demands upon us (sometimes of a most disagreeable kind).[9]

Violence then, according to Sen, is largely the result of people focusing too intently on one (radically different, adversarial) aspect of their identity. In the context of anti-Christian violence, and its putative naturalness, religion is clearly emphasized at the expense of other identities, and presumed to be, as Swami Dayananda Saraswati put it, the "deepest, most basic" part of an individual. But this assumption requires further justification that is never given.

One might be tempted to defend the assumption by arguing that historical factors peculiar to India have conspired, over its long history, to juxtapose Hinduism and "foreign" religions like Christianity, and to construct them as primordially "belligerent," such that no real "choice" in the matter of identity now remains for their adherents. And the historical analyses provided earlier of the progressive "disintegration" of many

---

[8] Amartya Sen, *Identity and Violence: The Illusion of Destiny* (New York: W. W. Norton, 2006), viii, 38.
[9] Ibid., xiii.

forms of Indian Christianity from the broader Indian religious landscape over the course of its fifteen-century history, might appear to provide some support for the argument. However, to admit that the current situation is a product of historical processes is to admit that it is contingent, and therefore mutable. Those who continue to insist, then, that religious identities are particularly strong and inevitably conflict-prone in the Indian context problematically parrot and perpetuate what Gyanendra Pandey has termed the "Colonial Construction of 'Communalism.' "[10]

While many Indians would reject the notion that India is particularly prone to communalism, both Hindu and Christian observers of anti-Christian violence often ascribe it to the ostensibly "simple," passionate, and unrestrained nature of India's rural low-caste and tribal peoples. It is, of course, true, as I have suggested, that anti-Christian violence is primarily a rural and small-town affair. The victims, moreover, are often low-caste and tribal people, as are many (but certainly not all) of the perpetrators. But even if all of those who attacked Christians were members of rural low-caste and tribal communities, to suggest that they could not but have responded violently to being offended religiously is to engage once again in blatant essentialism, this time of an elitist and rather condescending kind.

Violence among humans may be endemic, but that does not mean it is "natural." One of the more intriguing conclusions of Randall Collins's *Violence: A Micro-sociological Theory* is that humans are often quite hesitant to engage in it.[11] Violence, and situations conducive to the committing of it, must for this reason be "produced," as Paul Brass contends.[12] And to the extent, then, that Hindus, Christians, and even Pentecostals perpetuate the myth of the naturalness of a violent response to antagonistic evangelism, they participate in the production of anti-Christian violence.

And this leads us back, then, to the question of culpability, because it is to some extent the presumed naturalness of a violent response to evangelistic provocations that leads people to ask whether those who are responsible for the provocations should also be considered responsible for the violence. I have already, at various points, indicated my willingness

---

[10] Gyanendra Pandey, "The Colonial Construction of 'Communalism': British Writings on Banaras in the Nineteenth Century," in *Mirrors of Violence: Communities, Riots and Survivors in South Asia*, ed. Veena Das (Delhi: Oxford University Press, 1990).

[11] Randall Collins, *Violence: A Micro-sociological Theory* (Princeton: Princeton University Press, 2008).

[12] Paul R. Brass, *The Production of Hindu–Muslim Violence in Contemporary India* (New Delhi: Oxford University Press, 2003).

to condemn those who attack India's Christians with physical violence. I am, to be honest, quite sympathetic to Hindu concerns about the future of Hinduism, and I resonate, in many ways, with the critique of Christian missionizing. There is also a part of me, at least, that roots for the survival and growth of the Hindu faith, against all odds, in the face of the overwhelming strength of globalization, and its religion of choice: Christianity.

But to root for the survival and thriving of Hinduism and Hindus is not the same as to desire it by any means necessary. And though it might be a function of my inability to recognize the violence of globalization—we are all, after all, often blind to our preferred forms of violence, and to those from which we most directly benefit—I am incapable of accepting the argument that the association of India's Christians with western Christian power, and the competitive advantage in the religious marketplace that this association might entail, justifies a physically violent (as opposed to rhetorical, legal, etc.) response to Christian proselytization. There is no doubt, then—in my mind, at least—about the culpability of the criminals who engage in anti-Christian violence. Such violence is against India's laws, and I could not be convinced of the desirability of using violence to circumvent democratically established laws of the land.

But what about those who themselves engage in provocative acts of proselytization? Do they bear some responsibility for the violence they and other Christians experience? I have frequently been asked to weigh in on this question, and have, until this point, assiduously avoided it. One of the reasons I have avoided the question is because of my suspicion that it sometimes, at least, emerges from a place of prejudice. I have admitted, of course, that I personally find many aspects of Pentecostalism unappealing, and I have a particularly negative reaction to many of the more adversarial and pugnacious evangelical methods described in this book. Yet I sense in some Hindu nationalist calls for a condemnation of Pentecostal and Pentecostalized Evangelical practices a disquieting desire for affirmation, from a scholarly source, of their belief in the justifiability of a violent response to them.

Likewise, in the encouragement to blame Pentecostals I receive from my mainstream Christian interlocutors, both in India and elsewhere, I suspect a desire for affirmation of a more theological kind, that is, of their belief in the orthodoxy, respectability, and superiority of their own mainstream brands of Christianity, vis-à-vis those of Pentecostals and Pentecostalized Evangelicals. Even among non-Christian scholars of religion I sometimes sense the vestiges of this mainstream Christian prejudice in the general scholarly (and often unconscious) preference for "rational" over "emotional" or "ecstatic" faith. Not wanting to condone violence, then, and not wanting to engage in theological disputation, I have tried to avoid the question.

A second reason I have avoided the question is because I do not take it as my role to answer it. This is a book about India, and I am, it is obvious enough, not an Indian. The outsider's, or *etic,* perspective is not an inherently illegitimate one. And in fact I suspect that there are many ways in which the fact that I stand largely apart from and outside of the conflicts described in this book have aided my perception. But when, as a scholar, one moves from description and analysis (the focus of this book) to prescription, one moves into more complicated territory. There may be certain kinds of solutions implied, or even implicitly recommended, by the way this book tells the story of anti-Christian violence. But I hesitate to promote any of these solutions in particular. There are disciplinary reasons why I avoid being prescriptive. While other fields (e.g., Political Science) somewhat more frequently engage in prescriptive exercises, Religious Studies, my field, more regularly operates in a descriptive mode, particularly in its more sociological or ethnographic manifestations. But in addition to this fact, it ultimately strikes me as the responsibility of Indians themselves to address the issue of conversion and Hindu–Christian conflict as they see fit, whether through a crackdown on violence, the passing of laws banning conversion altogether (and not just conversion by "force, fraud, and inducement."), or some other solution beyond my own imagination.

But the other reason I have avoided the question is more scholarly. On what grounds, and from what perspective, as a scholar, could I assign blame? I am willing to condemn violent attacks on India's Christians because they contravene laws established by a democratically elected government, and therefore undermine that very government. The position from which I do so, then, is not neutral, since it implies a prior commitment to democracy, but the fact that most Indians themselves share that commitment makes me willing to take a stronger position on the matter of violence.

Certainly, as a scholar of religion, it is not my role to engage in theological disputation, and therefore I could not condemn Pentecostals on the theological grounds that other Christians sometimes do. The mainstream Christian condemnation of Pentecostals and Pentecostalized Evangelicals has multiple sources. It emerges at least partly from social tensions involving the moderately higher social status of most mainstream Christians in relation to most Pentecostals, and the desire of mainstream Christians to maintain that status, and to not have their reputation sullied by association with less "respectable" people (and this, of course, is also true in the relation of higher to lower status Pentecostal congregations). But the mainstream Christian execration of Pentecostalism also rests on theological and biblical arguments about what Christians are required to do and not do, how they are required to behave and not behave. And here, of course, the social and theological factors intermingle, for quite suspiciously, it seems to me, mainstream Christians, in India and elsewhere, often condemn as theologically or biblically unsound the very same things that they find socially unsophisticated and impolite.

But social prejudices will not do as a logic for condemning Pentecostals, nor will the argument that they are uncivil. Although a lack of courteousness may be annoying, it is, like evangelization, not illegal. Lots of people do lots of annoying things, all the time, and democracies like India's protect their right to do so. Moreover, though, as I said, I will not intervene in intra-Christian theological disputes, it does seem to me to be the case that Pentecostals have at least as much biblical support for their way of being religious in the world as do mainstream Indian Christians.

Earlier I applied the standard of legality to those who violently attacked Christians, and condemned them for contravening the democratically established laws of the land. What would happen if we applied this very same standard to Pentecostals? Do they in fact break the law? This is a question, unfortunately, which leads rather inevitably into brambles.

One of the problems, of course, is that Indian laws on proselytization and conversion are not nearly as clear as those restricting violence. The "Freedom of Religion" laws discussed in chapter 2, which were established in various Indian states beginning in the 1960s, were almost immediately challenged in court. In the suit brought against Odisha's law, the state's High Court declared the law *ultra vires*, or beyond the purview of the Indian Constitution, and therefore unconstitutional.[13] But a challenge to Madhya Pradesh's Dharma Swatantrya Adhiniyam Act of 1968 resulted in that state's High Court upholding its constitutionality.[14] When called upon, in 1977, to reconcile the contradictory verdicts in the case of *Stanislaus vs. The State of Madhya Pradesh*, India's Supreme Court upheld the Madhya Pradesh High Court's ruling, struck down that of Odisha's, and declared the acts constitutional. In its decision, the Supreme Court

---

[13] Sebastian C. H. Kim, *In Search of Identity: Debates on Religious Conversion in India* (Oxford: Oxford University Press, 2003), 78.
[14] Ibid., 79.

judges differentiated between propagation and conversion. Article 25 of the Indian Constitution grants all Indian citizens the right "freely to profess, practise and propagate religion." Nevertheless, what this Article guarantees, according to the judges:

> is not the right to convert another person to one's own religion, but to transmit or spread one's religion by an exposition of its tenets . . . there is no fundamental right to convert another person to one's own religion because if a person purposely undertakes the conversion of another person to his religion . . . that would impinge on the "freedom of conscience" guaranteed to all the citizens of the country alike.[15]

According to this judgment, then, there is in India no constitutionally guaranteed right to intentionally seek the conversion of another person. That said, there still are currently no laws on the books of any state, or at the national level, that make it illegal to try to convert another person to one's faith, so long as one does not engage in "force, fraud, or inducement," or contravene other directives of these laws. The mere fact that Pentecostals attempt to convert others to their faith cannot, therefore, be used as a reason to condemn them, or declare them implicated in the violence they experience.

Most Pentecostals, adversarial, disrespectful, and antagonistic as they may be in certain, usually rather limited situations, do not engage in "force, fraud, or inducement," or at least not if those terms are interpreted in a more restricted sense, following conventional usage. There are cases, of course, where in the act of proselytization Pentecostal and other Christians, of course, break the law. For example, those rare missionaries who do employ explicit, quid pro quo monetary (or other) inducement in states with "Freedom of Religion" laws are criminals and deserve to be prosecuted as such. Likewise, those who do not give local authorities advance notice of conversions in states where it is required are breaking the law.[16]

While those who break such laws deserve our condemnation, the vast majority of Pentecostals are not guilty of their transgression. Evangelization,

---

15. Ibid.

16. As this book went to press, Madhya Pradesh was considering such a law. Unfortunately, India's various state "Freedom of Religion" laws have been used mostly to harass Christians and have been unevenly applied. For example, though they all prohibit conversion by "force," they were not at all used in the aftermath of the Kandhamal riots, during and after which many Christians were actually physically forced to convert.

even public evangelization, is not illegal anywhere in India. Nor is it illegal to engage in ecstatic worship, and to do so noisily (in most spaces). So the legal and democratic argument that I have used to censure violent attacks against Christians cannot be used to condemn Pentecostals, at least not on the basis of these laws.

But the Indian Penal Code also includes, in section 153A, the threat of imprisonment, up to three years, or a fine, or both, for anyone who "promotes or attempts to promote . . . disharmony or feelings of enmity, hatred or ill-will between different religious . . . groups or castes or communities." Similarly, section 295A threatens the same punishment for anyone who "with deliberate and malicious intention of outraging the religious feelings of any class . . . insults or attempts to insult the religion or the religious beliefs of that class." These laws have been used in recent years, *inter alia*, to prosecute provocative artists who work with religious symbols (e.g., Maqbool Fida Husain), critics of the public nudity of Digambara Jain monks, two young women who, on Facebook, questioned the shutdown of Mumbai for controversial political (and Hindu) leader Bal Thackeray's funeral, and (fairly regularly) Christian evangelists. The laws have also been used, more famously (in the West, at least), as the basis of a lawsuit threatened against Penguin Press in India, as a result of which in spring 2014 the press agreed to pulp remaining copies of Wendy Doniger's *The Hindus: An Alternate History*, which it had published, and which was the target of the lawsuit.

We will leave aside, for the moment, the question of whether such laws are conducive to the efficient and humane functioning and flourishing of a secular democracy. If we are to evenly apply the standard of legality outlined above, we forfeit the right to choose to which laws it should be applied. The question that concerns us here, then, is whether common forms of Pentecostal evangelizing run afoul of these democratically established laws. There are some rather extreme evangelistic acts which certainly would. For example, the evangelist who instructs converts from Hinduism to defile or destroy their images of Hindus gods or goddesses would be guilty, it seems to me, of deliberately insulting the religious beliefs of others, particularly if the profaning happened publicly, or in a temple used by other Hindus.[17] So, too, would evangelists who engage in the public demonizing of Hindu gods and goddesses.

[17.] Defiling or destroying places of worship or objects "held sacred by any class of persons with the intention of thereby insulting the religion of any class of persons" is also forbidden by section 295 of the Indian Penal Code.

But what of those who engage in evangelism of a more irenic character? One of the more difficult questions related to this discussion is whether it is even possible to openly and intentionally try to convert another person to one's faith without outraging their religious sentiments. Any attempt to convert another person would, by implication, suggest something inadequate about their faith. And that alone, the person targeted for conversion might argue, is insulting, and an outrage to her or his religious feelings. One of the problems with these laws, of course, is that it is unclear how severe the insult or outrage must be to constitute a transgression against them. In any case, while there may be room for evangelism of the conversational, friend to friend variety within these laws, it seems to me that anyone who engages in public evangelism with the intent to convert others who have not invited their intervention, and particularly those who engage in such evangelism while aggressively criticizing other people's religious beliefs, would risk arrest under these laws. And because many Pentecostals, and Evangelicals more broadly, still (though decreasingly) engage in this kind of evangelism in India, we must admit that those who do so engage in criminal activity, and censure them accordingly. But in democracies like India's, criminals have the right to be prosecuted legally, and not through violent forms of vigilante justice. So while it would be difficult to argue that evangelists breaking such laws are "innocent" victims, when they are attacked, it would be quite another thing to say they deserve it, or bear responsibility for provoking it.

There is one context, however, in which it does perhaps make some sense to talk of Pentecostal culpability for provoking the violence they experience. As indicated in chapter 3, many Pentecostal and other Christian missionaries in India told me that missionaries who were doing their job should be "getting some slaps." And many of them also believe that the gospel is a necessarily disruptive force and read certain biblical passages as prophesying the persecution of those who engage in sharing it. In this regard, it bears mentioning that the word English-speaking Christians use for martyrs has its root in a Greek verb (*martyreo*), which means "to testify" or "to bear witness." (Incidentally, the Arabic term Muslims use for martyr, *shahid*, also has its etymological root in the idea of testimony.) The linkage of experiences of violence with Christian testimony and evangelization, therefore, has a very long history. Describing experiences of violence has become a regular form of testimony in Indian Pentecostal and Pentecostalized Evangelical circles, so much so that they have even become, like other forms of testimony, somewhat stylized. Experiences of violence now also function in these circles as badges of honor.

These facts should make us alert to the possibility of embellishment, even fabrication in testimonies about experiences of violence. Indeed, in at least one case I believe an evangelist I interviewed had manufactured a story about having been attacked for evangelizing in a remote village (about which, when questioned by my research assistant who was familiar with the village in which the attack allegedly occurred, the evangelist evinced a striking lack of knowledge). But even more importantly, because experiences of violence have become, in some circles at least, badges of honor, even a kind of credential, the temptation is no doubt real for some Christians to solicit them. Although it is surely not a widespread phenomenon, my own ethnographic research and interviews with Indian Christians suggest that some of them do occasionally intentionally court violence. And those that do, in my view, deserve our condemnation, for there appears to me little difference between violent action, and the conscious cultivation or instigation of it.

But the vast majority of India's Pentecostals, and Pentecostalized Evangelicals, even the antagonistically evangelistic among them, do not intend to provoke violence. Some of them are, in fact, quite surprised to experience it when they do. In such cases we find ourselves back again in frustratingly ambiguous territory. India's Pentecostals and Pentecostalized Evangelicals are, like many more fundamentalist Christians, often accused of being intolerant because of their soteriological exclusivism. And this then raises the question, of whether, how, and how far Indians should be expected to tolerate them. The notion of "freedom of religion" is far more complicated than it seems, and no secular democracy has worked out to all of its citizen's satisfaction how to preserve religious freedom without threatening the notion of tolerance itself (since some religious people, at least, promote deeply intolerant ideas).

It is true, of course, as Gerald Larson has recently put it, and as this book should make clear, that Pentecostals are implicated in India's "struggle to tolerate the intolerant."[18] But that struggle exists also in other secular democracies. In the United States, for example, many now advocate restricting Muslims' freedom of religion, expression, worship, and propagation because they believe that Muslims cannot be trusted to respect the notions of secular tolerance and religious freedom. And this should underscore the point that debates about Christian proselytization in India

---

[18] Gerald Larson, "India's Struggle to Tolerate the Intolerant: Some Problems with Proselytizing," *Exemplar: The Journal of South Asian Studies* 1, no. 2 (2012): 27–44.

are merely a species of another, broader set of debates about the appropriateness and ideal forms of secular governance, debates that are not unique to India, but which are, rather, nearly universal in countries calling themselves secular.

These debates emerge and derive their urgency from what it seems to me, borrowing the language of computer programming and cybersecurity, are two significant vulnerabilities in the code of democratic secularism. In what follows, I describe these vulnerabilities with reference to both India and the United States. The point of the comparison is not to suggest that everything is the same everywhere, for that, of course, would be folly. Rather, the point is to underscore the fact that these vulnerabilities do not affect India alone, but in various ways pose a challenge to secular governance more generally.

The first vulnerability has to do with the fact that democratic secularisms depend for their flourishing on the presence of majorities willing to self-limit their political power. "Freedom of religion" can only be established and assured if religious majority communities agree not to exercise their numerical power to restrict the freedoms of minority religious communities, or to gain special privileges for their own. To put it another way, for the idea of secularism to work, and for freedom of religion to become a reality, religious majorities must embrace the basic project of secularism.

The problem, of course, is that there is no way, in a democratic setting, to legally require that they do so. Coercing religious majorities to accept the secular project would contravene the very principles of "secularism," "democracy," and "freedom of religion." When the secular project is experienced as coerced, as it has at times been (e.g., in France, historically and today), the illusion that it is somehow neutral comes undone, and citizens begin to see it as an anti-religious ideology. (Of course, the putative "neutrality" of secularism is always only an illusion, since secular laws and governments intervene regularly in debates about appropriate and acceptable religion.)

The second vulnerability in the code of democratic secularism is in many ways the inverse of the first and has to do with the fact that secular, democratic forms of governance possess no mechanism for limiting the spread of intolerance by legal and democratic means. Changing demographics have significant electoral effects; laws can be changed, constitutions amended. The growth of religious minorities deemed intolerant is a threat to the idea of religious tolerance in democracies. And to the extent that religious majorities believe (rightly or wrongly) that their religion and its influence are essential to the preservation of secularism and religious tolerance itself (as is the case for right-leaning Hindus in India and their Christian counterparts in the United States), they have good reason to be concerned about the demographic growth of religious minorities.

It is obvious enough that which religious minorities get declared "intolerant" is a function of sociocultural context; "intolerance" is, to some extent at least, in the eye of the beholder, and most people are more concerned about manifestations of intolerance in other people's religions and ideologies than in their own. Yet there is at least some similarity between that which is considered "intolerant" in the United States, and that which is considered "intolerant" in India. Few in the United States would declare proselytization itself a form of "intolerance" that should be made illegal, in part because American understandings of "religion" have been so thoroughly influenced by and derived from the model of Christianity, a traditionally missionizing faith. Yet many Americans do share with their Indian counterparts a concern about religious "funda-mentalism," in both its Christian and Islamic varieties. And in both con-texts, the perception is that one of the defining characteristics of religious "fundamentalism" is its desire to impose itself on others. Proselytization is worrisome and worth prohibiting to some Hindus, then, not (or at least not merely) because it offends members of the non-proselytizing faiths that have so influenced Indian understandings of right and proper "religion," but rather because it advances, through democratic means, the political power of a religion deemed—again, rightly or wrongly—"fundamentalist" and "intolerant."

Some in both India and the United States contend that if left unchecked, "intolerant" religious minorities pose a threat to secular tolerance and free-dom of religion itself. To restrict the rights of those minorities in specific and targeted ways infringes upon the principles of secularism and freedom of religion, but some in both contexts would argue that limited and tar-geted infringements upon these principles are necessary to preserve and protect the principles of secularism and freedom of religion themselves.

Not surprisingly, then, there are fractures surrounding these issues within the religious majorities of India and the United States, and the fault line dividing them runs between those most concerned about threats exploiting the first vulnerability in the code (i.e., religious majorities unwilling to self-limit their political power and imposing their will on religious minori-ties) and those most concerned about threats that might exploit the second (i.e., "intolerant" groups using democratic means to expand their political power).

In India, those most concerned about the former vulnerability extol the virtues of Nehruvian secularism, criticize the putative atavism and bigotry of "Hindu nationalists," celebrate and make ample space for religious minorities, and vote against the establishment of laws that might unfairly target or be disproportionately applied to religious minorities (like the "Freedom of Religion" laws). Those most concerned about threats exploiting the latter vulnerability, conversely, criticize the secularism of the first group as "pseudo-secularism" (because, they contend, it disfavors Hindus and "panders" to minorities), while (1) warning that making too much space for religious minorities risks eroding the culturally and religiously "Hindu" foundations on which, they assert, true and ideal Indian secularism depends, and (2) attempting to erect legal barriers against what they consider the further erosion of that ideal.

Likewise, in the United States, those concerned primarily about threats exploiting the first vulnerability celebrate religious diversity, mock the ostensibly narrow-minded exclusivism of conservative Christians, and protest and/or vote against the establishment of laws that appear to disprivilege religious minorities or favor Christianity (e.g., "blue" laws restricting the sale of alcohol on Sundays, or religiously based exemptions to health-care laws). Meanwhile, those concerned about warding off threats exploiting the second vulnerability believe the former group is politically naïve and unwilling to confront the "threat" posed to the nation by the growth of religious minorities, who allegedly do not embrace the notions of democracy, secularism, or freedom of religion. For this reason, then, this latter group goes about trying to set up bulwarks against the continued growth of religious minorities and their influence, for example, by warning of the dangers of Islamic expansion (as in the shockingly politically incorrect 2012 Chick Tract, "Camel's in the Tent"[19]), pressing for the establishment of anti-shariah laws,[20] or protesting against the establishment of a "mosque" near Ground Zero.

Large-scale religious conversions, or rumors about them, then, are so momentous and politically charged because they set in motion (or at least exacerbate and accelerate) processes of social change that threaten democratic secularism by exploiting both of its vulnerabilities identified above, and this is particularly true if the religion to which there are large-scale conversions is deemed intolerant, as proselytizing Christianities in India

---

[19.] Available at http://www.chick.com/reading/tracts/1081/1081_01.asp.

[20.] See, for example, The Center for Security Policy, *Shariah: The Threat to America* (Washington, DC: The Center for Security Policy, 2010).

have been. Conversion to Christianity in India exploits the second vulnerability directly, expanding through democratic means, and thereby threatening Indian secularism (in the eyes of its critics) by radically changing, or threatening to radically change India's social and political landscape in ways that favor "intolerant" religions. In response to this perceived threat, at least some among India's majority Hindu community are tempted to exploit the first vulnerability that plagues democratic secularism and use their demographic and political power to restrict the growth of Indian Christianity in ways that are both anti-secular (as in the disproportionate and harassing application of "Freedom of Religion" laws to Christians) and (in the case of violence) anti-democratic, and do so believing that these limited infringements upon the principles of "secularism," "democracy," and "freedom of religion" will enable their broader preservation.

Given these dynamics, then, and as this book has argued in various ways, the disproportionate targeting of Indian Pentecostals in contemporary violence against Christians appears to be an acute and particularly tragic manifestation of a more chronic tension in secular democracies. Pentecostals are, in India, at the forefront of the conversion movement. They are out there, making converts, and in some cases bragging about or even exaggerating their successes. They therefore threaten to provoke radical social change and exacerbate fears about the impact of such social change by preaching a gospel of radical cultural discontinuity while at the same time appearing (to their critics) to introduce the cultural and religious norms of foreign patrons. None of this should suggest, of course, that the violence experienced by Pentecostals is inevitable or natural, or that Pentecostals are to blame for it (except, perhaps, when they intentionally provoke it). Nor should it be taken as a denial of the very significant external and intra-Christian factors enumerated throughout the book (e.g., transnational flows of wealth and power, the ways that mainstream Indian Christians blame and distance themselves from their Pentecostal co-religionists, etc.). But it should, I hope, at the end of these pages, make the disproportionate targeting of Indian Pentecostals in contemporary violence against Christians somewhat easier to understand.

WORKS CITED

Aaron, Sushil. *Christianity and Political Conflict in India: The Case of Gujarat*. Colombo: Regional Centre for Strategic Studies, 2002.

Aaron, Sushil. "Emulating Azariah: Evangelicals and Social Change in the Dangs." In *Evangelical Christianity and Democracy in Asia*, edited by David H. Lumsdaine, 87–130. New York: Oxford University Press, 2009.

Ali, Muhammad Mohar. *The Bengali Reaction to Christian Missionary Activities 1833–1957*. Chittagong: Mehrub Publications, 1965.

Anderson, Allan. *An Introduction to Pentecostalism: Global Charismatic Christianity*. New York: Cambridge University Press, 2004.

Anderson, Allan. "Introduction: The Charismatic Face of Christianity in Asia." In *Asian and Pentecostal: The Charismatic Face of Christianity in Asia*, edited by Allan Anderson and Edmond Tang, 1–12. Costa Mesa, CA: Regnum Books, 2005.

Anderson, Allan. "Pentecostal and Charismatic Movements." In *Encyclopedia of Mission and Missionaries*, edited by Jonathan J. Bonk, 331–35. New York: Routledge, 2007.

Anderson, Allan. "Revising Pentecostal History in Global Perspective." In *Asian and Pentecostal: The Charismatic Face of Christianity in Asia*, edited by Allan Anderson and Edmond Tang, 147–73. Costa Mesa, CA: Regnum, 2005.

Anderson, Allan. "Varieties, Taxonomies, and Definitions." In *Studying Global Pentecostalism: Theories and Methods*, edited by Allan Anderson, Michael Bergunder, André Droogers, and Cornelis van der Laan, 13–29. Berkeley: University of California Press, 2010.

Anderson, Allan, Michael Bergunder, André Droogers, and Cornelis van der Laan. "Introduction." In *Studying Global Pentecostalism: Theories and Methods*, edited by Allan Anderson, Michael Bergunder, André Droogers, and Cornelis van der Laan, 1–9. Berkeley: University of California Press, 2010.

Anderson, Robert Mapes. *Vision of the Disinherited: The Making of American Pentecostalism*. New York: Oxford University Press, 1979.

Apffel-Marglin, Frederique. *Subversive Spiritualities: How Rituals Enact the World*. New York: Oxford University Press, 2012.

Arora, Vishal. "Two Pastors in India Stripped, Beaten—Then Arrested." *Compass News Direct (Online)*, November 29, 2007. http://christianresponse.org/index.php?mact=News ,cntnt01,detail,0&cntnt01articleid=557&cntnt01origid=15&cntnt01returnid=15.

Baldauf, Scott. "A New Breed of Missionary: A Drive for Conversions, Not Development, Is Stirring Violent Animosity in India." *Christian Science Monitor (Online)*, April 1, 2005. http://www.csmonitor.com/2005/0401/p01s04-wosc.html.

Barrett, David B., George T. Kurian, and Todd M. Johnson. *World Christian Encyclopedia: A Comparative Survey of Churches and Religions in the Modern World*. 2nd ed. New York: Oxford University Press, 2001.

Bauman, Chad. *Christian Identity and Dalit Religion in Hindu India, 1868–1947*. Grand Rapids, MI: Eerdmans Publishers, 2008.

Bauman, Chad. "Conversion Careers, Conversions-For, and Conversion in the Study of Religion." *The Religion & Culture Web Forum*, May 2012. http://divinity.uchicago. edu/martycenter/publications/webforum/052012/bauman_response.pdf.

Bauman, Chad. "Does the Divine Physician Have an Unfair Advantage? The Politics of Conversion in Twentieth-Century India." In *Asia in the Making of Christianity: Agency, Conversion, and Indigeneity*, edited by Jonathan Seitz and Richard Fox Young, 297–321. Leiden: Brill, 2013.

Bauman, Chad. "Hindu–Christian Conflict in India: Globalization, Conversion, and the Coterminal Castes and Tribes." *Journal of Asian Studies* 72, no. 3 (2013): 633–53.

Bauman, Chad. "Identity, Conversion and Violence: Dalits, Adivasis and the 2007–08 Riots in Orissa." In *Margins of Faith: Dalit and Tribal Christianity in India*, edited by Rowena Robinson and Joseph Marianus Kujur, 263–90. Washington, DC: Sage, 2010.

Bauman, Chad. "Miraculous Health and Medical Itineration among Satnamis and Christians in Late Colonial Chhattisgarh." In *Miracle as Modern Conundrum in South Asian Religious Traditions*, edited by Selva Raj and Corinne Dempsey, 39–56. Albany: SUNY Press, 2008.

Bauman, Chad. "Postcolonial Anxiety and Anti-Conversion Sentiment in the *Report of the Christian Missionary Activities Enquiry Committee*." *International Journal of Hindu Studies* 12, no. 2 (2008): 181–213.

Bauman, Chad. "Review of *McDonaldisation, Masala McGospel, and Om Economics*, by Jonathan K. James." *Journal of Hindu–Christian Studies* 24, no. 1 (2011): 63–64.

Bauman, Chad, and Tamara Leech. "Political Competition, Relative Deprivation, and Perceived Threat: A Research Note on Anti-Christian Violence in India." *Ethnic and Racial Studies* 35, no. 12 (2011): 2195–216.

Bayly, Susan. *Saints, Goddesses and Kings: Muslims and Christians in South Indian Society 1700–1900*. Cambridge: Cambridge University Press, 1989.

Beita, Bei Chatlai. "Independence Day Prayers for India Disrupted, Barred." *Christian Post (Online)*, August 16, 2007. http://www.christianpost.com/news/independence-day-prayers-for-india-disrupted-barred-28915/.

Bergunder, Michael. "The Cultural Turn." In *Studying Global Pentecostalism: Theories and Methods*, edited by Allan Anderson, Michael Bergunder, André Droogers, and Cornelis van der Laan, 51–73. Berkeley: University of California Press, 2010.

Bergunder, Michael. "Miracle Healing and Exorcism in South Indian Pentecostalism." In *Global Pentecostal and Charismatic Healing*, edited by Candy Gunther Brown, 287–306. New York: Oxford University Press, 2011.

Bergunder, Michael. *The South Indian Pentecostal Movement in the Twentieth Century.* Grand Rapids, MI: Eerdmans Publishers, 2008.

Boel, J. *Christian Mission in India: A Sociological Analysis.* Amsterdam: Graduate Press, 1975.

Bonk, Jonathan J. *Missions and Money: Affluence as a Missionary Problem Revisited.* Revised and expanded ed. Maryknoll, NY: Orbis, [1991] 2006.

Brass, Paul R. *The Production of Hindu–Muslim Violence in Contemporary India.* New Delhi: Oxford University Press, 2003.

Caplan, Lionel. *Religion and Power: Essays on the Christian Community in Madras.* Madras: Christian Literature Society, 1989.

Center for Security Policy. *Shariah: The Threat to America.* Washington, DC: The Center for Security Policy, 2010.

Chakravarti, Sudeep. *Red Sun: Travels in Naxalite Country.* New Delhi: Penguin, 2008.

Chan, Simon. "Whither Pentecostalism?" In *Asian and Pentecostal: The Charismatic Face of Christianity in Asia,* edited by Allan Anderson and Edmond Tang, 575–86. Costa Mesa, CA: Regnum Books, 2005.

Chatterji, Angana. *Violent Gods: Hindu Nationalism in India's Present; Narratives from Orissa.* Gurgaon: Three Essays Collective, 2009.

Chowgule, Ashok V. *Christianity in India: The Hindutva Perspective.* Mumbai: Hindu Vivek Kendra, 1999.

Christian Solidarity Worldwide. *India: Religious Violence and Discrimination against Christians in 2007.* Surrey: Christian Solidarity Worldwide, 2008.

Clifford, James. "Introduction: Partial Truths." In *Writing Culture: The Poetics and Politics of Ethnography,* edited by James Clifford and George E. Marcus, 1–26. Berkeley: University of California Press, 1986.

CNN-IBN. "QOTD: Violence and Conversion in the Name of God." *CNN-IBN (Online),* January 2, 2008. http://www.ibnlive.com/news/qotd-violence-and-conversion-in-the-name-of-god/55440-3.html.

Collins, Randall. *Violence: A Micro-sociological Theory.* Princeton: Princeton University Press, 2008.

Copland, Ian. "Christianity as an Arm of Empire: The Ambiguous Case of India under the Company, c. 1813–1858." *Historical Journal* 49, no. 4 (2006): 1025–54.

Corrigan, John, and Lynn S. Neal, eds. *Religious Intolerance in America: A Documentary History.* Chapel Hill: University of North Carolina Press, 2010.

Csordas, Thomas J. "Catholic Charismatic Healing in Global Perspective: The Cases of India, Brazil, and Nigeria." In *Global Pentecostal and Charismatic Healing,* edited by Candy Gunther Brown, 331–50. New York: Oxford University Press, 2011.

Csordas, Thomas J. "Hammering the Devil with Prayer: The Contemporary Resurgence of Exorcism in the Catholic Church." Paper presented at the Department of Religious Studies, University of California, Santa Barbara, May 1, 2013.

Csordas, Thomas J. *Language, Charisma, and Creativity: The Ritual Life of a Religious Movement.* Berkeley: University of California Press, 1997.

Csordas, Thomas J. *The Sacred Self: A Cultural Phenomenology of Charismatic Healing.* Berkeley: University of California Press, 1994.

David, A. Maria. *Beyond Boundaries: Hindu–Christian Relationship and Basic Christian Communities.* Delhi: Indian Society for Promoting Christian Knowledge, 2009.

Dempsey, Corinne. "Selective Indigenization and the Problem of Superstition in Kerala." *Vidyajyoti: Journal of Theological Reflection* 69, no. 6 (2005): 404–14.

Dempsey, Corinne G. "Lessons in Miracles from Kerala, South India." In *Popular Christianity in India: Riting between the Lines*, edited by Selva J. Raj and Corinne G. Dempsey, 115–39. Albany: SUNY Press, 2002.

Droogers, André. "Essentialist and Normative Approaches." In *Studying Global Pentecostalism: Theories and Methods*, edited by Allan Anderson, Michael Bergunder, André Droogers, and Cornelis van der Laan, 30–50. Berkeley: University of California Press, 2010.

Durkheim, Émile. *The Elementary Forms of Religious Life*. Translated by Karen E. Fields. New York: Free Press, 1995.

Ellsberg, Robert, ed. *Gandhi on Christianity*. Maryknoll, NY: Orbis Books, 1991.

Engelke, Matthew. *A Problem of Presence: Beyond Scripture in an African Church*. Berkeley: University of California Press, 2007.

Express News Service. "Behead Those Who Convert Hindus: Togadia." *The Indian Express*, 2011. http://archive.indianexpress.com/news/behead-those-who-convert-hindus-togadia/872403/.

Foucault, Michel. *Power/Knowledge: Selected Interviews and Other Writings, 1972–77*. New York: Pantheon, 1980.

Freitag, Sandria B. *Collective Action and Community: Public Arenas and the Emergence of Communalism in North India*. Berkeley: University of California Press, 1989.

Freston, Paul. "Evangelical Protestantism and Democratization in Contemporary Latin America and Asia." *Democratization* 11, no. 4 (2004): 21–41.

Frykenberg, Robert. "The Gospel, Globalization, and Hindutva: The Politics of 'Conversion' in India." In *Christianity Reborn: The Global Expansion of Evangelicalism in the Twentieth Century*, edited by Donald M. Lewis, 108–32. Grand Rapids, MI: William B. Eerdmans Publishing Company, 2004.

Frykenberg, Robert Eric. *Christianity in India: From Beginnings to the Present*. Oxford History of the Christian Church. Edited by Henry Chadwick and Owen Chadwick Oxford: Oxford University Press, 2008.

Frykenberg, Robert Eric. "Introduction: Dealing with Contested Definitions and Controversial Perspectives." In *Christians and Missionaries in India: Cross-Cultural Communication since 1500*, edited by Robert Eric Frykenberg, 1–32. Grand Rapids, MI: William B. Eerdmans, 2003.

Gladstone, J. W. *Protestant Christianity and People's Movements in Kerala*. Trivandrum, Kerala, India: The Seminary Publications, 1984.

Goel, Sita Ram. *Catholic Ashrams: Sannyasins or Swindlers?* New Delhi: Voice of India, [1988] 2009.

Goel, Sita Ram. *History of Hindu–Christian Encounters AD 304 to 1996*. New Delhi: Voice of India, [1986] 2010.

Goel, Sita Ram. *Vindicated by Time: The Niyogi Committee Report on Christian Missionary Activities*. New Delhi: Voice of India, 1998.

Gooren, Henri. "Conversion Careers in Latin America: Entering and Leaving Church among Pentecostals, Catholics, and Mormons." In *Conversion of a Continent: Contemporary Religious Change in Latin America*, edited by Timothy J. Steigenga and Edward L. Cleary, 52–71. New Brunswick, NJ: Rutgers University Press, 2007.

Gooren, Henri. "Conversion Narratives." In *Studying Global Pentecostalism: Theories and Methods*, edited by Allan Anderson, Michael Bergunder, André Droogers, and Cornelis van der Laan, 93–112. Berkeley: University of California Press, 2010.

Gooren, Henri. *Religious Conversion and Disaffiliation: Tracing Patterns of Change in Faith Practices*. New York: Palgrave Macmillan, 2010.

Goslinga, Gillian. "Spirited Encounters: Notes on the Politics and Poetics of Representing the Uncanny in Anthropology." *Anthropological Theory* 12, no. 4 (2012): 386–406.

Gravend-Tirole, Xavier. "From Christian Ashrams to Dalit Theology—or Beyond: An Examination of the Indigenisation/Inculturation Trend within the Indian Catholic Church." In *Constructing Indian Christianities: Caste, Culture, and Conversion*, edited by Chad Bauman and Richard Fox Young, 110–37. Delhi: Routledge, 2014.

Grover, Vrinda. *Kandhamal: The Law Must Change its Course*. New Delhi: Multiple Action Research Group, 2010.

Hardiman, David. "Christianity and the Adivasis of Gujarat." In *Development and Deprivation in Gujarat: In Honour of Jan Breman*, edited by Ghanshyam Shah, Mario Rutten, and Hein Streefkerk, 175–95. London: Sage Publications, 2002.

Harding, Susan Friend. *The Book of Jerry Falwell*. Princeton: Princeton University Press, 2001.

Harper, Susan Billington. *In the Shadow of the Mahatma: Bishop V. S. Azariah and the Travails of Christianity in British India*. Grand Rapids, MI: William B. Eerdmans, 2000.

Hawley, John Stratton, ed. *Sati, the Blessing and the Curse: The Burning of Wives in India*. New York: Oxford University Press, 1994.

Hedlund, Roger. "Indigenous Pentecostalism in India." In *Asian and Pentecostal: The Charismatic Face of Christianity in Asia*, edited by Allan Anderson and Edmond Tang, 215–44. Costa Mesa, CA: Regnum, 2005.

Hill, Christopher. "Science and Magic in Seventeenth Century England." In *Culture, Ideology, and Politics: Essays for Eric Hobsbawm*, edited by Raphael Samuel and Gareth Stedman Jones, 176–93. Boston: Routledge & Kegan Paul, 1983.

Hindu American Foundation. "Hindu American Foundation Policy Brief: Predatory Proselytization and Pluralism." http://www.hafsite.org/sites/default/files/HAF_PolicyBrief_Predatory_Proselytization.pdf.

Hollenweger, Walter J. *Pentecostalism: Origins and Developments Worldwide*. Peabody, MA: Hendrickson, 1997.

Horowitz, Donald. *The Deadly Ethnic Riot*. Berkeley: University of California Press, 2001.

Human Rights Organisations. "From Kandhamal to Karavali: The Ugly Face of the Sangh Parivar." Nine Human Rights Organisations, 2009.

Hutchison, William R. *Errand to the World: American Protestant Thought and Foreign Missions*. Chicago: University of Chicago Press, 1987.

Inden, Ronald. *Imagining India*. Oxford: Blackwell, 1990.

Jaffrelot, Christophe. "Militant Hindus and the Conversion Issue (1885–1990): From Shuddhi to Dharm Parivartan: The Politicization and Diffusion of an 'Invention of Tradition'." In *The Resources of History: Tradition and Narration in South Asia*, edited by J. Assayag, 127–52. Paris: EFEO, 1990.

Jaffrelot, Christophe. "The Vishva Hindu Parishad: A Nationalist but Mimetic Attempt at Federating the Hindu Sects." In *Charisma and Canon: Essay on the Religious*

History of the Indian Subcontinent, edited by Vasudha Dalmia, Angelika Malinar, and Martin Christof, 388–411. Delhi: Oxford University Press, 2001.

Jaffrelot, Christopher, ed. *Hindu Nationalism: A Reader*. Princeton: Princeton University Press, 2007.

Jaffrelot, Christopher. *The Hindu Nationalist Movement in India*. New York: Columbia University Press, 1996.

Jain, Sandhya. *Evangelical Intrusions, Tripura: A Case Study*. New Delhi: Rupa & Co., 2010.

Jain, Sandhya. "Is There Imperial Design behind Conversion Overdrive?" *The Organiser (Online)*, 20 May 2007. http://www.organiser.org/dynamic/modules.php?name=Content&pa=showpage&pid=184&page=5.

Jain, Sandhya. "So the Caste Is a Convert's Nightmare Still! Let the Prodigals Return Home." *The Organiser (Online)*, April 8, 2007. http://www.organiser.org/dynamic/modules.php?name=Content&pa=showpage&pid=178&page=7.

James, Jonathan D. *McDonaldisation, Masala McGospel and Om Economics*. Washington, DC: Sage, 2010.

James, William. *The Varieties of Religious Experience*. New York: Mentor Books, 1958.

Johnson, Todd, and Kenneth Ross. *Atlas of Global Christianity 1910–2010*. Edinburgh: Edinburgh University Press, 2009.

Jones, Arun. "Faces of Pentecostalism in North India Today." *Society* 46, no. 6 (2009): 504–9.

Joshi, Sanjay. *Fractured Modernity: Making of a Middle Class in Colonial North India*. New Delhi: Oxford University Press, 2001.

Justice on Trial. *Kandhamal: Root Causes*. Ahmedabad: Justice on Trial, 2008.

Kant, Khajuria S. "Bajrang Dal Saves 42 Families." *The Organiser (Online)*, November 5, 2006. http://organiser.org/archives/historic/dynamic/modules6ef4.html?name=Content&pa=showpage&pid=155&page=11.

Keane, Webb. *Christian Moderns: Freedom and Fetish in the Mission Encounter*. Berkeley: University of California Press, 2007.

Kidambi, Prashant. *The Making of an Indian Metropolis: Colonial Governance and Public Culture in Bombay, 1890–1920*. Hampshire: Ashgate, 2007.

Kim, Kirsteen. "Theology." In *Encyclopedia of Mission and Missionaries*, edited by Jonathan J. Bonk, 436–41. New York: Routledge, 2007.

Kim, Sebastian C. H. *In Search of Identity: Debates on Religious Conversion in India*. Oxford: Oxford University Press, 2003.

Kooiman, Dick. *Conversion and Social Equality in India*. New Delhi: South Asia Publications, 1989.

Kurien, Prema. *A Place at the Multicultural Table: The Development of an American Hinduism*. New Brunswick, NJ: Rutgers University Press, 2007.

Larson, Gerald. "India's Struggle to Tolerate the Intolerant: Some Problems with Proselytizing." *Exemplar: The Journal of South Asian Studies* 1, no. 2 (2012): 27–44.

Lipner, Julius. *Brahmabandhab Upadhyay: The Life and Thought of a Revolutionary*. Oxford: Oxford University Press, 1999.

Lobo, Lancy. *Globalisation, Hindu Nationalism and Christians in India*. New Delhi: Rawat Publications, 2002.

Ma, Wonsuk. "Asian (Classical) Pentecostal Theology in Context." In *Asian and Pentecostal: The Charismatic Face of Christianity in Asia*, edited by Allan Anderson and Edmond Tang, 59–91. Costa Mesa, CA: Regnum, 2005.

Malhotra, Rajiv. *Being Different: An Indian Challenge to Western Universalism.* New Delhi: HarperCollins Publishers India, 2011.

Malhotra, Rajiv. *Breaking India: Western Interventions in Dravidian and Dalit Faultlines.* New Delhi: Amaryllis, 2011.

Mander, Harsh. "Barefoot: Remembering Kandhamal." *The Hindu (Online)*, December 17, 2011. http://www.thehindu.com/opinion/columns/Harsh_Mander/barefoot-remembering-kandhamal/article2723257.ece.

Mandryk, Jason. *Operation World: The Definitive Prayer Guide to Every Nation.* Colorado Springs: Biblica Publishing, 2010.

Mangham, Tom. "Encompassing the Globe: Reports from our Vice Presidents: Asia." *Multiply*, Summer 2008, 7.

Manshardt, Clifford, ed. *The Mahatma and the Missionary: Selected Writings of Mohandas K. Gandhi.* Chicago: Henry Regnery Company, 1949.

Martin, David. *Pentecostalism: The World Their Parish.* Oxford: Wiley-Blackwell, 2002.

Meyer, Birgit. "Pentecostalism and Globalization." In *Studying Global Pentecostalism: Theories and Methods*, edited by Allan Anderson, Michael Bergunder, André Droogers, and Cornelis van der Laan, 113–30. Berkeley: University of California Press, 2010.

Miller, Donald E., and Tetsunao Yamamori. *Global Pentecostalism: The New Face of Christian Social Engagement.* Berkeley: University of California Press, 2007.

Misra, Amalendu. "The Missionary Position: Christianity and Politics of Religious Conversion in India." *Nationalism and Ethnic Politics* 17, no. 4 (2011): 361–81.

Moffat, Michael. *An Untouchable Community in South India: Structure and Consensus.* Princeton: Princeton University Press, 1979.

Mosse, David. "Possession and Confession: Affliction and Sacred Power in Colonial and Contemporary Catholic South India." In *Anthropology of Christianity*, edited by Fenella Cannell, 99–133. Durham, NC: Duke University Press, 2006.

Mustafa, Faizan, and Anurag Sharma. *Conversion: Constitutional and Legal Implications.* New Delhi: Kanishka Publishers, 2003.

Narayanan, K. S. " 'The Attack is Only Natural'." *OutlookIndia.Com*, October 12, 1998. http://www.outlookindia.com/article.aspx?206325.

O'Flaherty, W. D. *The Origins of Evil in Hindu Mythology.* Berkeley: University of California Press, 1980.

Pandey, Gyanendra. "The Colonial Construction of 'Communalism': British Writings on Banaras in the Nineteenth Century." In *Mirrors of Violence: Communities, Riots and Survivors in South Asia*, edited by Veena Das, 94–134. Delhi: Oxford University Press, 1990.

Pandey, Gyanendra. *Routine Violence: Nations, Fragments, Histories.* Delhi: Permanent Black, 2006.

Parathazham, Paul. "Neo-Pentecostalism in India: Preliminary Report of a National Survey." *Word and Worship* 29 (May–June 1996): 81–101.

Pearson, M. N. *The Portuguese in India.* The New Cambridge History of India. Edited by Gordon Johnson, C. A. Bayly, and John F. Richards. Vol. I.1. New York: Cambridge University Press, [1987] 2006.

Prabhudesai, Sandesh. "BJP Ready to Probe VHP Funds, Says Minister." *Rediff on the Net*, October 5, 1999. http://www.rediff.com/news/1999/oct/05goa.htm.

Prasad, R. Guru. "Cash Prize for Hindus to Throw Photos of Hindu Gods: Extra Money for Wearing Cross Lockets." *The Organiser (Online)*, April 3, 2011. http://organiser.org/archives/historic/dynamic/modules4a3b.html?name=Content&pa=showpage&pid=391&page=7.

Preston, Andrew. *Sword of the Spirit, Shield of Faith: Religion in American War and Diplomacy*. New York: Alfred A. Knopf, 2012.

PUCL (Bhubaneswar), and Kashipur Solidarity Group. *Crossed and Crucified: Parivar's War against Minorities in Orissa*. Delhi: PUCL, 2009.

Rahman, Shafi. "Freelancers of God." *India Today International*, May 9, 2011, 36–39.

Rajan, Radha. "PIO Hindus—Gateway to White Imperialism." *VigilOnline.com*, July 31, 2011. http://www.vigilonline.com/index.php?option=com_content&task=view&id=1473&Itemid=71.

Rajan, Radha. "A Question of Identity." *VigilOnline.com*, July 31, 2007. http://www.vigilonline.com/index.php?option=com_content&task=view&id=879&I.

Rajan, Radha. "Tamil Nadu Politics: Cancerous Church Eats into Dravidian Parties." *VigilOnline.com*, March 30, 2011. http://www.vigilonline.com/index.php?option=com_content&task=view&id=1510&Itemid=71.

Rajendran, K. *Which Way Forward Indian Missions?* Bangalore: SAIACS Press, 1998.

Ram, Kalpana. *Fertile Disorder: Spirit Possession and its Provocation of the Modern*. Honolulu: University of Hawaii Press, 2013.

Rao, K. L. Seshagiri. "Conversion: A Hindu/Gandhian Perspective." In *Religious Conversion: Contemporary Practices and Controversies*, edited by M. Darrol Bryan and Christopher Lamb, 136–50. London: Continuum, 1999.

Robbins, Joel. "Anthropology of Religion." In *Studying Global Pentecostalism: Theories and Methods*, edited by Allan Anderson, Michael Bergunder, André Droogers, and Cornelis van der Laan, 156–78. Berkeley: University of California Press, 2010.

Robbins, Joel. "Continuity Thinking and the Problem of Christian Culture." *Current Anthropology* 48 (2007): 5–38.

Roberts, Nathaniel. "Anti-conversion Law in a Secular State: Religious Difference and the Threat to 'Public Order'." Paper presented at the Max Planck Institute for the Study of Religion and Ethnic Diversity, Göttingen, February 22, 2011.

Roberts, Nathaniel. "The Power of Conversion and the Foreignness of Belonging: Domination and Moral Community in a Paraiyar Slum." PhD diss. Columbia University, 2008.

Saraswati, Swami Dayananda. "Conversion Is an Act of Violence." *Hinduism Today (Web Edition)*, November 1999. http://www.hinduismtoday.com/modules/smartsection/item.php?itemid=4308.

Sarkar, Sumit. "Conversion and Politics of Hindu Right." *Economic and Political Weekly*, June 26, 1999, 1691–700.

Sarkar, Tanika. *Hindu Wife, Hindu Nation: Community, Religion, and Cultural Nationalism*. Bloomington: Indiana University Press, 2001.

Schmalz, Mathew. "A Space for Redemption: Catholic Tactics in Hindu North India." PhD diss. University of Chicago, 1998.

Sen, Amartya. *Identity and Violence: The Illusion of Destiny*. New York: W. W. Norton, 2006.

Shourie, Arun. *Harvesting Our Souls: Missionaries, Their Design, Their Claims.* Delhi: Rupa & Co., 2001.

Shourie, Arun. *Missionaries in India: Continuities, Changes, Dilemmas.* New Delhi: Rupa & Co., 1994.

Srivastava, Ajai. "The Pastor Reveals the Truth: Reconversion to Hinduism." *The Organiser (Online)*, March 11, 2007. http://organiser.org/archives/historic/dynamic/modulesb72e.html?name=Content&pa=showpage&pid=174&page=30.

Stoller, Paul. *In Sorcery's Shadow: A Memoir of Apprenticeship among the Songhay of Niger.* Chicago: University of Chicago Press, 1989.

Subramanian, Ajantha. *Shorelines: Space and Rights in South India.* Stanford, CA: Stanford University Press, 2009.

Sundar, Nandini. "Adivasi vs. Vanvasi: The Politics of Conversion and Re-conversion in Central India." In *Assertive Religious Identities*, edited by Satish Saberwal and Mushirul Hasan, 357–90. New Delhi: Manohar, 2006.

Swarup, Ram. *Hinduism vis-à-vis Christianity and Islam.* New Delhi: Voice of India, [1982] 1992.

Synan, Vinson. "A Healer in the House? A Historical Perspective on Healing in the Pentecostal/Charismatic Tradition." *Asian Journal of Pentecostal Studies* 3, no. 2 (2000): 189–201.

Thomas, Pradip Ninan. *Strong Religion, Zealous Media: Christian Fundamentalism and Communication in India.* Los Angeles: Sage, 2008.

Thomas, V. V. *Dalit Pentecostalism: Spirituality of the Empowered Poor.* Bangalore: Asian Trading Corporation, 2008.

Times News Network. "Jaganmohan Reddy's Tirumala Visit Kicks up a Row." *Times of India Online (Hyderabad)*, May 3, 2012. http://articles.timesofindia.indiatimes.com/2012-05-03/hyderabad/31555281_1_jai-jagan-ttd-executive-officer-temple-rules.

Turner, Edith. "A Visible Spirit Form in Zambia." In *Being Changed by Cross-Cultural Encounters: The Anthropology of Extraordinary Experience*, edited by David E. Young and Jean-Guy Goulet, 71–95. Toronto: Broadview Press, 1994.

Turner, Frederick Jackson. *The Frontier in American History.* New York: H. Holt and Co., 1920.

UCANews. "Protestant Bishop Criticized for Ordaining Pentecostal 'Archbishop'." *UCANews.com*, February 18, 2003. http://www.ucanews.com/story-archive/?post_name=/2003/02/18/protestant-bishop-criticized-for-ordaining-pentecostal-archbishop&post_id=22052.

van der Veer, Peter. *Gods on Earth: Religious Experience and Identity in Ayodhya.* New York: Oxford University Press, [1988] 1997.

van der Veer, Peter. *Religious Nationalism: Hindus and Muslims in India.* Berkeley: University of California Press, 1994.

Vandevelde, Iris. "Reconversion to Hinduism: A Hindu Nationalist Reaction against Conversion to Christianity and Islam." *South Asia: Journal of South Asian Studies* 34, no. 1 (2011): 31–50.

Viswanathan, Gauri. "Religious Conversion and the Politics of Dissent." In *Conversion to Modernities: The Globalization of Christianity*, edited by Peter van der Veer, 89–114. New York: Routledge, 1996.

Wagner, C. Peter. *Churchquake: How the New Apostolic Reformation is Shaking up the Church as We Know It*. Ventura: Regal Books, 1999.

Wagner, Kim. *The Great Fear of 1857: Rumours, Conspiracies and the Making of the Indian Uprising*. Oxford: Peter Lang, 2010.

Walls, Andrew F. "World Christianity, the Missionary Movement and the Ugly American." In *World Order and Religion*, edited by Wade Clark Roof, 147–72. Albany: State University of New York Press, 1991.

Weber, Linda J. *Mission Handbook: U.S. and Canadian Protestant Ministries Overseas*. 21st ed. Wheaton, IL: Evangelism and Missions Information Service, 2010.

Wilson, Everett. "They Crossed the Red Sea, Didn't They? Critical History and Pentecostal Beginnings." In *The Globalization of Pentecostalism*, edited by Marray Dempster, Byron Klaus, and Douglas Petersen, 85–115. Irvine, CA: Regnum, 1999.

Wuthnow, Robert. *Boundless Faith: The Global Outreach of American Churches*. Berkeley: University of California Press, 2009.

Yohannan, K. P. *Come, Let's Reach the World: Partnership in Church Planting among the Most Unreached*. Carrollton, TX: GFA Books, 2004.

Yong, Amos. "The Demonic in Pentecostal/Charismatic Christianity and in the Religious Consciousness of Asia." In *Asian and Pentecostal: The Charismatic Face of Christianity in Asia*, edited by Allan Anderson and Edmond Tang, 93–128. Costa Mesa, CA: Regnum Books, 2005.

Young, Richard Fox. *Resistant Hinduism: Sanskrit Sources on Anti-Christian Apologetics in Early Nineteenth Century India*. Vienna: Indological Institute, University of Vienna, 1981.

Zamindar, Vazira Fazil-Yacoobali. *The Long Partition and the Making of Modern South Asia: Refugees, Boundaries, Histories*. New York: Columbia University Press, 2007.

Zavos, John. "Conversion and the Assertive Margins." *South Asia: Journal of South Asian Studies* 24, no. 2 (December 2001): 73–89.

INDEX

Printed in the USA
CPSIA information can be obtained
at www.ICGtesting.com
CBHW030834121224
18797CB00018B/162